THE MEMORY MARKETPLACE

IRISH CULTURE, MEMORY, PLACE

Oona Frawley, Ray Cashman, Guy Beiner, editors

THE MEMORY MARKETPLACE

Witnessing Pain in Contemporary Irish and International Theatre

EMILIE PINE

INDIANA UNIVERSITY PRESS

This book is a publication of

Indiana University Press
Office of Scholarly Publishing
Herman B Wells Library 350
1320 East 10th Street
Bloomington, Indiana 47405 USA

iupress.indiana.edu

© 2020 Emilie Pine

All rights reserved
No part of this book may be reproduced or utilized in any form or by any means, electronic or mechanical, including photocopying and recording, or by any information storage and retrieval system, without permission in writing from the publisher. The paper used in this publication meets the minimum requirements of the American National Standard for Information Sciences—Permanence of Paper for Printed Library Materials, ANSI Z39.48-1992.

Manufactured in the United States of America

Cataloging information is available from the Library of Congress.

ISBN 978-0-253-04950-6 (hardcover)
ISBN 978-0-253-04952-0 (paperback)
ISBN 978-0-253-04951-3 (web PDF)

1 2 3 4 5 25 24 23 22 21 20

For Vanessa and Alex, and in memory of Elena

CONTENTS

Acknowledgments ix

Introduction: The Market for Pain 1

1. Tell Them That You Saw Us: Witnessing Docu-verbatim Memory 43
2. The Witness as Commodity: Autoperforming Memory 94
3. The Commissioned Witness, Theatre, and Truth 123
4. The Immaterial Labor of Listening: Presence, Absence, Failure, and the Commodification of the Witness 162
5. Consumers or Witnesses? Site-Specific Performance 189

Conclusion: Activism in the Marketplace 219

Index 241

ACKNOWLEDGMENTS

RESEARCHING AND WRITING CAN FEEL like solitary, and sometimes lonely, pursuits. I have been very fortunate that I have never felt alone in the task of making this book. I am thankful daily for the support of colleagues and students at the School of English, Drama, and Film at University College Dublin. Particular thanks go to my mentor Margaret Kelleher; my *Irish University Review* colleagues, John Brannigan and Lucy Collins; and to my colleagues in the school and across UCD: Ursula Byrne, Danielle Clarke, Nick Daly, Fionnuala Dillane, Kate Fama, Deirdre Flynn, Jane Grogan, Paul Halferty, Karen Jackman, Susan Leavy, Críostóir MacCárthaigh, Emily Mark-Fitzgerald, Naomi McAreavey, Mary McAuliffe, Gerardine Meaney, Niamh Pattwell, Paul Perry, Anthony Roche, Pauline Slattery, Maria Stuart, and Justin Synnott, friends and wise counselors every one. Thanks also to the support of Jennika Baines at Indiana University Press, to Guy Beiner for suggesting I send this work to them, and to the book's two readers, whose constructive feedback was an act of great intellectual and feminist generosity.

This book emerges out of the field of Irish theatre studies, and I would like to thank colleagues in IASIL, ACIS, ISTR, and WHA for their feedback on work in progress and for sharing their emergent work, in particular Guy Beiner, David Clare, Linda Connolly, Marguerite Corporaal, Mike Cronin, Eric Falci, Lisa Fitzpatrick, Miriam Haughton, Eamonn Jordan, Joseph Lennon, Patrick Lonergan, Claire Lynch, Ciara Murphy, Eve Patten, Alison Ribeiro de Menezes, Melissa Sihra, Brian Singleton, and Ian Walsh. For their inspiration and friendship, heartfelt thanks to Charlotte McIvor and Paige Reynolds. Recent years have allowed me to join the burgeoning field of memory studies, both in Ireland and internationally, and I am grateful to my partners in the Irish Memory Studies Network, Oona Frawley and Fionnuala Dillane, and to all the speakers at our lecture series since 2012. At the COST Network "In Search of Transnational Memory in Europe" and at the Memory Studies Association I would like to thank Tea Sindbæk Anderson, Silke Arnold-de Simine, Stef Craps, Astrid Erll, Paco Ferrandiz, Gunnþórunn Guðmundsdóttir, Marianne Hirsch, Sara Jones, Anna Reading, Ann Rigney, and Vered Vinitzky-Seroussi. Conferences and seminars represent the opportunity to share our work, and in that they are very valuable; but they are most precious for the friendships they foster.

Theatre is a collaborative enterprise, and I am grateful to the Dublin Theatre Festival and Dublin Fringe Festival for making international work available to me as an audience member and for all the support in contacting playwrights. Many thanks to the theatre makers who have shared their work with me, particularly unpublished and work in progress: La Conquesta del Pol Sud, Kabosh Theatre, the Nirbhaya Ensemble, Tiago Rodriguez, and Theater of Witness. Thanks also to the Waking the Feminists movement for waking up so many of us.

I have been extremely lucky in my friends, my chosen family, and I would like to thank them for their ongoing support: Emma Bradford, Sam Bufter, John Butler, Anna Carey, Kerri Chyka, Brian Cliff, Patrick Freyne, Sharon Jackson, David Long, Barry MacEvilly, Tara MacLoughlin, Alex Marrable, Jenny McDonnell, Brendan O'Connell, Niall O'Neill, Alan O'Riordan, Niamh O'Shea, Éadaoin Patton, Diana Pérez Garcia, Marni Rothman, Richard Rowland, Christine Ryan, Jim Shanahan, Anne Solari, and Pádraic Whyte.

My parents, Melanie Pine and Richard Pine, have been the wellspring of so many of the ideas and approaches in this book because of their mutual interest in the world and all the ways they inspire me to engage with a life full of art, music, literature, and theatre. I have been very fortunate, too, in being welcomed into a second family since 2001, and my sincere thanks and love to Peter and Sarah Kelly, Garvan Kelly, and Alessandro Loche. I will never be done being thankful to Ronan Kelly for his love, his unstinting support, humor, and kindness, and his example.

Finally, this book is dedicated to my sister, Vanessa Pine, and her two beautiful children, Elena Jane and Alexander. Thank you, Vanessa, for sharing your wonderful children with me, and for allowing me to watch over them with you; it is the great joy and privilege of my life.

THE MEMORY MARKETPLACE

INTRODUCTION

The Market for Pain

THIS BOOK IS INSPIRED BY my observation that public performances of painful stories are not simply formed, and told, and watched, and listened to, but are imagined, produced, and consumed in a cultural, social, and economic sphere that I call the memory marketplace. More than that, this book argues that in order to fully understand not just when and why we publicly tell stories about our pasts but how we perform as witnesses to painful pasts in general we have to consider the market dynamics of trade, which underpin how these stories are told, mediated, received, and re-mediated. In other words, we need to consider that stories of painful pasts are not just told but sold, not just received but bought, not just mediated and re-mediated but commodified.

The memory marketplace operates like any other form of market: in order to reach an audience and therefore to accrue value, public performances of pain require material and immaterial investment, labor, and a consumer willing to buy and promote them. And, just like items a consumer buys in the supermarket, the economic foundations and ramifications of memory performances are often invisible because they happen out of sight, or because we simply take them for granted. Though invisible, however, these economic factors determine not just how a performance happens, but whether it happens at all. Mirroring the economic dimensions of the memory marketplace, moreover, the symbolic functions of the marketplace are also key. In fact, I am most interested in the ways that reading performances of painful pasts through this framework can help us to interpret the performances themselves as transactions. For example, in reading how the producer's and performer's awareness of the audience as consumers influences the kinds of emotional engagement offered by a performance.

Why is it so rare that analyses of painful stories raise questions of commodity, value, and trade? Is it that we imagine the meaning of cultural performances exists in opposition to commercial evaluations, such as box office earnings? Are we afraid of confusing, or conflating, different forms of value? Memory and performance critics are sophisticated analysts of the material, historical, and political contexts and effects of memory, yet often critics stop short of interpreting memory performances themselves as commodity transactions. But in not pursuing the value of mnemonic capital to a reading of cultural memory, critics are missing an important part of the picture. My investigation of the memory marketplace is driven therefore by two major impulses. First, it is only by placing cultural memory in the context of the marketplace that the hierarchical and competitive structures guiding the production and consumption of cultural memory can be made visible. Second, in ignoring the engines of the marketplace we also ignore the material and immaterial labor (and the laborers) that actually produce mnemonic, symbolic, and social capital. My ambition in this book is to begin to make these necessary shifts in perception.

To ignore the marketplace for memory is to also disregard what the witnesses of painful pasts are telling us—these witnesses know there is a market for their memories, and they also know that they have to enter that market if they want to be heard. In *Land Full of Heroes* (UK/France/Spain, 2019), Carmen-Francesca Banciu, a Romanian writer based in Berlin, narrates for an audience the history of her life, in particular her involvement in the 1989 Romanian revolution and her escape to Berlin. In describing her migratory journey, Banciu considers the commodification of her emotions by others—and, given that she has no financial resources of her own, she knows that the expression of her feelings is her only form of currency:

> In March 1990 the world is no longer okay. Or it's just now on its way to being okay. I'm allowed to leave Romania. . . . From Romania to Hungary we drive across the Pusta. Across never-ending expanses that make the transition between one country and the next barely discernible. Dieter is also a writer and wants to write about me. About my experiences on this journey. He wants to capture the moment at the border with all of my emotions. But I don't feel anything. Or don't want to reveal my emotions to him. I feel mute and numb.
>
> They will pay the bills during the trip. This is a part of our deal. I should talk. Disclose. I'm not even aware that I'm selling my impressions. That I'm practicing for the first time for life in the market economy. In Capitalism.[1]

In this theatrical moment, there is a striking contrast between Banciu's historical reluctance to tell, and lack of awareness of the transaction, with the present moment in which she shares her feelings not with Dieter, but with a much larger audience. In both timeframes, Banciu's feelings are a commodity she trades. In the past, this trade secured her freedom from Bucharest and the socialist past; in the present, her articulation of her memories secures another valuable commodity—the audience's interest. Both Banciu and La Conquesta del Pol Sud (the company producing the show) acknowledge the voyeuristic, potentially exploitative nature of the audience's interest. They appear to give us what we want (the emotional content of Banciu's memories) while illustrating the knowingness of this performance by deliberately linking the selling of memory to capitalism. Despite this knowingness, however, Banciu's status as a controlling agent in the memory marketplace is debatable as, though she intentionally trades her mnemonic capital, in doing so she no longer owns it exclusively. This is the paradox that recurs throughout this book: that witnesses know what they trade—their memories for the value of being heard—but that the process of performing their testimony of painful pasts delivers them only temporary power in the marketplace. The fluctuations of witnessing can thus only be understood if we consider the "deal" that is being made between performer and audience; in other words if we recognise that cultural memory is a performance happening within a marketplace.

This book takes its cue from theatrical moments such as these, moments when the literal and symbolic memory marketplace becomes visible, moments when the commodity trading of performance becomes undeniable, moments that allow us to consider the power plays underlying different forms, and mobilizations, of mnemonic capital. The memory marketplace is particularly visible in testimonial "witness theatre," in which an onstage witness (either the original witness or an actor) performs painful memories for an audience. In return those memories are valued, and validated, by an audience who, in Paul Celan's terms, "bear witness for the witness."[2] This bearing witness, on both sides, is a transaction of different forms of capital. While Banciu's experience is unique to her, at the same time her life story is representative of a generation of artists and activists in Romania and across socialist countries more generally. In this way, Banciu's memories have significant social and cultural capital; this capital is added to by her status as an award-winning writer and her willingness to autoperform these memories herself on stage. *Land Full of Heroes* thus enables audiences to learn about the socialist past of Eastern Europe (at the thirtieth anniversary of the fall of the Ceaușescu regime), to gain insight into one woman's life, and to play the role of affective witnesses to Banciu's expression of her feelings.

Banciu's memory may be highly mediated, but nevertheless the emotional charge of "I was there, this was real" remains. This charge of the real or, in

Jean Baudrillard's term, the "hyperreal," gives her witness testimony value in the memory marketplace.[3] The production of *Land Full of Heroes*, funded by a grant by the UK Arts and Humanities Research Council as part of an academic project at the University of Birmingham, thus mobilizes both personal and institutional capital in order to create an authentic product that audiences will want to consume. Indeed, the premiere at Birmingham BE Festival (Birmingham Repertory Theatre, July 2019) was sold-out, and the show received a five-star review; it is currently scheduled for additional performances in Berlin, France, and London, illustrating the market impact of, and demand for, this kind of work.[4]

To read single performances like Banciu's and, more generally, to position witness theatre within a marketplace framework allows us as critics not only to understand the ways that witnesses create new narrations of the past, but also to spotlight how the immaterial labor of performing past experience creates and re-creates mnemonic capital. Focusing on the theatrical production of witnesses (both on and off stage), this book argues that painful memory is a commodity in a transactional exchange. This transaction has economic dimensions to it (e.g., institutional and commercial funding of theatre), making the value of pain traceable in the real economy. But witnessing is about producing more than economic value, and there are other forms of capital that require analysis—my argument in the chapters that follow thus engages with the idea of painful memory as a symbolic commodity. By expressing painful experience in witness plays, onstage witnesses gain status in the overlapping cultural, social, and political marketplaces. By producing testimonial work, companies and theatres not only create platforms to enable these witnesses, but also add to their own cultural status (as well as, potentially, their own commercial success given the expanding market for pain). In turn, in attending witness theatre, audiences can confirm themselves as good spectators (and perhaps good citizens) for their own exercise of labor in witnessing the performance of painful memory. These are the infrastructures, commodity chains, and transactional exchanges that lie, so often invisibly, behind every performance of painful memory.

Witnessing: Tell Them That You Saw Us

We get bored easily these days it would seem. Our phones are never off, and rarely out of sight. Our to-do lists are long and varied. The demands on our time and attention are never ending. But in the theatre we leave that behind. It's not just that theatre provides a break from modern life, it's that going to the theatre involves a contract in which audiences pledge their *attention*. This attentiveness flows both from and onto the stage. The person on the stage pays attention to the audience, performing for that audience, and in return the audience pays attention to the performer(s). This may seem too obvious to be worth spelling out here—but, here's the thing, if we notice that attention is the silver thread binding performer and audience to each other, then the next step is to think about what that attention produces. The performer onstage is always keen to tell their story (despite the challenges this may involve for them). In narrating their memories, the onstage person asserts the importance of their voice, of their identity as a witness. But it is the audience who grants the witness the space and time to perform, who frame their testimony as worthwhile, and who establish their authenticity and authority through their acts of attentive listening. Without the audience, nothing would be *produced* because there would be no transaction of labor or capital.

In theatre, there are, broadly, two types of witness—those onstage and those in the auditorium. We can better understand the relationship between types of witness, and between memory and witnessing if we look at another play, *Waiting for Godot* by Samuel Beckett. In Act 1, Vladimir and Estragon wait for Godot to arrive and impart some information, or meaning, which they are lacking. They wait to be witnesses and to be witnessed. But this desire is constantly frustrated as Godot does not arrive, and those who do—Pozzo and Lucky—do not bring them any closer to either enlightenment or salvation. At the end of the first act, a Boy appears to tell them that Godot will come tomorrow. The Boy then asks if Vladimir has a message for Godot:

> **Boy:** What am I to say to Mr Godot, sir?
> **Vladimir:** Tell him... [*He hesitates*] ... tell him you saw us. [*Pause.*] You did see us, didn't you?
> **Boy:** Yes sir.[5]

But the following day—Act 2—Godot is again a no-show, and again a Boy comes to tell the pair to wait again tomorrow. The second Boy (played by the same actor) claims not to know Vladimir and Estragon, and says he is the other Boy's brother. Again the Boy asks for a message for Godot:

> **Boy:** What am I to tell Mr Godot, sir?
> **Vladimir:** Tell him... [*He hesitates*] ... tell him you saw me and that... [*He hesitates*] ... that you saw me. [*Pause. Vladimir advances, the Boy recoils. Vladimir halts, the Boy halts. With sudden violence.*] You're sure you saw me, you won't come and tell me tomorrow that you never saw me![6]

Throughout *Waiting for Godot* the characters strive to be witnessed, in an enactment of Bishop Berkeley's maxim that "to be is to be perceived."[7] Self-perception does not count here, not least because Vladimir and Estragon have no confidence in their own powers of witnessing (they doubt what day it is, what place it is, what has happened). Instead, they require an external witness to validate them. In the second act, Beckett pushes this further—it is not enough for the Boy to see them and to relay that message to Godot, he must *remember* having seen them. The link between witnessing and memory thus illustrates that witnessing is an ongoing and active task, where repetition and remediation are *as important* as the first encounter in the creation of meaning. The Boy's actions are analogous to the audience's—where the audience is asked not only to spectate (to see), but to transform that act of spectating into witnessing, which is understood as an active role that continues after the act of seeing (remembering). The real meaning of a play, then, is the agglomeration of acts of witnessing: that which happens on the stage, projected outward to the audience; and that which happens internally as the audience sees, listens to, and processes the performance; and finally that which happens as the audience relates their experience and their insights in the future, whether that is for themselves, or to others who have not seen the show. The compulsion to tell becomes the compulsion to retell. In simple terms, this is how the past is witnessed; in a more complicated sense it is also how future memory banks are formed. As Astrid Erll and Ann Rigney assert, cultural memory "is as much a matter of acting out a relationship to the past from a particular point in the present as it is a matter of preserving and retrieving."[8] Through performance a relationship is built that links past and present—and that, through repetition, projects into the future.

Before I expand on the processes of witnessing, it is important to understand the context in which these performances happen. Witnessing—being a witness and being witnessed—is both a necessity and a luxury. The *violence* of Vladimir's insistence that he and Estragon be seen and remembered emerges from vulnerability; their precarity means that they struggle to be witnessed and increases the stakes to the extent that a young Boy can become the arbiter of their identity. That a child is elevated above two grown men indicates how witnessing is always performed within social and cultural power structures, in which some witnesses have power and some witnesses have little to none. This exemplifies Anna Reading's contention that in the capitalist marketplace different agents have "uneven memory capital."[9]

How can we read these different agents in this context? How can we interpret performances of witnessing in relation to both the top-down organization of memory culture, and the bottom-up drive for expression and understanding? What relationship is there between the scarce resource of witnessing-attention, and the current "memory boom"? What role do memory gatekeepers play, and what agency do spectators really have? The marketplace is a powerful framework for considering these questions.

THE MEMORY MARKETPLACE

The memory marketplace as both a real market and a metaphoric space of exchange helps us to consider how power and memory intersect: who owns memory, how it is traded, and how it is consumed. The marketplace framework enables us to think in broader terms of memory not just as a performance on both individual and collective levels, but as a product or commodity. Moreover, to follow Pierre Bourdieu, this book suggests that we think of the memory marketplace beyond financial and monetary terms, instead considering the marketplace as a symbolic space where values are produced and consumed. This book thus argues that the market is both "an institution of power" and a "site of contest" within which actors seek to have their memories witnessed in order to generate and maximize both cultural and social capital.[10]

We already have a language in memory studies that borrows from economics—memory entrepreneur, Holocaust industry—and much of the scholarship in this field emerges from recognition of the ways that processes of memorializing often overlap with processes of commodification. Yet the analysis of the economic dimensions of culture has largely been restricted to the heritage sector; as a result, the broader applicability of market concepts has not yet made significant impact. As Reading argues, "the mnemonic economy has largely been overlooked within memory studies and feminist memory studies."[11] Indeed, as Jonathan Bach argues, there is a tendency in memory studies to discuss cultural memory in terms of the production of "narrations of the past"; Bach's approach instead analyzes—alongside narrative—the ways that mnemonic capital circulates in "overlapping economies."[12] Tanya Notley and Reading argue that as critics we should pay attention to the labor as well as the objects of memory, as it is this labor that "becomes accumulated in [the] materialised states of memory capital."[13] Memory is thus both energetic and material. Through a focus on mnemonic capital and the labor of memory work, Reading highlights the otherwise invisible role of precarious workers and activists, often women. Hence one of the compelling reasons for considering the dynamics of the marketplace at play in the cultural sphere is the increased visibility of the investment of effort, emotion, and time by producers, performers, and audiences in the cocreation of "mnemonic capital." The cocreation aspect of mnemonic capital is also important to note because, as Matthew Allen argues, there has been a problematic identification of memory as "private property" without sufficient attention to the public ownership, differentials in valuation, and the exchangeability of memory.[14]

Building on this conceptual groundwork, this book argues that we exploit the marketplace as a framework in order to gain insights into how witnessing painful memory operates as a transaction of both real and symbolic capital. This examination considers how the memory marketplace subjects witnesses to different forms of gatekeeping, how audiences (read as consumers) exert agency, whether consumption is active or passive, and whether witness theatre can lead not only to empathic catharsis, but social change.

The memory marketplace frames the kinds of cultural exchange we already analyze—the interactions of what "Adorno scornfully called 'the culture industry,'" or, in Jen Harvie's terms, the "entertainment market."[15] Highlighting the role of market dynamics in these spaces foregrounds how memory functions as a commodity, both as an economic asset and, more broadly, as Reading terms it, "mnemonic capital."[16] Reading's use of mnemonic capital is an important addition to Bourdieu's framework for cultural capital, which notes three different forms: embodied, objectified, and institutionalized.[17] Reading draws on Bourdieu's recognition of how each of these forms contributes to what he terms "symbolic capital," the value accrued by generating or owning particular products (e.g., the social status conferred upon house owners).[18] Reading's development of this framework, to include mnemonic capital and mnemonic labor, thus recognizes that cultural memory involves a significant degree of work by a range of mnemonic actors (who is making it, who is transmitting it, who is receiving it). Moreover, building on Bourdieu's framework helps us to understand the *overlapping* of the literal capital benefits to memory work (e.g., many of the plays discussed here are commercially successful) with the symbolic capital generated by particular kinds of cultural prestige often associated with memory plays that shed light on painful or troubled pasts.[19] Drawing on Bourdieu's framework also illustrates the roles of time and accumulation—these plays may take years to come to fruition, as their subjects gain public traction or support; the performances may be either the apex of the struggle to speak out, or (in the case of activist work) may be hoped to contribute toward the struggle. Capital is not easily generated, the marketplace is not an "imaginary university of . . . perfect equality" but rather, as Vladimir and Estragon find to their cost, a stratified sphere of different power relations.[20] The frequent hope, then, underpinning the process of witnessing is that symbolic capital can work to reverse some of the marketplace inequalities.

As will become clear over the course of this book, in recent decades the performed memory of troubled pasts has taken on a certain market cachet and thus symbolic capital of its own, so that plays that share in this trend may enjoy an enhanced status in the marketplace (a result of trend scouting). By highlighting the role of capital we can perceive how memory functions not only as a signifier of a relationship to the past, but as a commodity in a marketplace that can be sold and bought, produced and consumed. Theatre is an unparalleled space on which to center these questions and discussions, not only because of how the past is put into form and performance, but because theatre represents a joint site of immaterial—"energetic"—production and consumption. Highlighting the role of immaterial labor is a political act, making visible the mnemonic, emotional, intellectual, and physical labor that are necessary to the witnessing event.

Memory products, from heritage sites to commemorative parades to memory plays, circulate in local and global markets. As Alison Landsberg argues, the commodification of memory enables "images of the past to circulate on a grand scale," making them "available to all who are able to pay."[21] Memory is thus both the marketing device and the product being marketed, both of which contribute to the creation of what Harvie identifies as "consumer allegiance," which generates "a more profitable bottom line."[22] While both Harvie and Landsberg point to the social good generated by memory culture—solidarity, connection, empathy—they each also emphasize the role of economic considerations in mediating how culture is transmitted—for example, the need to appeal to an audience "on a grand scale" will determine what kinds of memories are given space within the market (e.g., through corporate sponsorship, state/civic cultural programming, subsidies and grants, or heavy marketing).[23] As Jean Baudrillard argues, "distress, misery and suffering have become the raw goods" that attract the largest audiences.[24] Further, as Terri Tomsky outlines, trauma circulates as a commodity, "analogous to social and economic capital"; and, crucially, Tomsky illustrates how the scale of modern suffering (and knowledge of that suffering via the media) has resulted in the creation of a hierarchy of suffering as trauma is valued and revalued.[25] As this book will argue, the market is thus a key determinant of what memories are deemed to generate consumer allegiance and thereby drive profit, and what memories are devalued by the market hierarchy.

The memory marketplace is hence a vital framework, shedding light on the circulation and exchange of different forms of capital and how memory performances are produced and consumed. The theatre audience is not, after all, spontaneously turning up and listening. They peruse a season brochure, schedule plans, buy a ticket. They invest in hearing the memory. They leave a review, recommend the show, buy tickets for others to attend the show or for subsequent performances. Or not—perhaps instead they leave a bad review, share no positive word of mouth, never buy a ticket for the theatre again. The successful transmission of memory in culture has to be understood as a transaction in order to fully understand how an audience chooses to support or invest in a particular memory narrative product. This transaction may be directly financial (buying a ticket) or it may be suprafinancial (recommending it to a friend), either way it represents the outlay and generation of different forms of capital by an audience, who choose how they will invest in the value of that memory in performance. The audience thus represents one more layer of gatekeeping in a complex commodity chain of funders, producers, and marketers.

Using the term "gatekeeper" raises the issue of power—who has the power to gain entry to the marketplace, who controls others' entry, who regulates it, and who owns the "invisible hand"?[26] This can be answered in a literal sense—memory is produced by, and circulates within, cultural and economic infrastructures. Memory commodities that are popular in the market will receive infrastructural support. For example, public and private funding enable theatres to run, to program shows, and to offer discounted tickets for particular shows; programmers decide what will fill the theatre's stage; writers and directors decide on the final shape of the show; marketing campaigns seek to brand shows in ways that will appeal to consumers; successful shows will have extended runs and be booked in subsequent venues and festivals; tours will create transnational consumers; successful producers (writers, directors, performers, and companies) will gain support for their next venture, and their work will be highly promoted. This is how the industry works, driven by profit—as Carol Martin argues, "who decides who speaks . . . although ideally driven by ethics, is mostly a commercial and ideological decision."[27] Developing this idea, this book argues that the decision to represent particular stories in the theatre is not random, but a direct result of gatekeepers seeking to accrue cultural, social, and economic capital through selected "valuable" stories.

Though many of these decisions are based on "the bottom line" and respond to commercial trends, within each layer of the production process other kinds of marketplace decisions are made about what characters, subjects, and voices will be granted a platform. Gatekeepers are therefore empowered by both economic and social capital and use this power in multivalent ways—they can choose how to respond to wider market demands (e.g., to write/direct/program shows that aim for escapism, or that seek to confront), they can choose which social groups are prioritized (dominant top-down, or bottom-up), and they can choose how to market them (a three-day run in a studio theatre for a niche audience, a month-long main stage run for a national audience). Not all gatekeepers are created equal though: just as there are power differentials for witnesses, major public institutions—such as the national theatre—often have greater market access and impact than local or fringe theatres and, due to longer runs and funding for archiving, greater longitudinal impact. This book thus considers the differences between institutional—and institutionalized—witness theatre and smaller-scale productions that, while not totally ephemeral, are more likely to remain at the level of embodied capital

Gatekeeping is often determined by economic trends. In Ireland, the turn toward a more inclusive public memory culture coincided with the greater affluence of the "Celtic Tiger" period (1993–2007). From this, we can see how economic context informs remembrance policy. One result, for example, is the 1994 official opening of the Irish War Memorial in Dublin commemorating the Irish soldiers who died fighting for the British Army in World War I. The memorial, initially completed in the 1930s, had its official opening delayed due to the outbreak of World War II; it was further delayed by both economic and postcolonial anxieties in the wake of the declaration of the Irish republic in 1949. In the 1990s the new national economic confidence created a context in which remembrance could become more inclusive, and the state became willing to expend national resources to recognize marginal memories and, through this investment, increase the marginal memory community's mnemonic and social capital.

More recently the Irish "Decade of Centenaries" (2012–22), covering the revolutionary period from insurrection to civil war and independence, has been avowedly inclusive of previously overlooked narratives of the national past, including women's suffrage and the 1913 workers' lockout, alongside Irish participation in World War I. Indeed, the "unheard" status of many of these personal and national stories has been one of the features selling them to an audience who might be assumed to be fatigued by the monolithic anticolonial narrative. The inclusion of other marginal narratives is not, however, to suggest that the mainstream narrative has been displaced—indeed, the Decade of Centenaries budget tells another story. With €48.6 million of the approximately €60m budget for the entire decade spent on 2016—the centenary of the 1916 Rising against the British—its scale is a clear demonstration that this event is the most important in terms of the top-down state-led commemoration program. Even the expansion of that narrative to include female combatants and civilian casualties did not undermine the importance of this central event, rather it seemed a canny marketing tool to make new the old story of the rebellion. The success of the 2016 program, which resulted in huge crowds attending the commemorative parades and other family-related events (making hotel bookings skyrocket in cost[28]), demonstrates that the combination of state expenditure and the festivalization of history results in significant public buy-in. The combination of public spending with national remembrance (what Bourdieu terms the coincidence of economic and social investment[29]) thus carries significant dividends for both the state (the confirmation of a national narrative of progress and of Irish identity) and the market (new consumers for new stories[30]) incentivizing gatekeepers to make "transmissible heritage" a high profile and prestigious product in the marketplace.[31]

When it comes to the work this book discusses, I focus on how gatekeepers decide which witnesses are allowed to have a voice in the market. As Vered Vinitzky-Seroussi and Chana Teeger put it, "the narration of certain memories and the silencing of others can oftentimes be conceptualized as the attempts of those with power to set the limits on what is speakable or unspeakable about the past."[32] As suggested by the example of the First World War in Ireland, cultural gatekeepers with this kind of power thus shape the memory marketplace. What I explore in this book is how gatekeepers can use their power to transform what has been previously held to be "unspeakable"—child abuse, sexual violence, torture—by deliberately creating platforms for the voices of previously silenced cohorts. In fact, the witness plays discussed here highlight how two dimensions of the marketplace *converge*—the commercial desire for audiences, with a balancing desire for authenticity (itself a market-friendly concept).

The "social turn" in the culture industry, of which witness plays are a major aspect, promotes performances that enhance the social good, which seek to combat "fake news," and which promise contact with the "real." Witness plays, which focus on voices of victims and survivors, meet both needs as they market themselves as socially conscious plays where audiences can both enjoy a theatrical catharsis and fulfil their responsibilities as citizens to bear witness. The popularity of this medium (a new cultural hegemony?) has been marked in recent years, so that at times it seems it's not just a memory boom, it's a witnessing boom—with a seemingly endless supply of producers and consumers.

Gatekeepers and competition are fundamental features of the marketplace—without some element of selectivity, the memory marketplace becomes an overwhelming space of excess. After all, as Bourdieu warns, "it is taken for granted that maximum growth and therefore productivity... are the ultimate and sole goal of human actions," and it is the same for the memory industry.[33] This excess, however, is not a sign of complete remembering, but rather a kind of forgetting. While growth in the memory field may mean the expansion of platforms for unheard and untold stories, particularly by those with marginal memories, at the same time, expansion leads to the risk of saturation. As Gunnthorunn Gudmundsdottir argues, the logic of total recall is a kind of forgetting—if we remember everything without any selectivity, nothing is nominated as being particularly memorable or meaningful.[34] We can find an echo of this sentiment in Brian Friel's play *Translations* (1980) as Hugh advises his anxious son Owen that "to remember everything is a form of madness."[35] We may, then, need competition as a mechanism for cultures to reflect what is most important to remember and, yes, to forget what is less important. It's also worth noting that the opposite—a lack of competition—is a feature of totalitarianism, a kind of "organised forgetting" and remembering.[36]

Competition is thus not a sign of the scarcity of memory, but a result of its abundance. What is in shorter supply is audience attention. The results of competition in the attention economy are therefore often unfair, mirroring the stratification of the social marketplace. The term "free market" thus misappropriates the term "free," given that the market is determined by preexisting social and political factors, from state regulation to private investment. As Rosanne Kennedy and Gillian Whitlock argue, we need paradigms that can account for how "social and institutional structures, and political and economic power, shape and produce individual and collective experiences [and narratives] of suffering."[37] At a cultural level, we know well that powerful producers determine the narrative; in Walter Benjamin's words, that powerful historical discourses "silence the memory of the defeated and powerless for whom the past is an uneven succession of fragmented and interrupted moments."[38] Moreover, we also know that consumption, "is a class institution."[39] Consumption in a stratified marketplace means that, as Baudrillard puts it, "the purchase, choice and use of objects are governed by purchasing power ... in short not everyone has the same objects, just as not everyone has the same ... chances."[40] As a counterpoint to competition, Michael Rothberg advances the principle of multidirectional memory—suggesting that through solidarity and connectivity, memory culture can create enhanced platforms for multidirectional articulations of remembrance. This is a powerful way of understanding the solidarity that can be produced between different kinds of witnesses and, in the theatre, between the performer and the audience (and, indeed, between audience members). Rothberg's multidirectional model of memory culture, however, does not fully acknowledge the role of market forces in both production and consumption. Financial investment—whether it's the money to buy the land that a museum stands on, the backing to create a play, or the disposable income to purchase a theatre ticket—propels, shapes, and limits the articulation of remembrance. Likewise, audiences have to be selective—they cannot attend everything—and marketing departments are well aware of the need to capture their attention, investing financial and cultural resources in building audience share. If a play about twenty-first-century refugee memories, which also evokes the post–World War II migration crisis, cannot find a company to produce it, or a theatre to back it, or a grant to support it, or a catchy advertising campaign, or audiences to attend it, then its articulation and enactment of multidirectional remembrance is shut down because of its failure to accrue either economic or social capital. Competition is thus inherent within the market, whether it is competition for limited economic resources or for equally limited audience attention. Inequality in capital and the disproportionate power of certain social groups are thus major barriers in the cultural memory marketplace, undermining, just as in the social and political marketplaces, ethical principles of equality of representation and access. Indeed, as we will see, plays embody this competitive dynamic, often staging the competition between victims and perpetrators for both cultural and symbolic capital. Gatekeepers—whether funders, theatre makers, or witnessing audiences—are thus key in adjudicating how those competitions play out.

The Audience Consumer vs the Audience Witness

Given the role of social and political capital in shaping and mediating the marketplace, how can it avoid becoming a reflection of the desires and outlook of only an elite band of gatekeepers and consumers? The role of the consumer is key here—if the marketplace is not simply a space of top-down practices, but is driven by consumer demand and bottom-up practices, then there remains the possibility for consumers—who are not a homogenous group, and who are marked by power differentials themselves—to direct or counteract top-down investment and practices.

Lizabeth Cohen outlines distinctions between types of consumers, identifying two general types: the "customer consumer" and the "citizen consumer." Cohen argues that the customer consumer is motivated by the desire to consume, and their activity and output are summed up as "shopping" (pure economic capital). In contrast, the citizen consumer is motivated by the desire that their consumption can generate a social good, so that their activity may be consuming (or shopping), but their output is consuming plus social impact (the transferral of social capital).[41] Cohen's model is an important development in understanding how consumers operate, and a necessary move away from the view of consumers as "passive human resources."[42] In terms of the specifics of how memory performances are consumed, I deploy Cohen's binary and add two more terms relevant for discussing theatre: the "audience-consumer" and the "audience-witness." The audience-consumer is there to watch and enjoy the show, to have a good time, to expend their economic power investing in cultural performances that make them feel good. The audience-witness is driven by many of the same motivations, but with the added dimension of a sense of performing a public duty—this is less joyless than it sounds; as I explore in the following chapters, there is a feel-good dividend for audiences who invest in performances that make the world a better place.

The recent explosion in authenticity in culture (marking not only theatre but, notably, the whole heritage sector), may be read as a way for consumption and ethical witnessing to intersect, through the creation of more spaces for bottom-up initiatives and unheard stories. Though arguably this has the potential to make the marketplace a fairer place, it is doubtful that consumption in itself can change the structural imbalances of power within either the memory marketplace or the larger society. The philanthropic consumption model, embodied by initiatives such as Fair Trade, may set up the consumer, and the act of consumption, as a force for social good, but it can be ameliorative at best. It's also not the case that all audience consumers will invest in an ethical model of consumption, and it is thus far from automatic that all audience members attending a show that brands itself as ethical will become witnesses. We must assume, then, that plays will always have an audience made up of both consumers and witnesses (and all those in between).

Even in a marketplace full of citizen consumers/audience-witnesses, the marketplace is not necessarily a fair or stable place. Indeed, fluctuation and instability are inherent features of the market. After all, the market is driven by constant renewal, through a process of "creative destruction" (innovation),[43] whereby old narratives are discarded and new narratives introduced. The downside, then, of assuming a model in which the consumer has power, is that consumer trends will always change—and since novelty and competition are defining features of all consumption, access to the marketplace for minority voices is therefore always dependent on changing demands. Though creative destruction can lead to the overturning of oppressive narratives, for example in the case of the emergence of a new collective memory of institutional child abuse by the Catholic Church in Ireland in the 1990s and 2000s, just as quickly, the market can move on to yet another story, again limiting the space available to particular memory groups and disempowering those who are not currently in demand.

Often the individual consumer and the mass market are driven not by the principle of social good but by the allure of authenticity. As Gilmore and Pine put it, authenticity is what consumers really want.[44] Authenticity is a tricky object—on the one hand it suggests a veracity that cannot be bought or sold, yet on the other hand the "authenticity brand" is a driver of major commercial trends. This brand has multiple meanings that consumers attach to it, including the ability to secure identity through the careful curation of their consumption of authenticity, and the attraction of making consumers feel safe while simultaneously in contact with "the real."[45] Yet authenticity is not a stable concept, indeed both authenticity and the demands that shape it shift with market trends (creative destruction, again). As Christopher Howard states, "both the age of authenticity and consumerism centre on a restless individualism and the value of choice in an ever-changing market of consumable objects and experiences."[46] Indeed, as this book argues, even when a theatrical show is highly "authentic" this does not guarantee attracting an audience to make it commercially viable (which is vital even when a show is subsidized). Market awareness thus always mediates the kinds of aesthetic and performance strategies used to engage and satisfy an audience—and authenticity, while a major branding device in itself, is just one element of marketing theatre. Other strategies include the promise of novelty, the performance of trauma, creating a space for catharsis, marketing the show as culturally prestigious and/or as satisfying a social or political need (e.g., for knowledge or public accountability), and downplaying the potentially negative impacts on audiences by limiting the narrative or creating an uplifting ending.

As behavioral economics has demonstrated, consumers make decisions led by their emotions rather than purely based on rational calculations[47]—in the case of plays that witness painful memories, the promise of emotional expression/catharsis/fulfilment is combined with the expectation of social engagement, thereby suggesting that this form of theatre can deliver on both grounds, in theory being doubly attractive to consumers as a powerful mode of identity-signaling.[48] I make this point knowing at the same time that the reactions of many friends when I suggest going to see one of these plays—"sounds a bit depressing"—means that the double hit of emotion plus politics is not necessarily attractive to all consumers. When consumers do buy into the cultural trend for witnessing memory, then we see the full impact of consumption as an active influencer of market trends. Audiences are the target for the performers' acts of witnessing, and audiences are the ones who will remediate the memories being performed (creating what's known as market "surplus value").[49]

The Active Consumer and the Question of Power

The question of audience power is a knotty one. Does, for example, the idea of the citizen consumer/audience-witness mean the consumer is a powerful actor in the marketplace? Arjun Appadurai argues not: "merchandising is so subtle that the consumer is consistently helped to believe that he or she is an actor, where in fact he or she is at best a chooser."[50] Appadurai locates the "real seat of agency" and power with the producer and other actors within the market who decide what to produce, how to market it, and so on, all of which are behind-the-scenes actions that contribute to the illusion of consumer agency.[51] I have a mixed reaction to the view of consumers as "choosers." On the one hand, consumers do not have input into what cultural work is promoted to them, and how—indeed the rise of authenticity as a marketing tool alone should make us suspicious of how the outcome consumers desire (contact with "the real") is actually not the outcome, but the medium of the real message (the world is a consumer playground). As I discuss throughout the book, consumer agency in choosing which theatres to visit, and which shows to patronize, should not be mistaken for real social or political action or activism. As Baudrillard scathingly puts it, when audiences consume suffering all too often what happens is that "they swap their distress with the misery of the poor, both of them sustaining each other."[52] This is not a relationship productive of social good, but of social exploitation. On the other hand, at the very least, audiences *do exercise choice*. I am biased here, I realize—as a critic and teacher, I am a major consumer of theatre and so, for the sake of retaining passion in what I do, I have to believe that audiences are not powerless: I believe we can be active witnesses.

Exercising consumer power is not restricted to choosing which show to buy a ticket for and thus influencing the real economy of the cultural memory marketplace. Consuming, or even witnessing, a show does not mean being uncritical about it. On the contrary, critical witnesses add surplus value and further capital to a production by interpreting and responding to what they see and hear. Jacques Rancière argues against the view that the spectator is passive because they are "immobile" in their seat—instead recognizing the "activity peculiar to the spectator. Every spectator is already an actor in her story."[53] The audience as not just witness, but also actor, takes the idea of the active spectator further. This formulation understands that the audience-witness always interprets what they are seeing and hearing via their own story, their own subjectivity, their own position in the marketplace. John Durham Peters interprets the spectators' subjectivity as being vital to their act of witnessing, because for Peters it is only in retelling or reproducing the original act of witness that the spectator themselves witnesses: "an active witness must first have been a passive one."[54] This view chimes with Stuart Hall's reception theory of media, in which audiences not only receive but actively construct identities in relation to media; Jukka Törrönen terms this the "mutual modelling" of media and audiences.[55] This audience-forward reading of reception does not equate to the power to set the agenda, it is a reactive, "soft" power; yet in the moment of the performance, and in its aftermath, it is nevertheless a performance of consumer agency. It is thus not as simple as labeling some consumers active and others passive—with power or without power—but instead identifying the multiple ways in which audiences perform different roles, consecutively and concurrently, in the marketplace.

Reflecting on consumers as agentic, and the performance of witnessing as an active role, leads us to acknowledging that audiences also carry out labor: the work of watching, listening, processing, and reacting to what is being performed. The labor entailed in spectating a show, often most obvious in experimental or avant-garde theatre, means that the audience are (to different degrees) cocreators of the mnemonic capital that the show produces. The labor of the audience—what Harvie calls "prosumerism"[56]—demonstrates how vital the consumer is, not just to the marketplace, but to the production of meaning and thus capital; without the audience, the performance is not only unseen, but unproductive.

Audience agency also means that spectators may choose not to witness. One reason for this choice is that they may not invest their belief or trust in the testimony being performed. Paul Ricoeur points to the role of the audience in determining which testimony is seen as trustworthy,[57] while Elizabeth Jelin points out that audiences only accord authority to certain witnesses.[58] While gatekeepers can influence how an audience encounters a firsthand witness, it is ultimately up to the audience how well the show does in the marketplace.

When Jay Winter asks "Who has the right to speak of the violent past?"[59] he seems to address the ethical issue of rights (who grants this right, who guarantees it?). But he is also raising, of course, a series of questions about the marketplace: is there a market for stories of "the violent past," which firsthand witnesses and gatekeepers have the capital to command consumer investment in those stories, and how does consumer investment create the necessary memory capital to institutionalize those stories in remembrance culture? The agency of both the audience-consumer and the audience-witness is therefore not only necessary to the operation of the market, but to who gets remembered and who forgotten.

From Consumers to Witnesses?

The debate around the relative activity and passivity of audiences emerges from the question of what kinds of witnessing audiences perform. As Lisa Fitzpatrick argues, the "increasing emphasis on trauma and traumatic experience in arts practice" has led to an equal rise in the "use of the term 'witness' in place of spectator."[60] No longer do we ask audiences to simply watch or listen, now the expectation is that audiences will provide a much larger service—that of witnessing, a term and identity that, as Fitzpatrick points out, emerges from the relatively new dominance of trauma in the arts. We are in an era of witnessing others' pain.

Dori Laub defines witnessing as having three levels: from the firsthand witness of subjective experience, to secondhand witnesses to others' subjective experience, to thirdhand witnesses who observe the testifying process.[61] Laub argues for the importance of testifying and witnessing in the wake of painful experience, and the importance of being an "authentic witness" by recognizing the truth of the experience being testified to. Without all three levels of witnessing functioning authentically, Laub argues, there is a "collapse of witnessing" whereby neither the experience nor its subjective pain are recognized.[62] Tamar Ashuri and Amit Pinchevski, likewise, view witnessing as a complex field in which there are three zones: (1) the eyewitness, (2) the mediator, and (3) the audience.[63] This tripartite schema demonstrates that successful witnessing involves the event being seen by one person, who then testifies about their experience to a second person (who did not experience the event), and that second person then choosing how to mediate the testimony for the third form of witness, the audience. This is a complex performance chain, akin to the making of theatre in fact, as the information about the event must go through two stages in order to be communicated to the audience. It is also a perpetuating performance, in which the audience further mediates the testimony to another person, creating new audiences in turn (surplus value). Laub adds an additional requirement to the definition of witnessing: positing the witness as someone who can step outside the totalizing and dehumanizing frame of reference in which the event takes place.[64] The witness must therefore not only be able to identify what is happening within the frame, but also, in stepping outside it, be able to achieve a greater understanding and perspective on the suffering caused by the event. Acknowledging these different levels to, and articulations of, witnessing is important to understanding how these performances function—and also to identifying how they may become blocked if one or more of the levels does not flow smoothly or clearly. As Peters argues, "witnessing is an intricately tangled practice."[65] Naming the audience as "witnesses" then demands not only that they be active, but that they pursue a particular agenda in how they spectate and what their response will be.

Aleida Assman's definition of the "moral witness" explicitly emphasizes this ethical dimension, defining witnessing as an act that goes beyond the body of the victim testifying to include the secondary witnesses in the audience.[66] As Pat Palmer argues, "the community of compassionate spectatorship which pain creates is a partisan community, united in solidarity against those inflicting pain."[67] Peters inflects this further, stating that "to witness an event is to be responsible in some way to it."[68] The entanglement of witnessing is thus imagined by these critics as more than a stratified field—instead reading it as a collaborative and communal practice. How does this apply to theatre specifically? Does its communal nature automatically create the setting for witnessing? Diana Taylor suggests it does, arguing that "witnessing is transferable—the theater ... can make witnesses of others."[69]

What does this actually mean? In the theatre, we tend to sit surrounded by others, but is that truly communal? Bourdieu's frame for economic and social exchanges suggests yes: "a two-way relation is always in fact a three-way relation, between the two agents and the social space within which they are located."[70] Becker and Murphy argue that consumer behavior is always led by others, whether fashion-setting or simply because consumption is always a social interaction.[71] So do these social settings necessarily convert the audience into witnesses? Karine Shaefer asks this important question, "Does listening to testimony ... [create] spectatorial witnesses"? The answer may not live up to our ideal wish for the moral witness—as Shaefer puts it, "any attempt to unilaterally equate spectators with witnesses collapses under the multivalency of audience reactions."[72] Likewise, Caroline Wake objects to the automatic titling of spectators as witnesses, in particular the way "the word witness is becoming a generalised, semi-sacralised term" employed "to emphasise the historical importance or emotional impact of a particular performance."[73] Wake calls attention to the emotive power and marketability of the word "witness" and its connotations of ritualized attention and catharsis: "In our eagerness to promote the ethical potential of performance [we ignore that] though primary witnessing is implicated in the ethics of vision and visibility, it is not necessarily an ethical mode of spectatorship per se."[74] Blanket use of the term witnessing distorts the multivalent realities of audiences and the performance of spectating. In order to avoid this distortion, Wake, like Peters, argues that we should more accurately think of witnessing as something that happens after the performance—it is through remediation of the testimony that the ethical level of witnessing is achieved. Whether or not that remediation occurs cannot be controlled but only guessed at.

The interaction between audience and stage, spectator and performer is thus not a definite or controlled interface. Yet it is essential that we consider how the presence of the audience functions as a key determiner of meaning. As Alan Filewood argues, we need to start to ask "whether audiences are local communities in formation, legitimising communities summoned by the performance, or metonymic agents."[75] We can extend that to challenge, as Rancière does, the automatic assumption that theatre represents a site of community at all—though the auditorium may be filled with people, they do not necessarily cohere into a single "we."[76]

Asserting that being an audience member is, as Gareth White says, a "social process" has direct implications for *how* we witness, as White argues that during a show "audience behaviour is guided as well as audience perception."[77] It may be then that the feeling of being "allied" that Jill Dolan hopes for is what guides audiences to perform as moral witnesses.[78] Solo, in the marketplace, individuals might act in one way, but in the context of a group where particular norms are developed (responding sympathetically, laughing, applauding) individuals can be influenced in particular ways (analogous to Jan Assmann's concept of "social mediation"[79]). Very little work on this exists in relation to theatre, but both consumer research and social psychology suggest that group behavior is a significant determining factor in an individual's adherence to "ethical" norms.[80] Rosanne Kennedy also points to how cultural texts "educate" the public in how to respond appropriately.[81] Viewed this way, theatre is perhaps the ultimate modality to create what Marianne Hirsch terms "an affiliative space of remembering" in which performers and audiences each strive to successfully perform the second and third levels of witnessing.[82] However, it is debatable how voluntary this performance is, as Susan Sontag contests, "strictly speaking there is no such thing as collective memory—part of the same family of spurious notions as collective guilt. But there is collective instruction."[83] Is the communal just a context, then, for compulsory collective instruction? This sense of top-down direction also underscores Attilio Favorini's statement that theatre "organize[s] us into a group of rememberers."[84]

Against this background of guided behavior we must acknowledge that the theatrical organization of the audience is always in dialogue with their preexisting beliefs (which may be either aligned with, or oppositional to, the show they are attending), so that audience members' social position "including the intersectionalities of race, class, gender, and age, significantly inform how they read" and interpret what they are being presented with, or asked to witness to."[85] This point brings us back to consumer agency and the power of choice—because while it is valuable to recognize how powerful the communal setting of theatre is, and the power of the call to witnessing created by being part of a group, audience choice remains. In other words, however coercive the social setting of the theatre, the possibility remains that audiences will actively choose not to be instructed, not to witness, or to witness divergently.

What Are We Witnessing?

What is it that a theatre audience is witnessing? This book takes as its subject a genre of witness theatre that can broadly be termed documentary or, following Carol Martin, "the theatre of the real."[86] As will be discussed in chapter 1, this form of theatre aims to present documentary stories, often through verbatim testimony, to an audience who will bear witness to its truths and, through their collective presence, validate those stories and experiences being performed. The sharing of testimony allows the person whose story is being performed—whether by an actor, through a veil of anonymity, or by the person themselves—to move away from being portrayed as an object of representation, toward instead portraying their experience as an agent of their own lives and memories. This firsthand contact with "the real" is what gives this form its social, cultural, and political power, generating multiple forms of capital through a complex balancing of authenticity (the witness) and mediation (the performance). Testimonial witness plays often, as discussed further below, involve witnesses and audiences in performances of painful memory. As such, testimony, as Anne Cubilié and Carl Good state, "emerges not merely *as a result of* the destabilization of narrative, memory, identity and history by trauma, but also *as a response to* trauma, a response which evokes—and ventures—the possibilities of language, literature and ethical community in a resistance to effacement from juridical, literary, psychic and cultural fields."[87] What I appreciate in this theorization of testimony is the refusal to equate painful experience with silence. As this book will show, testimonial witness plays enable fulsome articulation of varieties of memory and experience from pain to joy, devastation to resilience, loss to growth. And this, perhaps, is where the appeal lies for consumers who are not only seeking in the theatre to "find pleasure in the un-pleasurable" but who seek to invest in narratives and performances that access the breadth of another person's experiences.[88]

In some senses memory plays perform the relationship between memory and identity itself—in that memory and identity are both inherently performative and discursively constructed and depend on, following Judith Butler, repetition in order to become inscribed as normative.[89] Freddie Rokem argues that audiences for memory plays are witnessing the time lapse of history as they eavesdrop on testimony about past events.[90] Rokem calls this a "'ritual' of resurrection."[91] In *Memory in Play*, Favorini describes theatre "as a placeholder for memory," suggesting that theatre performs a social function in remembering on behalf of the audience—so that they may revisit, through ritual, past events they may not have the capacity to remember themselves.[92] These rituals however are only validated by the presence of the audience—and so in some ways what is being performed and witnessed is the presence of the audience. Without an audience, as theatre-maker Teya Sepinuck argues, there is no testimony.[93] So we attend the theatre to be reminded of our own existence.

Is this always the case? Is the same call upon the audience being made by Beckett as it is by a documentary play in which women testify about having been raped? In fact, can we even say that a memory play necessarily calls an audience to action? (Are there plays that ask for our passivity? Plays that do not, perhaps, even require an audience?)

In writing this book, it has been difficult to resist the word "should" (audiences *should* do particular things). In discussions about how we might witness injustice it is easy to slip into moralizing. Indeed, it's hard to resist using the term "we" (even when that imagined communal identity stretches across national and temporal boundaries) simply because of the rhetorical imperative invoked by the moral imperative of witnessing.

Allen Feldman is suspicious of many memory performances that depend on the inevitable "moralizing periodization" of postevent depictions of violence, pain or injustice.[94] These moral positions may call for simplified reactions and affects. One particular pitfall of this trend is that the emotive nature of so many witness plays means that audiences may feel they are being called on to react emotionally rather than intellectually. There is thus a tight line for theatre makers to walk, so that, in Hirsch's terms, the work of art can "touch us without paralyzing us ... galvaniz[ing] memory in the interest of activist engagement for justice and social change."[95] The sustained focus of this book is thus on the aesthetic strategies chosen by theatre makers: how they create witnesses, how and why they call on audiences to behave in particular ways. Paramount here is whether, as Peters puts it, performances of witnessing "call for our aid [or] our appreciation; our duty [or] our pleasure."[96] If the audience is allotted subjectivity, then does that also hold true for the onstage witness? Because, as

Feldman argues, "no matter how empathic the gaze" of the audience member, the process of witnessing is inevitably often an objectifying one. This brings us to the risk of witnessing—that the witnessing dividend accrues not to the person being witnessed, but to the person consuming.[97]

The Real Inequality

Perhaps these questions of consumer power actually divert attention away from the real subjects of disempowerment—those being represented. We cannot assume that just because someone, or their story, is represented on stage that they have power as witnesses. As many critics of discourses around victimhood argue, power is distributed unequally between those who are represented and those doing the representing. The important question about power and exploitation does not center on the consumer, but pivots on how often, in fact, the subject of the performance is exploited. In the desire for authenticity, "the real," and stories of personal hardship, the experiences of survivors of abuse, victims of sexual violence, and protestors against injustice, become market commodities. As Jasbir Puar argues, performances of empathetic or charitable selfhood are used by gatekeepers to accrue symbolic cultural and social capital without any proper recompense or benefit to the survivors themselves.[98] This is not to be undersold, as Allen states, "the cultural production of memory depends increasingly" on the "intensification of immaterial, precarious and forced labour."[99] A witness's labor may be rewarded by consumer interest in their stories and the validation and potential support this generates, but the real benefit is to the gatekeepers' profit margins and the already-privileged consumers' performance of being a good citizen. Precarity in the marketplace is thus not solved, but actually worsened, by some performances of witnessing.

In an ideal world, we can hope to set against the inequalities and disempowerments engendered by the competitive, top-down, and profit-driven nature of the marketplace, the citizen consumer's desire to exercise their critical faculties, and to see change enacted—and the possibility that they may further enact those changes themselves outside the boundaries of both theatrical and remembrance cultures, thus shifting the balance of power in the marketplace. As Jill Dolan encouragingly argues, we must believe in "the potential of different kinds of performance to inspire moments in which audiences feel allied with each other, and with a broader, more capacious sense of a public, in which social discourse articulates the possible rather than the insurmountable obstacles to human potential."[100]

It is also important to note the possibility for work that does not speak on behalf of the survivor, but that is made by the survivor. This book includes discussion of performances in which different stakeholders get to speak—from victims of physical, sexual, and state violence who script and perform their own narratives, to activists who campaign for social justice. Overall, however, it is important to acknowledge that most of the culture we consume is made by one group, about another group. The stakes of aestheticizing another's pain, and the risk of appropriating suffering, are thus very real concerns, and I set out to examine them in the context of power and capital. Appropriation does not have to be a destructive process; there is potential for audience witnesses to make the problem their own without, in the process, appropriating the moral capital of the victim/survivor.

It is vital that we acknowledge the inequalities—social, political, and economic—of the marketplace and the ways that market practices entail the silencing of the memories of particular social groups in order to amplify and bolster others, or that exploit the suffering of some in order to generate economic and social capital for those who already hold power. However, so that we do not despair, we also need at the same time to remind ourselves that these inequalities do not preclude the potential for positive change. Indeed the starkness of the market inequalities around not just social issues, but also memory issues, may call on the audience to do the opposite—to become activists. In this reading, we can salvage precarity as a potential ground for new political subjectivities and solidarity, though, as Rosalind Gill and Andy Pratt acknowledge, that is itself "a precarious project,"[101] one that risks not only instrumentalizing the disenfranchised, but further burdening this cohort with insatiable expectations of their immaterial labor.

The Witness to Pain

Identifying that the audience is being called on does not quite answer the question of *what* it is that a theatre audience is being asked to witness, or indeed why audiences are being cast in the role of witnesses at all. As suggested by Fitzpatrick above, the rise of the term witness is linked to the rise of trauma: albeit witness theatre offers audiences a range of experiences, more and more audiences are being asked to witness pain. Indeed, Sepinuck argues that this has reached such a level that many potential theatrical witnesses fear they have not "suffered enough" and that they should therefore not testify as their stories do not "count."[102] Indeed, in some instances it may be that consumers are simply attracted by, and marketers exploit, what has become a "trauma brand." This brand is linked to positive social values, such as empathy and the production of social relations, but it is also at risk of flattening and commodifying personal experiences, leading us to ask more questions of how trauma operates in performance. Is our concept of witnessing linked exclusively to painful memory? Do we expect, or even demand, performances of suffering? Is this the real impact of the consumer?

And what is the effect on the audience of being asked to witness pain—either firsthand (in the case of autoperformance) or secondhand (via actors)? It is troubling to consider these effects because, as Michal Givoni asserts, witnessing so often entails being "overtaken by a performance of trauma and loss."[103] Givoni is referring here to firsthand witnessing where an individual testifies to their own experience of trauma—but if we expect an audience to enter into a collaborative witnessing relationship, and to remediate the testimony they have heard, does this description of witnessing not also apply to the audience?

I am wary of the idea of secondary trauma because it is important to recognize the distance between the event and the secondhand witness and hence the relative safety of that second witness—nevertheless, in transferring the responsibility of witnessing from performer/testifier to audience, something of the performance of pain must also be transferred. In the auditorium, audience members may react with fear, or tears, or anger—a range of emotions linked to trauma—and when it comes to remediating the testimony their reactions may equally be to be afraid again, or to cry again, or rail again at the injustice they have witnessed. These may only be surface-level emotions, exhausted by the performance, but, still, they affect the kind of witnessing that is happening. This leads to what Carol Martin argues is the key problem with memory plays that "instead of offering [audiences] analysis or responsibility, [leave them] to sentimentally weep."[104] As Carole-Anne Upton also argues, staging trauma can lead theatre makers to opt for "a sympathetic portrayal of victims of injustice rather than an interrogation of [social] responsibilities."[105] Given the tendency for sympathy over criticism, the expected activity of the audience thus becomes about emotional expiation rather than political action—meaning that trauma theatre's potential, as Fitzpatrick puts it, "is often limited [as] the desired transformation is actually interpersonal" not political.[106] This form of personal transformation is a worthwhile dividend of the labor that spectators perform at the theatre, but it is a benefit that primarily profits the individual, not the collective, and the witnessing that occurs will primarily drive further consumption, rather than social change. Moreover, the assumption that affect always entails "pleasant" emotions of solidarity and other "affirmative feelings" stubbornly ignores the fact that affect in fact often involves less pleasant emotions—anxiety, frustration, competitiveness—and that while it can be used to mobilize positive forces for change, it can also be used to "collude and reproduce" negative social attitudes such as racism.[107]

The empathic response by an audience is often assumed to be a necessary context or prerequisite for witnessing, but the recent dominance of empathy not as a tool, but as a *mode*, of witnessing actually limits the range of audience engagement. Many of the case studies in this book are based on documentary sources, or performed using autoperformance—where the performer onstage is actually a firsthand witness. This allows me to discuss the connections between the performance and the world outside, and to argue that witnessing by both performer and audience member is capable of making a link between the aesthetic representation of injustice and actual injustice. But empathy can be a stumbling block. Though Rokem argues that the awareness of an actor mediating the character's victimization enables both identificatory and critical responses, I would argue that the turn toward "the real," combined with the "complete absorption" that characterizes empathy, make it difficult for audiences to avail of any critical distance in making judgements about the performances they see.[108] This is why Kabosh Theatre Company in Belfast, though they base their work on documentary and verbatim research, always translate this into a fictional framework, in order to create critical space for both the original memory and the audience to interrogate that memory as a kind of public history (which is more available for critical discussion than someone's personal memory).[109] This is a tricky maneuver as fictional plots and characters, in losing the impact of "the real," have to work differently in order to establish the authority of the witness text—so that audiences don't simply dismiss what is being performed as fictional and therefore not applicable to life outside the theatre, or requiring witness. Of course, theatre productions—no matter how real—always go through multiple stages of mediation, so that audiences are always only seeing the outcome of firsthand witnessing, a witnessing text, and never the "real thing." Nevertheless, the "live" dimension of theatre, in which audiences watch a real person on stage and not via a screen, can occlude the function of mediation, particularly in the case of testimonial theatre, as its reliance on verbatim material and autoperformance produces a kind of invisibly mediated firsthand witnessing. The pain being performed onstage hence has an unavoidable affective power—this really happened, and now it's happening again, *right in front of me*. The emphasis on trauma and the real thus makes it easier for the producer to create impact, but harder for the audience to think about how they are being impacted, and to translate their spectatorship into acts of *critical* witnessing.

The Victim as the Perfect Witness and
Affective Witnessing in the Marketplace

In this cultural moment, it is easy to see how victimhood and suffering have become the currency of so much popular culture, and a route to establishing the authority of the witnessing work of art in the memory marketplace. Indeed, Rothberg argues that trauma as a universal condition has become "a form of cultural capital that bestows moral privilege."[110] The victim thus becomes the perfect moral witness. This is a turn from the previous treatment of trauma, which silenced victims in a marketplace that privileged nostalgia on the one hand and progress on the other. Now we live in an "empire of trauma."[111] The shift in the status of the victim has led to the rise of the victim as a valuable commodity—as Peters puts it, "Not surprisingly, there has been something of a scramble to capture the prestige of the victim-witness."[112] Victim prestige is produced by a combination of their testimony as a novelty product in the market and the symbolic capital conferred by their firsthand presence and suffering.

The market dominance of sympathy and empathy can thus be read as both enabling and disabling witnessing. Lauren Berlant's work on compassion is illuminating here, as she argues that calls to action that utilize these emotions depend on privilege: "In operation, compassion is a term denoting privilege: the sufferer is *over there*. You, the compassionate one, have a resource that would alleviate someone else's suffering."[113] It is a generous impulse to want to alleviate another's suffering, but the question then becomes—how? Berlant goes on, "When we want to rescue X, are we thinking of rescuing everyone like X, or is it a singular case that we see?"[114] Further, as Rosanne Kennedy argues, the risk of compassion is that it may "displace efforts that could be more productively put into working for social justice."[115] These empathic dynamics thus make the outcomes of even citizen-consumer witnessing ambivalent.

Let me give an example: in *Sanctuary*, a verbatim production by Theatre of Witness (2013, Northern Ireland), several asylum seekers testified to an audience about their reasons for seeking asylum—including familial breakdown, death threats, and gang rape. At the end of the show, which was obviously highly emotive, postcards were distributed to the audience to write to the UK home secretary so that each of us could remediate the testimony we'd received, and call on the officials with hard power to grant asylum to these particular individuals. These postcards were a way for audiences to act in a meaningful way in response to what they had witnessed—to become witnesses themselves. It held the promise of political action, a way to balance the emotional reaction during the moment of the play. Direct political actions like these can be highly effective—yet the worry remained for me that as witnesses we were not making a decision based on the political facts, nor were we protesting the structural inequalities of the system, but merely making a plea for one person (X) based on our sympathetic response to her plight (but not all people like X). And in answering the call to sympathize, and then signing the postcard, were we also appropriating her story to enrich our own—in Puar's terms, was cultural capital accruing to us, rather than to the "other"?[116] And if we turn to Landsberg's model of prosthetic memory, which gives us the feeling of memory as an extra "limb," we need to ask—are we, as consumers, simply shopping for feel-good limbs?

At one point in *Sanctuary*, during the female asylum seeker's testimony, she became unable to deliver her lines and another performer had to take over. The woman's onstage silence provoked many people in the audience to cry—and I couldn't help but think that this was not either fair to her (clearly she was still traumatized) or fair to the audience (in the wake of such an emotional performance, it is very difficult to say "I want to think about it before signing the postcard"). And this brings us back to agency—was the postcard signing an indication of being an active or a passive audience, was it an act of witnessing or not? And once the card had been signed and given to a volunteer, were we *done*? Was that, as Berlant puts it, "the apex of affective agency among strangers"?[117]

Like Berlant, Givoni questions the capability of witnessing to solve political problems, suspicious of how witnessing is currently marketed as "the most available solution for an increasingly pressing need to cope with political evil."[118] Both these critics instead see affective witnessing not as the solution but a form of amelioration. This is doubly the case when we consider the relatively small scale of the theatre audience—as Upton argues, theatre "does not constitute the public sphere in the way that mass media and particularly television can."[119] Indeed, the theatre of painful memory represents a potentially even smaller-scale market segment. Even a popular show, which tours and enjoys high market impact, cannot change the market structures—or the political and social inequalities beyond the memory marketplace. In fact, if we return to the idea that each "untold story" derives much of its popularity from consumers who constantly crave novelty in content and form, we can then understand why the rise in, for example, theatre shows that perform stories of injustice based on gender or racial inequality do not change the dominance of white patriarchal culture. Instead of actually changing the marketplace, these narratives create new niche market segments for audiences that want to consume those narratives—thereby expanding, but not fundamentally changing, the market.[120] Segmentation has been a feature of markets for many decades, as a response to overcapacity that, in turn, creates a need for "market differentiation and for the discovery of new niche" market segments.[121] In this model, then, consumer demand leads to the creation of market segments, rather than the decentralization of power.

Hope, Witnessing, and the Marketplace

Do all these limits make theatrical witnessing redundant? I point to all the potentialities of witnessing with a sense of optimism, and I note all the contradictions with a heavy heart. But overall, I believe that even in a crowded and consumption-driven marketplace, witnessing memory can make a difference. I love theatre, and I believe in its transformative power; I believe that we do have the opportunity for community at the theatre; and I believe that theatre can make us better citizens, as well as witnesses. Like Dolan, I see in the choice of audiences to watch live performances as a group "potential for intersubjectivity not only between the performer and spectators, but among the audience as well."[122] Out of that intersubjectivity may grow the grounds of real change. I offer two examples of effective memory plays as a way of gesturing toward the utopian possibilities of theatrical witnessing in practice.[123]

In *By Heart* (2015), the Portuguese theatre maker Tiago Rodriguez enlists the audience in a memory collaboration. Rodriguez invites ten audience volunteers to sit onstage with him, and to learn "by heart" one of Shakespeare's sonnets: "Sonnet 30," which begins "When to the sessions of sweet silent thought, I summon up remembrance of things past." Though only ten individuals move onto the stage (each entrusted to memorize a single line) the entire audience is involved in this project, as we recite each line with Rodriguez and the volunteers, until at the end of the show, the full poem is memorized and recited. Interspersed with the repetition of each line, Rodriguez tells other stories of the importance of memory and witness: the story of the Russian writer Boris Pasternak, who was threatened with arrest, and who risked disaster by standing up at a public congress in Russia. Yet instead of giving a speech, or reciting his own work, all Pasternak said was a number, the number of the Shakespearean sonnet he had translated from English to Russian. And when Pasternak said "30," the audience at the Stalin congress stood and recited the poem in Russian. This action, as Rodriguez puts it, "said everything. It said—you can't touch us." Instead, touch is mobilized in positive ways—through the solidarity of the audiences, then and now.

In *By Heart*, Rodriguez does not tell his stories of memory as abstract or historical parables. Instead, he involves the audience as active witnesses and cocreators of meaning. The collaborative witnessing achieved, through listening to stories and reciting the poem, has the effect of expanding the meaning of collective memory to acknowledge the trauma of fascism and also hope: the ability of people to unify in a common purpose and achieve something larger than the sum of their parts through the joint act of memory and witnessing. The memorization and recitation of "Sonnet 30" by the end of the show felt like an achievement, and every time I have recited it since, it invokes my memory of that act of witnessing, as well as summoning to mind the potential for audiences who want to remember to make a difference.

By Heart embodies and enacts so many of the principles of witnessing that underpin my optimism about theatre, and memory plays in particular. Yet it is in many ways a very different play from those discussed in this book: though there are stories in *By Heart* about oppression and sadness, it is a comic show. Rodriguez enlists the audience's support through humor and the shared experiences of laughter, rather than tears. This is deliberate—indeed, one of the funniest jokes of the show is when a volunteer's memory falters and his line is forgotten; Rodriguez turns to the volunteer and says "if you forget something, don't worry—it's very good for the performance; the audience always loves to watch failure." The laugh of recognition (and culpability) resounds in the theatre. So it is perhaps salutary to note that this witness play relies for its impact on the joyful practice of creativity and collective remembering. Does this mean we were not witnesses, though, in the sense I have discussed up until now? Does witnessing only count if it is to suffering? I think not—the principle of *By Heart* is the recognition of the joint importance of attention and memory, and so while it may not ask us to witness current injustice, it does answer Vladimir's painful demand in *Waiting for Godot* that the powerless be witnessed with compassion and care. And it also provides the audience with evidence of their own ability and power as witnesses, rather than simply as consumers.

By Heart revolves around making the audience visible—as a core part of what is being performed, and how that performance is witnessed. Another theatrical moment that made the audience visible came on November 19, 2016, during a curtain call to the US Broadway hit musical *Hamilton* by Lin-Manuel Miranda. Actor Brandon Victor Dixon stepped forward on the stage and quieted the audience's applause. Speaking directly to the auditorium, and deliberately going "off script," Dixon spoke on behalf of the cast of *Hamilton* to address one of the show's spectators: US vice president-elect Mike Pence. Dixon called on Pence, saying: "We, sir—we—are the diverse America who are alarmed and anxious that your new administration will not protect us, our planet, our children, our parents, or defend us and uphold our inalienable rights. . . . We truly hope that this show has inspired you to uphold our American values and to work on behalf of all of us."[124] Dixon's statement was greeted with a further standing ovation and went viral via traditional and social media. Clearly this was another moment when the audience realized their role as witnesses and the concomitant necessity for them to cocreate and remediate the theatrical message.

The next day US president-elect Donald Trump responded on Twitter: "The Theater must always be a safe and special place. The cast of Hamilton was very rude last night to a very good man, Mike Pence. Apologize!" The cast did not apologize. It is significant that the cast of *Hamilton*, as makers of a hit Broadway show, have a platform in the loud and crowded cultural marketplace that allows their voices to be heard, and that they choose to use this platform, and their symbolic capital, to speak up for the diverse others who are not enfranchised in the same way. It is also significant that they understand the potential of a history play to "inspire" future action, implicitly identifying the power of cultural memory to act as an ethical catalyst. Most of all, they recognize the importance of making theatre an "unsafe" space where radical things can happen. My point here is not just that theatre matters but that *witnessing* matters as an act in itself. Certainly, neither Pence nor Trump have showed any signs that this theatrical intervention was meaningful to them—but *for the audience* Dixon's act of witness from the stage, and their witnessing of this moment, was meaningful. So while this moment does not demonstrate that theatre can change the political sphere, it does show how theatre can positively shape the witnessing sphere. And since this moment has now taken on iconic status, it has not only shaped cultural memory (both of *Hamilton* and of the weeks following the US presidential election) but continues to act as an exemplar of how artistic intervention, voice, and witnessing are vital in the cultural and memory marketplaces.

Witness plays call on their audiences to act as moral witnesses, and to assume the responsibility for collective memory and thereby to shape and define the memory marketplace along ethical lines. As the examples of *By Heart* and *Hamilton* demonstrate, these calls to action do not have to be based on trauma. However, as this book will explore, these are exceptional moments—as pain and suffering are the current default modes for memory work in the theatre (and arguably culture more generally). The ethics of how painful memory is deployed as a tool for generating ethical remembering, and as a marketing tool, will be debated in the chapters that follow. There is a fine line between witnessing and appropriation, between ethical memory and entertainment consumption, and much depends on the aesthetic and performative decisions and strategies used by the theatre companies as to where on the line their depictions of pain fall. As Winter argues, not only silence, but also speech, can be used in "morally deplorable ways."[125]

It is valuable to note here that responsibility works in two directions—memories of brutality and injustice deserve to be heard and witnessed, but we must not forget that scenes that depict brutality are a burden to the audience. The performance of painful memory creates an ethical imperative to remember and an equal need to forget. In a crowded marketplace, novelty and increasingly intense physical and emotional experiences drive consumption. Yet these experiences, which are the very ones that need witnessing, may become so normalized that they blend into a generalized trauma culture that reduces the capacity for witnessing as traumatic cultural memory reaches a saturation point. In some senses, then, it is not simply that these plays act out past trauma, but that they actually enact a traumatized relationship to the past. This relationship also requires witnessing.

THIS BOOK

This book focuses on the production and consumption of painful memory in contemporary Irish and international theatre. The chapters that follow examine how memories of pain are staged by playwrights and theatre companies, how they are communicated to audiences, and how that audience, in turn, both consumes and witnesses. Each chapter considers the message being sold to the audience, the possibilities for reception and remediation, the effects of different levels of social and cultural capital on the status of the witness, and how theatrical strategies can highlight competition, or create solidarity, through recognizing different forms of capital, and involving the audience in mnemonic labor. In deciding what plays to discuss, I have chosen to focus on testimonial and memory plays—witness plays—that stage the personal experiences of subjects who traditionally do not enjoy social and economic capital, as a way of understanding whether theatre can function as an intervention in the marketplace. As such, this book takes its cue from a long history of feminist performance (both in theatre and performance art), which has used the autobiographical as a mode to "reveal otherwise invisible lives, to resist marginalisation and objectification and to become, instead, speaking subjects with self-agency."[126]

Over the course of the two opening chapters, I establish many of the practices of "theatre of the real" and the performances—and risks—of witnessing. Beginning with documentary and verbatim theatre, chapter 1 discusses two examples of that genre—*No Escape* (Ireland, 2010), compiled by Mary Raftery and created by the Abbey, Ireland's national theatre, an example of subsidized theatre with a limited audience; and *The Laramie Project* (US, 2000) and *The Laramie Project Ten Years Later* (US, 2010) by Tectonic Theater Company, both of which were massive commercial successes with national US tours. These plays open the book's discussion of how theatre can provide a powerful ensemble platform for experiences of the marginalized—victims of sexual abuse and violence—to be testified to. Though the productions are on very different scales, they each illustrate how mnemonic capital can be witnessed—and institutionalized—through the actions of key gatekeepers in the marketplace.

In chapter 2, the discussion turns to autoperformance plays, a form of documentary verbatim work in which the performer is the firsthand witness. The chapter highlights how *I Once Knew a Girl* (2010), by Theatre of Witness in Northern Ireland (2010), and *Nirbhaya* (India and UK, 2013), by Yael Farber and the ensemble at once show how victims can be empowered to perform their own stories, and also illustrate the risk of empathy as a dramaturgical strategy that commodifies the victim and enables the too-easy consumption of their suffering. These plays further illustrate the value of considering funding streams—public subsidy via grants, online marketing campaigns—demonstrating the tension for producers between creating platforms for marginalized voices and creating prestigious and instrumentalized cultural products.

Chapter 3 develops the analysis of the staging of witnessing, both within and outside institutionalized memory contexts, focusing on three plays based on and around the concept of truth and reconciliation commissions: *Ubu and the Truth Commission* by Jane Taylor and Handspring Puppet Company (South Africa/UK, 1997), *Claudia* by La Conquesta del Pol Sud (Spain/Argentina, 2016), and *Death and the Maiden* by Ariel Dorfman (Chile/UK, 1990). Through these plays, I consider how testimony, as a particular form of cultural capital, becomes a tradeable commodity and the dimension that transnational witnessing adds to the market. Chapter 4 shifts the focus to modes of witnessing, to consider active listening as a way that audiences can engage in witnessing as a performance of immaterial labor. Discussions of *Twilight—Los Angeles, 1992* (US, 1994) by Anna Deavere Smith, *Come Out Eli* (UK, 2003) by Alecky Blythe, *Annulla (An Autobiography)* (US, 1985) by Emily Mann, and *Krapp's Last Tape* (Ireland/France, 1958), *Footfalls* (Ireland/France, 1976), and *Come and Go* (Ireland/France, 1965) all by Samuel Beckett, ultimately suggest how dramaturgical strategies around listening may resist the commodification of the firsthand witness.

Taking theatre out of the auditorium in chapter 5's consideration of site-specific theatre allows us to look at other forms of resistance—and the full role of the audience as "prosumer" and collaborator in the construction of meaning. This chapter focuses on *Proximity Mouth* (Ireland, 2015) by Dominic Thorpe, the work of Dublin-based company ANU Productions (in particular their Monto cycle, Ireland, 2010–14), and audio performance walks *Quartered: A Love Story* (N. Ireland, 2016) by Kabosh Theatre Company; *Echoing Yafa* (Palestine/Israel, 2014) by Miriam Schickler; and *And While London Burns* (UK, 2007) by Platform. Each of these productions requires the audience to step out of the comfortable role of passive consumer and suggests the role of space and movement in the creation of mnemonic capital.

Finally, the conclusion considers the #MeToo movement as a new form of collective memory performance, and analyzes how in Ireland, feminist theatre movements such as "Waking the Feminists" and "Speak Up and Call It Out" show the activist power of mobilizing mnemonic capital in progressive ways, staging painful pasts for political ends rather than consumer empathy. This chapter responds to many of the ethical questions raised in the book about the consumption of others' pain, asking us to notice how collective movements often require enormous labor from individuals, and finally considering how to balance the need to address inequalities in power and capital with the need to withdraw at times from the marketplace in order to preserve a sense of self.

Throughout the book, my analysis focuses on how producers exploit scripted and production strategies in the hope of directing audience attention to painful memory in particular ways, thereby shaping their behavior as both consumers and witnesses. I consider how audiences may have multivalent reactions and what the possibilities are for the citizen consumer to act in transgressive ways to become audience-witnesses and perhaps even activists. Witnessing memory of painful pasts is, in this iteration, not just a performance, but a performance of responsibility that occurs within, and draws attention to, the power strata of the marketplace.

NOTES

1. Carmen-Francesca Banciu and La Conquesta del Pol Sud, *Land Full of Heroes* (2019), unpublished script courtesy of La Conquesta del Pol Sud.

2. Dori Laub and Shoshana Felman, *Testimony: Crises of Witnessing in Literature, Psychoanalysis and History* (London: Routledge, 1992); Paul Celan quoted in Marianne Hirsch, *The Generation of Postmemory* (New York: Columbia University Press, 2012), 89.

3. See Jean Baudrillard, *Symbolic Exchange and Death* (London: Sage, 1993), 85 and passim, for definition of hyperreality.

4. "Our BE Festival Review Round-up," What's On Birmingham, accessed October 12, 2019, https://www.whatsonlive.co.uk/birmingham/news/our-be-festival-review-round-up/44721.

5. Samuel Beckett, *Waiting for Godot*, in *The Complete Dramatic Works* (London: Faber, 1986), 50.

6. Beckett, *Waiting for Godot*, 86.

7. George Berkeley, *A New Theory of Vision and Other Writings* (London: J M Dent, 1938), 114–15.

8. Astrid Erll and Ann Rigney, quoted in introduction to *Performing Memory in Art and Popular Culture*, ed. Liedeke Plate and Anneke Smelik (London, New York: Routledge, 2013), 4.

9. Anna Reading, "Seeing Red: A Political Economy of Digital Memory," *Media, Culture & Society* 36, no. 6 (2014): 748–60, see esp. 753.

10. John Brewer and Frank Trentmann, eds., introduction to *Consuming Cultures, Global Perspectives* (Oxford: Berg, 2006), 4.

11. Anna Reading, "The Female Memory Factory: How the Gendered Labour of Memory Creates Mnemonic Capital," *European Journal of Women's Studies* (2019): 1–20, see esp. 4.

12. Jonathan Bach, *What Remains: Everyday Encounters with the Social Past in Germany* (New York: Columbia University Press, 2017), 3.

13. Anna Reading and Tanya Notley, "Globital Memory Capital: Theorizing Digital Memory Economies," in *Digital Memory Studies: Media Pasts in Transition*, ed. Andrew Hoskins (London: Routledge, 2018).

14. Matthew Allen, "The Poverty of Memory: For Political Economy in Memory Studies," *Memory Studies* 9, no. 4 (2016): 371–75, see esp. 371.

15. Jen Harvie, *Fair Play* (London: Palgrave, 2013), 8.

16. I am grateful to Anna Reading for her use of this term, discussed during the "Activist Memory" workshop at Columbia University, November 2–3, 2018.

17. Pierre Bourdieu, "Forms of Capital," in *Handbook of Theory and Research for the Sociology of Education*, ed. John G Richardson (New York: Greenwood, 1986). For a discussion of the influence of these forms of capital on tourist consumer decisions, see Erdinç Çakmak, Rico Lie, and Tom Selwyn, "Informal Tourism Entrepreneurs' Capital Usage and Conversion," *Current Issues in Tourism* (2018): 2250–65.

18. See Pierre Bourdieu, *The Social Structures of the Economy* (London: Polity, 2000).

19. Anna Reading defines mnemonic capital in her article "The Female Memory Factory: How the Gendered Labour of Memory Creates Mnemonic Capital," *European Journal of Women's Studies* (2019): 1–20.

20. Bourdieu, "Forms of Capital," 241.

21. Alison Landsberg, *Prosthetic Memory* (New York: Columbia University Press, 2004), 18.

22. Harvie, *Fair Play*, 8. Harvie draws on Joseph Pine and James Gilmore's work on the "experience economy." See Pine and Gilmore, *The Experience Economy: Work Is Theatre and Every Business a Stage* (Boston, MA: Harvard Business Review, 1999).

23. For a discussion of how community versus public/private funding creates a particular market-driven narrative, see Robyn Autry, "The Political Economy of Memory: The Challenges of Representing National Conflict at Identity-Driven Museums," *Theory and Society* 42, no. 1 (2013): 57–80.

24. Jean Baudrillard, "No Reprieve for Sarajevo," *Liberation*, January 8, 1994, republished on CTheory.net, http://ctheory.net/ctheory_wp/no-reprieve-for-sarajevo/, September 28, 1994.

25. Terri Tomsky, "From Sarajevo to 9/11: Travelling Memory and the Trauma Economy," *Parallax* 17, no. 4 (2011): 49–60, see esp. 49.

26. The idea of the "invisible hand" of the market is discussed in Mark Bevir and Frank Trentmann, "Markets in Historical Contexts: Ideas, Practices and Governances," in *Markets in Historical Contexts* (Cambridge: Cambridge University Press, 2004).

27. Carol Martin, "Living Simulations: The Use of Media in Documentary in the UK, Lebanon and Israel," in *Get Real*, ed. Alison Forsyth and Chris Megson (Basingstoke, UK: Palgrave Macmillan, 2009): 74–90, see esp. 82.

28. See Fiona Gartland, "Dublin Hotels Fully Booked for Easter 1916 Commemorations," *Irish Times*, March 9, 2016, https://www.irishtimes.com/news/ireland/irish-news/dublin-hotels-fully-booked-for-easter-1916-commemorations-1.2566748.

29. Pierre Bourdieu, *The Social Structures of the Economy* (Oxford: Polity, 2005), 21.

30. For a discussion of the relative appeal of popular history books in 2016, see John Spain, "Coogan Blows Ferriter Away," Independent.ie, January 10, 2016, https://www.independent.ie/entertainment/books/book-reviews/coogan-blows-ferriter-away-in-explosion-of-1916-books-34344713.html.

31. Bourdieu, *The Social Structures of the Economy*, 19.

32. Vered Vinitzky Seroussi, "Unpacking the Unspeakable: Silence in Collective Memory and Forgetting," *Social Forces* 88, no. 3 (2010): 1103–22, see esp. 1107.

33. Pierre Bourdieu, *Acts of Resistance* (New York: The New Press, 1999), 30–31.

34. Gunnthorunn Gudmundsdottir, *Representations of Forgetting in Life Writing and Fiction* (London: Palgrave, 2017), 9–10.

35. Brian Friel, *Translations* in *Plays One* (London: Faber, 1996), 445.

36. Paul Connerton, *How Societies Remember* (Cambridge: Cambridge University Press, 1989), 14.

37. Rosanne Kennedy and Gillian Whitlock, "Witnessing, Trauma and Social Suffering: Feminist Perspectives," *Australian Feminist Studies* 26, no. 69 (2011): 251–55, see esp. 252. Michael Rothberg echoes this, acknowledging that, "all articulations of memory are not equal; powerful social, political and psychic forces articulate themselves in every act of remembrance." See Michael Rothberg, *Multidirectional Memory: Remembering the Holocaust in the Age of Decolonization* (Stanford, CA: Stanford University Press, 2009), 16.

38. Walter Benjamin, as quoted in Jeanette Malkin, *Memory-Theater and Postmodern Drama* (Ann Arbor: University of Michigan Press, 1999), 26.

39. Jean Baudrillard, *The Consumer Society: Myths and Structures* (London: Sage, 1998), 59.

40. Baudrillard, *The Consumer Society*, 59.

41. Lizabeth Cohen, "Citizens and Consumers in the United States in the Century of Mass Consumption," in *The Politics of Consumption: Material Culture and Citizenship in Europe and America*, ed. Martin Daunton and Matthew Hilton (Oxford: Berg, 2001), 203–22.

42. Bevir and Trentmann, "Markets in Historical Contexts," 3.

43. See George M. Zinkhan and Richard T. Watson, "Advertising Trends: Innovation and the Process of Creative Destruction," *Journal of Business Research* 37, no. 3 (1996): 163–71.

44. James Gilmore and Joseph Pine, *Authenticity: What Consumers Really Want* (Boston, MA: Harvard Business School Press, 2009).

45. See S. Banet-Weiser, "Branding Consumer Citizens," *Authentic: The Politics of Ambivalence in a Brand Culture* (New York: New York University Press, 2012).

46. Christopher Howard, "Touring the Consumption of the Other: Imaginaries of Authenticity in the Himalayas and Beyond," *Journal of Consumer Culture* 16, no. 2 (2016): 354–73, see esp. 362.

47. For an overview of emotion and consumer behavior research, see Fleur J. M. Laros and Jan Benedict E. M. Steenkamp, "Emotions in Consumer Behavior: A Hierarchical Approach," *Journal of Business Research* 58, no. 10 (2005): 1437–45.

48. Identity-signaling is a key part of decisions about consumption, meaning that the social-good dimension of attending social-justice plays may play a large role in people's ticket-buying patterns. See Jonah A. Berger, Benjamin Ho, and Yogesh V. Joshi, "Identity Signaling with Social Capital: A Model of Symbolic Consumption" (working paper, SSRN, April 15, 2011) https://ssrn.com/abstract=1828848.

49. Adam Arvidsson, "Brand Management," *Consuming Cultures*, 71–94, see esp. 87.

50. Arjun Appadurai, *Modernity at Large: Cultural Dimensions of Globalisation* (Minneapolis: University of Minnesota Press, 1996), 42.

51. Appadurai, *Modernity at Large*, 42.
52. Baudrillard, "No Reprieve for Sarajevo," http://ctheory.net/ctheory_wp/no-reprieve-for-sarajevo/.
53. Jacques Rancière, *The Emancipated Spectator*, trans. Gregory Elliott (London: Verso, 2009), 2, 16.
54. John Durham Peters, "Witnessing," in *Media Witnessing*, ed. Paul Frosh and Amit Pinchevski (Basingstoke, UK: Palgrave, 2008), 26.
55. Jukka Törrönen, "Between Public Good and the Freedom of the Consumer," *Media, Culture & Society* 23, no. 2 (2001): 171–93.
56. Harvie, *Fair Play*, 29–61.
57. Paul Ricoeur, *Memory, History, Forgetting*, trans. Kathleen Blamey and David Pellauer (Chicago: University of Chicago Press, 2004), 162.
58. Elizabeth Jelin, *State Repression and the Struggles for Memory* (2003), 23, quoted in Berthold Molden, "Power Relations of Collective Memory," *Memory Studies* 9, no. 2 (2016): 134.
59. Jay Winter, "Thinking about Silence," in *Shadows of War*, ed. Efrat Ben-Ze'ev, Ruth Ginio, and Jay Winter (Cambridge: Cambridge University Press, 2010), 6.
60. Lisa Fitzpatrick, "Gender and Affect in Testimonial Performance: The Example of *I Once Knew a Girl*," *Irish University Review* 45, no. 1 (2015): 126–40.
61. Dori Laub, "An Event without a Witness," in *Testimony: Crises of Witnessing in Literature, Psychoanalysis and History*, ed. Shoshana Felman and Dori Laub (London: Routledge, 1992), 75.
62. Laub, "An Event without a Witness," 80.
63. Tamar Ashuri and Amit Pinchevski, "Witnessing as a Field," in *Media Witnessing*, ed. Paul Frosh and Amit Pinchevski (Basingstoke, UK: Palgrave, 2008), 133–55, see esp. 137.
64. Laub, "An Event without a Witness," 81.
65. Peters, "Witnessing," 23.
66. Aleida Assmann, "Truth and Memory" (lecture, UCD Humanities Institute, February 6, 2018), https://soundcloud.com/ucd-humanities/aleida-assmann-truth-and-memory.
67. Pat Palmer, *The Body in Pain in Irish Literature and Culture*, ed. Fionnuala Dillane, Naomi McAreavey, and Emilie Pine (London: Palgrave, 2017), 21–38, see esp. 23.
68. Peters, "Witnessing," 23.
69. Diana Taylor, "Staging Social Memory," in *Psychoanalysis and Performance*, ed. Patrick Campbell and Adrian Kear (London: Routledge, 2001), 16.
70. Bourdieu, *The Social Structures of the Economy*, 148.
71. Gary S. Becker and Kevin M. Murphy, *Social Economics: Market Behaviour in a Social Environment* (Cambridge, MA: Harvard University Press, 2000).

72. Karine Shaefer, "The Spectator as Witness?" *Theatre & Performance* 23, no. 1 (2003): 5–20, see esp. 7, 17.

73. Caroline Wake, "Towards a Taxonomy of Spectatorial Witness in Theatre and Performance Studies," in *Visions and Revisions*, ed. Caroline Wake and Bryoni Tresize (Copenhagen: Museum Tusculaneum Press, 2013), 34.

74. Wake, "Towards a Taxonomy of Spectatorial Witness," 42.

75. Alan Filewood, "The Documentary Body," in *Get Real*, ed. Alison Forsyth and Chris Megson (Basingstoke, UK: Palgrave Macmillan, 2009): 55–73, see esp. 69.

76. Rancière, *The Emancipated Spectator*, 16.

77. Gareth White, *Audience Participation in the Theatre: Aesthetics of the Invitation* (London: Palgrave, 2013), 57.

78. Jill Dolan, *Utopia in Performance* (Ann Arbor: University of Michigan Press, 2005), 2.

79. Jan Assmann, "Collective Memory and Cultural Identity," *New German Critique* 65 (Summer, 1995): 125–33, see esp. 127.

80. See, for example, E. Kromidha, "Social Identity and Signalling Success Factors in Online Crowdfunding," *Entrepreneurship & Regional Development* 28, no. 9–10 (2016): 605–29; Roland Benabou and Jean Tirole, "Incentives and Prosocial Behavior," *The American Economic Review* 96, no. 5 (2006): 1652–78; Rachel Croson, Femida Handy, and Jen Shang, "Keeping Up with the Joneses: The Relationship of Perceived Descriptive Social Norms, Social Information, and Charitable Giving," *Nonprofit Management & Leadership*, 19, no. 4 (2009): 467–89; Deborah J. Terry, Michael A. Hog, and Katherine M. White, "The Theory of Planned Behaviour: Self-Identity, Social Identity and Group Norms," *The British Journal of Social Psychology* 38 (1999): 225–44.

81. Rosanne Kennedy makes this argument in relation to apologies to the Australian Stolen Generation. See Rosanne Kennedy, "An Australian Archive of Feelings," *Australian Feminist Studies* 26, no. 69 (2011): 257–79.

82. Hirsch, *The Generation of Postmemory*, 93. Favorini argues that theatre is "a connectionist rather than a storage model for memory," Atillio Favorini, *Memory in Play: From Aeschylus to Sam Shepard* (New York: Palgrave Macmillan, 2008), 180.

83. Susan Sontag, *Regarding the Pain of Others* (London: Penguin, 2004), 66.

84. Favorini, *Memory in Play*, 135.

85. Louise Woodstock, "It's Kind of Like an Assault You Know," *Critical Studies in Media Communication* 33, no. 5, 399–408, see esp. 406.

86. Carol Martin, *Theatre of the Real* (Houndmills, UK: Palgrave, 2013).

87. Anne Cubilié and Carl Good, "The Future of Testimony," *Discourse* 25, no. 1/2 (2003): 4–18, see esp. 7.

88. Patrick Duggan, *Trauma-Tragedy: Symptoms of Contemporary Performance* (Manchester, UK: Manchester University Press, 2012), 1.

89. See Judith Butler, *Gender Trouble* (London: Routledge Classics, 2006), 2–4.

90. Freddi Rokem, *Performing History* (Iowa City: University of Iowa Press, 2007), 19, 204.

91. Rokem, *Performing History*, 205.

92. Favorini, *Memory in Play*, 7.

93. Interview with Teya Sepinuck by Playhouse as part of the Playhouse Theatre of Witness program, Derry. July 10, 2013. https://www.youtube.com/watch?v=hJNWzN5mdTE.

94. Allen Feldman, "Memory Theaters, Virtual Witnessing and the Trauma Aesthetic," *Biography* 27, no. 1 (2004): 163–202, see esp. 164.

95. Marianne Hirsch, "Connective Histories in Vulnerable Times," *PMLA* 129, no. 3 (2014): 330–48, see esp. 334.

96. Peters, "Witnessing," 39.

97. Feldman, "Memory Theaters," 166.

98. Jasbir Puar interprets Foucault's idea of "speaker's benefit" to discuss this kind of cultural capital. See Jasbir Puar, "Celebrating Refusal: The Complexities of Saying No," Bully Bloggers, June 23, 2010, https://bullybloggers.wordpress.com/2010/06/23/celebrating-refusal-the-complexities-of-saying-no/. I am grateful to Anne Mulhall for this reference.

99. Allen, "The Poverty of Memory," 373.

100. Dolan, *Utopia in Performance*, 2.

101. Rosalind Gill and Andy Pratt, "In the Social Factory: Immaterial Labor, Precariousness and Cultural Work," *Theory, Culture & Society* 25 no. 7–8 (2008): 1–30.

102. Teya Sepinuck, *Theatre of Witness* (London: Jessica Kingsley, 2013), 157.

103. Michal Givoni, *Care of the Witness* (Cambridge: Cambridge University Press, 2016), 44.

104. Carol Martin, "Living Simulations," 78.

105. Carole-Anne Upton, "Northern Ireland: The Case of Bloody Sunday," in *Get Real*, ed. Alison Forsyth and Chris Megson (Basingstoke, UK: Palgrave Macmillan, 2009): 179–94.

106. Fitzpatrick, "Gender and Affect in Testimonial Performance," 132.

107. Gill and Pratt, "In the Social Factory," 15–16.

108. See Rokem, *Performing History*, 204, 192. "Complete absorption" is why advertisers in particular engage empathy in their "drama-based" ads. See Jennifer Edson Escalas and Barbara B. Stern, "Sympathy and Empathy: Emotional Responses," *Journal of Consumer Research* 29 (2003): 566–78, see esp. 573.

109. Conversation between author and Paula McFettridge, artistic director of Kabosh Theatre Company, Dublin, April 2018.

110. Rothberg, *Multidirectional Memory*, 87.

111. Didier Fassin and Richard Rechtman, *The Empire of Trauma* (Princeton, NJ: Princeton University Press, 2009).

112. Peters, "Witnessing," 31.

113. Lauren Berlant, ed., "Compassion (and Withholding)," in *Compassion* (London: Routledge, 2004), 4.

114. Berlant, "Compassion (and Withholding)," 6.

115. Rosanne Kennedy, "An Australian Archive of Feelings," 259.

116. See Jasbir Puar, "Celebrating Refusal," https://bullybloggers.wordpress.com/2010/06/23/celebrating-refusal-the-complexities-of-saying-no/. On the risks of trauma and appropriation, see also Dominic LaCapra, *Writing History, Writing Trauma* (Baltimore: Johns Hopkins University Press, 2001).

117. Berlant, "Compassion (and Withholding)," 9.

118. Givoni, *Care of the Witness*, 4.

119. Upton, "Northern Ireland," 192.

120. See the discussion of market segmentation (the creation of new niche markets targeting particular consumer groups) in Art Weinstein, *Market Segmentation* (London: McGraw Hill, 1994).

121. Arvidsson, "Brand Management," 78.

122. Dolan, *Utopia in Performance*, 10. See also Landsberg, *Prosthetic Memory*, for belief that cultural memory has the ability to shape subjectivity and politics (p. 2); and that memory can consolidate important group identities (p. 4).

123. Throughout this book when I refer to "utopian" possibilities, I am following the example of Jill Dolan in *Utopia in Performance*.

124. Clarisse Loughrey, "Read Hamilton Cast's Surprise Statement to Vice President-Elect Mike Pence," *Independent*, November 21, 2016, https://www.independent.co.uk/arts-entertainment/theatre-dance/news/hamilton-mike-pence-booed-statement-in-full-watch-new-york-vice-president-elect-a7429251.html.

125. Winter, "Thinking about Silence," 11.

126. Deirdre Heddon, *Autobiography and Performance* (Basingstoke, UK: Palgrave Macmillan, 2008), 3; see also pp. 20–25 for an overview of feminist and queer consciousness-raising performances.

ONE

TELL THEM THAT YOU SAW US

Witnessing Docu-verbatim Memory

SOCIAL AND MNEMONIC CAPITAL ARE intimately linked. This chapter considers this statement in relation to the emergence of previously unspeakable memories into the marketplace as the social capital of marginalized groups begins to shift. These shifts are inextricably linked to cultural representation, and this chapter analyzes how theatrical gatekeepers use their influence within the cultural marketplace to raise both the memory and social capital of formerly powerless stakeholders—the victims of child abuse, sexual violence, and murder—through the form of docu-verbatim work, in order to create a more ethically balanced culture. Continuing the focus on the audience as a consumer in this dynamic, however, the chapter also highlights the risks inherent in marketing painful memory. Indeed, docu-verbatim theatre's construction of the audience as witnesses creates a product and brand that generates memory capital for the firsthand witness, but whose ultimate dividend is the accrual of moral capital by the audience. As Roberta Sassatelli argues, "a growing variety of discourses, both within the marketplace and outside it, in politics and civil society, is calling into being the 'consumer' not only as an active subject but also, and above all, as a moral and political subject."[1] This chapter argues that docu-verbatim theatre is one such discourse, which not only calls into being, but depends on the idea of the moral consumer and audience-as-witness. But it also argues that the outcomes of this positioning have not yet been sufficiently analyzed in relation to how docu-verbatim theatre's use of trauma as a catalyst for witnessing—what Ann Cvetkovich has called "an archive of feelings"—creates a consumer commodity out of painful memory.[2] The chapter explores the tension between witnessing and shame, the interventionist role of biased mediation, the use of intolerable images, and the institutionalization of memory capital in order to engage with the fraught question of how theatre stages difficult histories.

DOCU-VERBATIM

Docu-verbatim theatre is not the best known form of Irish, or indeed international, theatre. But it is a genre increasing both its market share and its symbolic impact, and as such urgently requires analysis as an "alternative product," a commodity that, as defined by Sassatelli, embodies "a critical dialogue with many aspects of commoditization as we know it."[3] In other words, this is a form of theatre that makes visible the cycle of production, distribution, and consumption through foregrounding the mechanisms of theatre-making and witnessing and highlighting the role of theatre as a joint site of production and consumption.

Docu-verbatim, my blended term designed to encompass documentary (based on documents) and verbatim (word-for-word) theatre styles, has experienced a recent market resurgence, its popularity broadly a response to the form's attempt to represent some of the ethical crises of recent decades.[4] It may be understood as a response to what Cvetkovich has defined as the need for nonmainstream social groups, without cultural capital, to have their memories and experiences represented through nonmainstream forms of performance, including "new genres of expression, such as testimony, and new forms of monuments, rituals, and performances that can call into being collective witnesses and publics."[5] Docu-verbatim is thus a "new form of... ritual" that responds to the consumer demand for art to react to crisis and to make the intricacies of those crises available, via a combined presentation of the relevant facts and an agreed message. Its recent popularity represents, as Alison Forsyth and Chris Megson put it, "a remarkable mobilisation and proliferation."[6] While many docu-verbatim plays are based on material (such as court transcripts) that is already publicly available, the form's advantage is its mobilization of this information into a more accessible and performative medium. This action is attractive to a cultural and social marketplace that is constantly flooded with information, as these plays promise to distill what is important in a consumer-friendly format. In one sense, then, docu-verbatim's contemporary market success is based not only on its seeming response to ethical crises, but to a crisis of knowing—or rather, a feeling of not-knowing. As Carol Martin argues, docu-verbatim "both acknowledges a positivist faith in empirical reality and underscores an epistemological crisis in knowing truth," a feeling of crisis that, perhaps, an evening at the theatre can allay.[7] Insecurity, as any analyst will tell you, is bad for the market—unless, that is, the market can create a brand to simultaneously address and feed off that insecurity.

The "art" of docu-verbatim is to transform complex ethical and social debates into a theatrically powerful moment, harnessing the emotive power of crisis and controversy in order to do so. In championing the disenfranchised, and highlighting abuses of power, these plays derive their edge from challenging the status quo and saying the unsayable. In this sense docu-verbatim theatre goes beyond "holding the mirror up to nature," instead actively attempting to intervene in the world outside the theatre—the social, cultural, and memory marketplaces. What is particular to this form is its rooting in "the real"; docu-verbatim theatre gives direct access to untold stories of the unheard. I say "gives" and "direct," with the obvious caveat being that docu-verbatim gives the *impression* of granting access to authenticity, through what is a highly stylized and highly selective form. We need to consider the dialectic between witnessing the authentic voice and the exigencies of shaping the message; through examining this tension we will see how docu-verbatim theatre negotiates the marketplace, positions the witness within the marketplace, and mediates the witness's voice in order to create a powerful connection between the witness and the audience, a connection that creates significant cultural, social, and memory capital.[8] Ultimately, theatre makers who privilege the voice of the unheard work as gatekeepers, who transform not only the cultural but hopefully also the social capital of the person or group whose testimony is being witnessed.

Is consuming docu-verbatim theatre a different experience to consuming fiction theatre? The short answer is yes. While the performers of mainstream fiction theatre relate their narratives to an implied audience, docu-verbatim is generally characterized by a direct address style, which creates an uninterrupted relationship, removing the security of the fourth wall entirely. Though there are obviously theatrical personas being performed in docu-verbatim, many of the "roles" portray real people or, in the case of autoperformance (considered in the next chapter), the "actor" and the "real" person are one and the same. Moreover, the sense that these productions address urgent and moral crises also serves to increase the feeling of consuming something real and important, shifting the audience member toward the role of citizen consumer and audience-witness. Since this genre of performance projects itself differently, it makes sense to consider how the audience may react differently. For example, in watching an actor perform a true story of abuse, is the audience more engaged, more impacted, more affected? If the story of abuse is due at least in part to inequality in social, political, and economic capital, is the audience inspired to leave the theatre and to join a campaign for greater equality? Does the communal nature of hearing this testimony inspire theatre audiences for docu-verbatim shows to situate themselves in a social dynamic whereby each individual sees their responsibility to the collective? Conversely, does the setting of the theatre and the use of theatrical strategies of scripting and mediation work to separate this "reality" from the outside world, thereby preventing the translation of the ethical feelings produced by the play within the theatre into ethical action outside the theatre? Docu-verbatim theatre may create the potential for both collective and individual ethical witnessing, but it does not automatically lead to ethical action outside the theatre, in the larger market.

The Market for Docu-verbatim:
The Starving Man

Playwright David Hare said of the appeal of documentary theatre "What is a painting, a painting of a starving man? What is a painting of a corpse? It's the facts we want. Give us the facts."[9] The popularity of docu-verbatim theatre rests on the idea that this form of theatre will "give us the facts." The veracity of the form is integral to its appeal, yet since one show could never, and we would not want it to, give us *all* the facts, it must necessarily be selective. Just as a painting is, docu-verbatim theatre is composed, crafted, and framed, an artistic mediation. The facts, however, grant the docu-verbatim play an atmosphere of legitimacy, which in wearing its mediation lightly, seems to offer a refreshingly unswerving contact with its subject: suffering. This may not be the most obviously appealing or popular form; when presented with crises, audiences often crave escapism. Yet the success of London's Tricycle Theatre, which pioneered tribunal theatre in the UK,[10] and the success of individual artists such as Anna Deveare Smith, who has made a career in the US out of her one-woman shows based on verbatim testimony (discussed in chap. 4), illustrates that Hare is right—there is substantial consumer demand for the starving man.

What is it that the fact of the "starving man" gives the audience? In basing itself on archival history or personal, often oral, testimony, the docu-verbatim show derives a value from its proximity to "the thing itself." The actor portraying the firsthand witness, using their words, can declare "I was there" and the audience can declare "I was there to witness the person who experienced this," seeming to put the primary and secondary witnesses into a new relationship.[11] There is a certain frisson attached to this proximity and also a potential visceral thrill for the audience in coming close to suffering, a thrill that is made safe by the environs of the theatre. Though the subject matter may be violence and its consequences, the staging of docu-verbatim is nonviolent and it may be perceived indeed as an alternative for audiences who want a dose of reality but do not desire the confrontation of in-yer-face theatre. There is also a clarity offered by docu-verbatim theatre, based on its proximity to, but difference from, the archive or event. The process of docu-verbatim sifts the "important" facts from the irrelevant or messy, creating a more straightforward narrative and message with which audiences can engage. As Martin has described it, "theatre of the real participates in how we come to know and understand what has happened."[12] It may be that docu-verbatim shows play to the converted, but there is also the possibility that the docu-verbatim show can change minds too. In being presented with different sides of the debate, or being granted access to the verbatim words of the original witness, the audience member may be newly convinced (or reconvinced) of the case that is under presentation. And this highlights a feature of docu-verbatim: that it so often has a case to present, which I would summarize as the case to champion the disenfranchised or otherwise voiceless.

In championing the disenfranchised, docu-verbatim theatre promises to create a platform for the many voices that otherwise have no social capital and thus no access to the theatre, or to the cultural marketplace in general. This promise is appealing to an audience, in the same way that "untold stories" have a novelty and discovery value. The promise is also, of course, appealing to those whose stories are to be dramatized as it offers the potential to amplify their voice in an otherwise loud and crowded marketplace. Unlike the television documentary, there is no screen or commercial break to come between the spectator and the subject (though the screen may, in fact, be a welcome diversion for audiences averse to such a close identification). And, finally, in selecting one story to tell—or personalizing through drawing out, however basically, "characters" from the messiness of all the facts—the docu-verbatim show offers the promise not only of making the archive or experience intelligible, but knowable. In this way, docu-verbatim shows promise audiences that in the process of witnessing the production, they will gain an authority over the subject matter and attain a sense of ownership over an archive or experience that did not, initially, belong to them. This promise is a potentially valuable commodity.

If these are some of the reasons why audiences buy a ticket to hear the facts or to see "the thing itself," then what happens once they are in the theatre? As I discuss in detail below in relation to specific productions, there are various answers to this question. As mentioned, there is the possibility that audiences can be inspired (or not) by the production to act as witnesses themselves in the marketplace outside the theatre. But there are multiple other dimensions to the relationship between the docu-verbatim stage and the auditorium. The agency of the audience is never an easy question to consider, but it is possible to see how productions themselves hope to construct and affect that agency. Ownership of, or authority on, an experience or event is one way that docu-verbatim can create a sense of agency for an audience. Crucially, however, not all perspectives on that experience or event are valued equally within the docu-verbatim play. Frequently, the docu-verbatim show prioritizes the voice and experience of the victim over the perpetrator. The docu-verbatim play, as a result, configures some onstage witnesses and witnessing texts as more valuable or more factual than others. The symbolic capital of the victim is created through the same strategies of editing, scripting, and performance style that are used in fiction plays. The agency of an audience in deciding whose testimony to value is thus circumscribed by the way that docu-verbatim playwrights and companies act as gatekeepers of memory capital. Overall then, the docu-verbatim show grants the audience a feeling of independent agency and being "in the know" while actually strongly guiding their judgement and limiting their knowledge.

Gatekeepers of Memory

Docu-verbatim theatre is always a mediated form. The material being presented comes from archival or testimonial sources but, in its presentation on stage, it is always a limited version of that material. Though this act of limiting may be framed as a socially useful intervention, it nevertheless mediates the material via an ideological agenda with major implications, for example, for what a particular archive is then taken to mean, and how its memory capital is used to support particular subject positions within the political and cultural memory marketplaces. Various strategies of mediation—from where and how statements are positioned within thematic segments, or by telling the audience some pieces of information before others—have direct impact on the reception of the onstage witnesses. How questions are framed and whether the questions are visible or audible to an audience is also a major factor affecting how the testimony being performed—testimony which is often given in response to a question—is itself mediated by the witness and then received by an audience. These strategies are partly driven by necessity—with docu-verbatim theatre there is usually a very large amount of information that needs to be selected from and structured in order to be relayed in any meaningful way.

And so at every stage of the process, there are decisions made about what is meaningful and what should be conveyed, from the self-scripting of the witness or testifier, to the selection, editing, and scripting of the playwright, to the direction of actors or the witnesses themselves, to the production decisions on lighting, sound, and so on. These decisions affect how witnesses are given performance time, and how they are positioned (sympathetically or unsympathetically), and what testimony is included versus what testimony is left out. Technically, as mentioned above, it may be possible with a purely documentary play, based on an accessible archive, to determine what has been excised, but this is not an easy nor, I would imagine, a frequently performed exercise. And where the play is based on oral testimony, often gathered specifically for this purpose, it is impossible to access and know what has been removed from that archive in order to make the performed version. Recognizing inclusion and exclusion as not merely aspects of process, but highly political issues for the docu-verbatim play, is also to recognize that docu-verbatim playwrights, directors, and companies are not so much mediums of memory but gatekeepers. The effect of this gatekeeping is more than telling an audience that some memories or perspectives are important, it results in giving the audience a potentially partial (or slanted) version of the experience—the opposite of "the facts" that are the audience's initial motivation to see the show. This is particularly important in the cases where the play stands in for the archive; though Brian Friel could declare that "We don't go to *Macbeth* for history" this is not the case for plays that actually market themselves as factual approaches to the past.[13]

Witnesses to Painful Experience

We might not go to *Macbeth* for history, but we do go for heightened drama, conflict, and catharsis. So what can the docu-verbatim play offer its consumer? The answer is: access to the voice of the disenfranchised, victimized, traumatized individual. In isolating the voices of the disenfranchised, this platform nominates them as particularly important and gives the audience time to consider their memories apart from the usual social context. While this can increase attention, it's also possible that this apartness can make it difficult for audiences to then connect what they are prepared to listen to appreciatively in the theatre, with the social world outside, with other issues competing for their attention and sympathies.

These plays are not easy to witness. The memories and histories of vulnerability discussed in this chapter make for uncomfortable watching and listening. Many of the experiences described—child abuse, rape, and murder—are still taboo social facts that are hard to hear and, as a result, are all too often underlistened to. However, as these productions, and their reception, show, audiences can be attentive and responsive. We can therefore identify these shows as potential utopian moments of ethical and collective witnessing, moments that are not usually available in the marketplace. Yet in buying a ticket for these kinds of productions, the audience may be self-selecting consumers with an interest in the area, who are particularly amenable to listening to vulnerability. Are these then taboo issues for the audience, or is it—more likely—that the docu-verbatim play is pushing at an already open door? We will also see, in relation to plays that deal with suffering, that audiences respond empathetically, and so a follow-up question is whether the way that audiences respond to painful memories of suffering is temporary catharsis or whether the utopian moment can continue outside the theatre, after the show? These docu-verbatim productions thus offer important opportunities for us to consider how to stage and respond to vulnerability.

This chapter considers three productions. In part one, I focus on the Irish play *No Escape* (2010) by Mary Raftery, first produced by the Abbey Theatre, which dramatizes the story of institutional child abuse in Ireland. This is a traditional documentary play based on a public archive that stages the testimony in a combination of direct address and tribunal-style interviews. In part two, I consider two plays by New York–based Tectonic Theater Company, *The Laramie Project* (2000) and *The Laramie Project: Ten Years Later* (2010). These two shows, created by the ensemble, respond to the homophobic hate-crime murder of Matthew Shepard in Laramie, Wyoming, in 1998. Both plays are based on interview material created by the company, with small elements of other documentary material, such as court records. Like *No Escape*, these two plays are staged as a blend of direct address and onstage interview scenarios, though Tectonic takes a different approach in constructing its own testimony archive. In linking these three plays, I aim to show the international appeal and applicability of docu-verbatim theatre, as well as divergences in subsidized versus commercial theatre. Though they emerge from different national contexts, what unifies these three plays is the consistent use of docu-verbatim theatre as a style to respond self-consciously and ethically to violence against vulnerable individuals in order to deliberately build social and memory capital for the victims.

PART ONE

Capital in the Marketplace: No Escape

No Escape (2010) is the first-ever documentary play commissioned by the Abbey, Ireland's National Theatre. Compiled by Mary Raftery, the play is traditionally documentary in its approach, based on the archival material and published text of the 2009 *Report of the Commission to Inquire into Child Abuse* under Judge Ryan (henceforth the Ryan Report), which investigated the abuse of children in residential institutions administered by the Catholic Church in Ireland over a seventy-year period. Raftery's play combines the tribunal approach in staging some of the interviews between the commission's legal team and the religious congregations, presided over by Judge Ryan, with the direct address more common to verbatim theatre, as individual abuse-survivor testimony is delivered face on to the audience. The play's dependence on the official report suggests what Caroline Wake has described as a version of "history as it has been recorded in the archive."[14] What the docu-verbatim play brings to the archive, though, is the further potential for representation and explanation.

No Escape is a highly interventionist version of the archive and, as such, reflects a particular political agenda, and equally political representation and explanation of this history. Raftery's work on this archive refutes any idea of these documents as a static or fixed narrative of the past; indeed Raftery's editing technique profoundly illustrates the ability to make the archive seem a contested and lively space from which multiple and conflicting histories can emerge. Though the weight of written material in the archive, including records and log books and so on, belongs to the religious congregations, the play's script moves this quantitative material to the background, bringing the voices of the survivors and their oral histories to the foreground, consistently prioritizing their voices, embodied experience, and formerly suppressed memories.

The set for the first production (Abbey Theatre 2010), directed by Róisín McBrinn, bisected the stage with two glass screens onto which Judge Ryan (played by Lorcan Cranitch) wrote place names, dates, and figures. This schoolroom aesthetic affirms the didactic approach of the play, with Ryan playing the role of teacher as much as judge. Behind the screens, stacked boxes of files represented the original interviews and research conducted by the commission, and the historical records of the religious congregations and the state, so that the audience saw onstage part of the material history of the abuse. This didacticism and the "weight of history" connoted by the stacked file boxes both support the truth claims of the docu-verbatim play and reinforce its message and investment in the voice and memory capital of the victims.

The commissioning of *No Escape* illustrates a significant shift in the marketplace status of the play's constituent witnesses—religious congregations and abuse survivors—and further indicates the relative *and constantly shifting* value of social capital in the marketplace; as public confidence in the Catholic Church decreases, so the investment in survivors' stories increases. This is not a story that is limited to Ireland, as internationally we have seen a widespread shift of cultural capital and status—both of which equal credibility—from religious figures to survivors with the direct effect that allegations of abuse are now believable in ways that they weren't two decades ago.[15] This effect is, of course, in part due to the accumulation of proven cases of clerical abuse, which render new allegations increasingly believable, and in part due to the connected shift in attitudes to abuse that mean these memories are no longer unspeakable. In the case of *No Escape*, the legitimacy of the play is guaranteed by the generic authority of the official state report while the Ryan Report's social and juridical capital also creates an audience amenable to hearing these stories in the forum provided by the National Theatre.

In Ireland, the momentum behind the revolution in market status of the survivor-witness had a long development from the 1980s and 1990s, when perceptions of narratives of institutional child abuse began to change due to the growing body of memories and stories of abuse available in the public sphere. In 1999, the government issued an apology to institutionalized children for the state's "collective failure to intervene, to detect their pain, to come to their rescue,"[16] signifying an official authorization that led to memories of institutional abuse becoming increasingly normalized and accepted.[17] As a result of this shift, the pattern of social memories related to these institutions, and the groups of people incarcerated within them, has changed significantly. We might argue then that this docu-verbatim play is simply confirming a linked change in both memory culture and social capital that has already happened. Yet docu-verbatim theatre and the witnessing it produces is still a necessary step in the process of changing social attitudes and the power dynamics in the memory marketplace, and this is where the enactment of representation and explanation is most productive.

Docu-verbatim Responds to the "Big Lie"

After the publication of the Ryan Report, the Abbey directors met to discuss how best the National Theatre could respond to its significance; their decision was to commission a documentary play. The Abbey had previously hosted the Tricycle's touring production of Richard Norton-Taylor's *The Saville Inquiry* (2005), but had never before commissioned documentary work. Aideen Howard, then literary director of the Abbey, suggested that the documentary form would do justice to this history in a more direct way than a fictionalization could.[18] Though the media coverage was widespread and thorough, the Ryan Report itself was twenty-six hundred pages long, so this theatre piece was a chance for audiences to access in more depth some of the detail and individual testimony of the report.

The Abbey was astute in asking Mary Raftery to create the play, as Raftery, an investigative journalist whose work over the previous two decades had pioneered and championed the case of survivors of abuse, had an exhaustive knowledge of the institutional system and an authoritative public identity and cultural capital as a campaigner. Raftery's 1999 television documentary series, *States of Fear*, was a major factor in the government's official recognition of the abuse and then Taoiseach (Prime Minister) Bertie Ahern's historic apology for the state's "failure," which led to the establishment of the Commission to Inquire into Child Abuse.[19] Though the resulting play is a tiny slice of the vast data in the Ryan Report—the report includes evidence from 1,712 complainants and 1,090 witness statements, yet the play is just under ninety minutes long—Raftery worked with the National Theatre team, including Howard and McBrinn, to make this tiny slice feel representative of the whole history.

Raftery used a dramatic editing technique, imported from her experience in television production, combining information from different sections of the Ryan Report into unified scenes, and alternating testimony between survivors, the religious congregations, and civil servants. Raftery also themed the sections of the play so that, roughly speaking, the first scenes are concerned with physical abuse of boys and girls, the next section is concerned with sexual abuse, and the final sections are concerned with the institutional system and its legacy for survivors. Raftery also concentrates the play on a small number of institutions that exemplify the problems of the general system. Though Raftery was a trusted pair of hands, it is still worth emphasising that her role in compiling the play was a highly interventionist one, manipulating the particular archive of the Ryan Report, as discussed below. The purpose of this manipulation was to create an accessible format, or digest, of the report itself, which Catriona Crowe, in a review of the play, argued was achieved, as *No Escape* is "a very successful way of dealing with a huge public issue that convulsed... and is still convulsing the country."[20]

Creating a Timeline: "Hindsight Is Grand, Of Course"

The docu-verbatim play must situate itself clearly in time and space in relation to the subject that it seeks to represent. *No Escape* locates itself firmly within a combined discourse of social history and personal memory. The contrast between these two versions of the past is shocking and worth quoting in some detail:

Dept of Education: 1933 Department of Education Rules and regulations for Certified Industrial Schools—

> Rule 13
>
> ...
>
> (c) Chastisement with the cane, strap or birch.
> Referring to (c) personal chastisement may be inflicted by the Manager, or, in his presence, by an Officer specially authorised by him.... No punishment not mentioned above shall be inflicted.
>
> **Sean Ryan:** [Children were] hosed down with cold water before being beaten, beaten while hanging from hooks on the wall, being set upon by dogs, being restrained in order to be beaten, physical assaults by more than one person, and having objects thrown at them.
>
> ...
>
> There were accounts of boys being hit or beaten with a variety of sticks, including canes, ash plants, blackthorn sticks, hurleys, broom handles, hand brushes, wooden spoons, points, batons, chair rungs, yard brushes, hoes, hay forks, picked and piece of wood with leather thongs attached... bunches of keys, belt buckles, drain rods, rubber pram tyres, golf clubs, tyre rims, electric flexes, fan belts, horse tackled, hammers, metal rulers, butts of rifles, t-squares, gun pellets and hay ropes.
>
> **Dept of Education:** Circular No11/1946—"Discipline and Punishment in Certified Schools":
> Corporal punishment should only be used as a last resort, where other forms of punishment had been unsuccessful as a means of correction.[21]

The duration and extent of these lists being read onstage is an early shock to the audience. The inclusion of the regulations is also significant for the years from which they date. In Act 4 Brother Reynolds states that "I would say the understanding of the abuse and its effect on the young people wasn't known."[22] And in Act 5, Mr. Black, a former principal officer of the Department of Education says "it was a crime, but it wasn't regarded in that light at the time."[23] Mr. Black is actually referring to an incident that occurred in 1980, yet there is a clear attempt at "archaicization" where the distance between the present and the past is exaggerated in order to explain the aberration of past events or views. Indeed, Mr. Black also comments in relation to 1980 that women working within the department were not shown files on abuse as "there was a rule at one time that girls were not to see any things like that, they were very sensitive creatures."[24] Mr. Black counters the suggestion that he, or the department, were remiss by asserting "hindsight is grand, of course."[25] Raftery is careful to resist this reimagining of recent Irish history as a premodern era. The regulations, in their careful elucidation of what represents acceptable punishment, and what does not, demonstrate that punishment by being beaten while "hanging from hooks," for example, would have been equally unacceptable in 1946 as it is seventy years later.

In teaching this play (as a read script, not in performance), I find that students are always shocked and often overwhelmed by these lists. In each class there is also at least one student who, as a result, cannot read any further or who finds the material so disturbing that they choose not to come to class; this is always the risk in teaching emotionally difficult plays. The students who choose to write on this play show great insight into it as a constructed work, calling attention to the ways that this scene functions to contrast the regulations on the one hand and the experience of punishment on the other, and to identify the "rules" as one version of history and the survivors' embodied remembrance of physical abuse as an alternate version. The students' reactions thus demonstrate both the risk of alienating or abjecting an audience by confronting them with emotionally overwhelming material, and the possible intellectual reward of the same confrontation. This is not a criticism of those students who do not, or cannot, engage with the text but an observation of the different impacts of docu-verbatim representations of painful memory. Though there are other highly emotive plays in this course, this is the only play that stimulates this adverse reaction, and it is the only docu-verbatim play, which suggests that fictional plays (about suicide, infant death, and so on) are more easily processed.

The Purpose of Competing Witnesses: The Individual and the "Record"

In "selling" a message to an audience, sympathy is a valuable commodity and tool for theatre makers. The catalog of horrific punishments is certainly one visceral way of eliciting audience sympathy for the children who suffered under such a regime. In order to move sympathy to something stronger, Raftery alternates testimony between competing witnesses: survivor-witnesses who allege abuse, and religious witnesses who claim the abuse allegations are unfounded. By reinforcing the truth claim of the survivor-witness, Raftery generates more than sympathy—audiences are encouraged to side with, or at least acknowledge the truth claims of, the abuse survivor.

An idea of how this works can be gauged from this scene:

Sean Ryan: One witness spoke of arriving at Goldenbridge as a six-year-old child . . . after her mother had died. . . . She said she used to lie in her bed at night and wished that she didn't wake up in the morning. She said that she would sob her heart out crying for her mother.

Witness 2 (female): I used to scurry around. I used to try to dodge and weave to get away from the beatings, the abuse. You didn't. You were helpless. Wherever you were you were a helpless victim. You couldn't get away from them. They used to clatter you, they used to batter you. The names you were called. The stuff you had to go through. The thing was you were always so alone. There was never anybody there for you. Nobody was there this is what I find so hard to tell you. You were lumped together and you were one of a many, many.

[Public hearing (from Phase 3 hearing, 15 May 2006)—scenario as above]

Sr O'Donoghue: Well . . . from all of the material that we have examined and all of the people that we have talked to over the past ten years we are of the conviction that Goldenbridge was . . . a reasonably efficient and caring school, that the managers and Sisters there were committed and worked long and hard in the interest of children, and that it was both committed and dedicated and progressive in very many ways. We believe that having examined some of the, certainly, serious allegations we have not been able to find grounds that would convince us that they were part of the reality.[26]

Here we see how the two types of witness statements alternate competitively. Ryan functions as an intermediary in this competition, to highlight significant points, leaving little room for an audience to sympathize or identify with Sister O'Donoghue, as Raftery's editing strategy works to validate the survivor testimony and to set up an emotional connection between the survivor witnesses and the audience.

It need not be the case, however, that emotion positively attaches to direct statements over interview testimony; it is easy to imagine a reverse of this scenario, where the stark direct-address statements would have a less sympathetic effect in contrast with a fuller and more complex representation of the witness via interview. The inclusion of onstage interaction might have given the interviewed witnesses a more humane quality or given more opportunity for the demonstration of emotion. The intercutting of the survivor testimony with an evasive religious spokesperson, however, creates affective impact and, combined with Sister O'Donoghue's lack of remorse, gives that affective capital to the survivor-witness. In a way, then, the purpose of Judge Ryan's onstage role is in educating and guiding the audience to understand that compassion is the correct witnessing response.[27]

The performance of memory in *No Escape* is consistently structured to ensure that audiences sympathetically witness the victim, while condemning the religious spokesperson. In relation to one boy's school, for instance, Raftery alternates again: Brother Reynolds, argues that "the picture that was presented at Artane [industrial school] was one that was predominantly negative and I would certainly say that the record shows that that is not true" and that the view of that industrial school as "an abusive institution" is "seriously unbalanced."[28] This comment immediately follows two survivor testimonies that describe the nighttime terror of being "beat up and down the dormitory."[29] Raftery's editing technique, putting contradictory testimony side by side, allows the audience the apparent opportunity to come to their own conclusions. I say "apparent" because of course, as I have suggested, the play structurally encourages an audience toward particular conclusions; though there is always the option that an audience, individually or as a group, may identify with the religious congregations, in order to do so the audience would have to resist the structure of the play, which works to support the truth claims of the testimony of the survivors over those of the religious congregations and the state.

Not all witnesses have equal power or capital. Indeed, survivor testimony, while eliciting sympathy, only derives its full impact once confirmed by the conclusions of Judge Ryan. Raftery's deployment of competing witnesses highlights how subjective memory is; in one sense, the competition in these scenes might simply be read as a disagreement between two versions of the past, both of which are delivered with conviction. However, it is the inclusion of Ryan as the central mediator and narrator of the docu-verbatim play that gives credibility, and thus memory capital, to the victims' testimony.

The central role of Ryan, as the arbiter of truth, further illustrates that, given the choice between the two voices, audiences do not always automatically "side with" the victim. Indeed, Raftery's editing practice seen in this light serves to highlight both the competitiveness of the memory market, and the shifting outcomes of that competition: the audience's previous lack of ethical witnessing of the abuse victim.

Social Capital in the Marketplace: "They Were Gods" vs. "Everyone Knew"

The implicit question of *No Escape* is how, given the scope and extent of children's suffering within the system, this level of abuse went undetected for so long. The failure to intervene earlier in this violent system was not necessarily because of a complete lack of abuse reporting, but more likely because of the social capital and status of those reporting it. As novelist John Banville succinctly puts it, "Everyone knew." Banville goes on, "Surely the systematic cruelty visited upon hundreds of thousands of children incarcerated in state institutions in this country from 1914 to 2000 . . . would have been prevented if enough people had been aware of what was going on? Well, no. Because everyone knew."[30] Yet if everyone knew, if the testimony being presented in the report and *No Escape* is not news to audiences, then why was this knowledge not acted on in the past? The only answer is, as suggested above, that the power, status, and capital of the respective stakeholders have fundamentally changed in the social, cultural, and memory marketplaces. The vast majority of children who were sent to residential institutions were working class. Their social position, contrasted with the high status of religious brothers, priests, and nuns, meant that their allegations of abuse were viewed as either unfounded or socially dangerous.[31]

One witness's statement puts the link between disparities in social capital and the continuation of abuse in stark terms, when discussing how a priest sexually abused her, she says: "I couldn't tell anyone. They were Gods, the priests were God, no one would believe you. I was about 11."[32] Witnesses need audiences. This witness's claim that no one would believe her applies not only to the time when the abuse happened, but also to the future years in which she still could not tell anyone. Each individual's and group's understanding of itself in relation to its past is also formative of its sense of its future self and status. Victims, as a marginalized memory community, are prevented from having authoritative control over their own past by the refusal of any audience to support them ("no one would believe you"), and this marginalization continues as this subordinate memory community then also struggles in other social fields, for example, in the "accumulation of power or... influence."[33] Paul Connerton attributes the subordination of certain individuals and groups to the idea that their memories represent a particular social danger: "The oral history of subordinate groups will produce another type of history: one in which not only will most of the details be different, but in which the very construction of meaningful shapes will obey a different principle."[34] On the other hand, the narrative exclusion of subordinate memory groups, such as survivors of abuse, serves to maintain a cohesive social narrative. The link between cultural memory and social power partly explains why subordination within the memory and social marketplaces functions cyclically—how one's experiences and memory are perceived by the dominant group affects not only how one perceives one's own past and thus also one's future, but one's cultural power in arenas outside of memory too, and thus the (im)possibility of changing either the memory or the social narrative and marketplace hierarchy.

Raftery shows that when family members outside the institution made official complaints on the part of institutionalized children, their allegations were also discredited.

Sean Ryan: In February 1963, a Mrs McCarthy brought her grandson to Artane [residential industrial school] to discuss with the Superior his difficulty in keeping jobs and to see if he could help in finding employment. What happened in the course of this meeting is in dispute. The grandmother gave her version of what happened in a letter written later that month 26th February to the Minister for Education.

Mrs. McCarthy: I could not believe my eyes, without word or warning the Superior, closed his fist + struck the boy a most brutal blow on the side of the jaw...[35]

When Mrs. McCarthy went to her local priest for "assistance with her complaint" the priest wrote to the Superior General of the Christian Brothers (who ran Artane), but the priest represented Mrs. McCarthy as "a mental case with a strong antipathy against Artane School.... It is easy to note that she is a very dangerous type of woman."[36] Mrs. McCarthy followed up her complaint with a letter to the Department of Education, but that investigation concluded "it is clear that the charges of brutality and sadism made by Mrs. McCarthy are without foundation."[37]

In teaching this play, this is one of the moments that we focus on in class. I ask students who in this scene they believe. Many of these students will have been educated in religious schools (given that the Catholic Church still runs 92 percent of primary education in the Irish Republic). Despite this background, the students routinely assume that the allegations of abuse are true. This is one indication of the complete about-face in Ireland in the past twenty years, as the social capital and credibility of the Catholic congregation—as a group—has radically decreased, to the point where it is now normal for accusations of wrongdoing against priests, nuns, and brothers to be automatically believed. Prior to this major cultural shift, the reverse would have been true, with allegations of religious wrongdoing automatically discredited or rejected, representing not only a shift in the perception of the Catholic congregations, but a complete shift in the relative status and capital of witnesses, so that the formerly discredited witness now becomes the arbiter of truth, and the formerly authoritative witness now becomes the perpetrator and liar. Memory capital thus increases—and decreases—in tandem with parallel changes in social capital.

Knowledge in the Marketplace: How Do We Know?

How do we know? Often, as shown above with the religious testimony denying abuse, it is because we are told by someone in authority, with recourse to "the record" and to the power connoted by high social status. Yet despite this top-down instruction, other forms of knowledge are available, and Raftery gives us evidence that people were indeed aware of the abusive reality:

> **Ryan:** One witness stated that when one of the sisters sent her to the local shop to get a dozen new canes the shopkeeper broke the canes on his knee in front of her and told her to tell the Sisters he had none left.[38]

This incident indicates the subterranean awareness of abuse, which cannot be articulated except through gesture and denial. This subterranean awareness cannot be transmitted (or transacted) because of its inherent incommunicability and lack of social credibility. Thus the major distinction between the timeframe in which this act took place and the current, post–Ryan Report timeframe can be characterized as the difference between "awareness of abuse" and "knowledge of abuse," a knowledge that is now open and overt, and actively circulating within the marketplace.

Yet culturally it can still be a taboo (albeit one that provokes sympathy rather than antipathy) to have been incarcerated in one of these industrial schools, so it would be an overstatement to claim that these memories are no longer problematic or unsettling. Whereas previously survivors would not have been listened to or believed, in the post-2009 climate, although these witnesses now have a degree of memory capital, a power generated via a combination of social acceptance and their continued mnemonic labor, it would be an exaggeration to convert this cultural recognition into either hard social or economic capital—real markers of social status. You can be remembered and yet remain powerless. Indeed, the survivor-witness, though now accorded credibility, can still struggle to be heard. This struggle includes the difficulty of testifying about abuse and the painful memories this forces the witness to remember/reexperience, and the fraught dilemma of what to do with that testimony once it has been given. This is complicated further by the Irish process of redress, which required witnesses to sign a confidentiality document in order to access financial compensation. The silencing of the witness was an inbuilt part of the government's response—as a result, the Ryan Report is the only access we have to survivors' stories. Again this highlights the importance of theatre, as the translation of the report into a docu-verbatim play illustrates both the ability to belatedly recognize the suffering of the survivors, as well as the need to continue to create platforms for their voices so that their suffering is not simply forgotten.

Legacies of Trauma and Not-Trauma

The final section of *No Escape* is a series of thirteen witness statements, each of which testifies to the personal—and national/international—legacy of institutional abuse. For witnesses, this legacy includes the inability to form close family relationships and the continuation of feelings of shame and stigma: "It's a darkness they gave me. I live alone, my family don't come near me."[39] Other witnesses are no longer able to testify: "I knew seven people who after leaving [the school] committed suicide.... I know an awful lot of people who just cannot come forward to this day, an awful lot are dead."[40] By ending the play with this collection of witness statements, Raftery ensures that survivors have the last word—and by highlighting the ongoing damage of childhood abuse, the play brings the memories of the past into the audience's present.

Within this final section, however, Raftery also strikingly includes some positive memories:

> **Sean Ryan:** Many witnesses who complained of abuse nevertheless expressed some positive memories: small gestures of kindness were vividly recalled. A word of consideration or encouragement, or an act of sympathy or understanding had a profound effect. Adults in their sixties and seventies recalled seemingly insignificant events that had remained with them all their lives.
> **Witness (male) 1:** That Br ... he seemed to have an understanding of us, he was the best one I met in my life. I felt safe with him.... He was able to help with my reading and he would put a mark saying "well done!"
> **Witness (female) 2:** The kindest thing that ever happened to me was a nurse ... we were all around saying the Rosary and she put a sweet in my hand, one sweet. I didn't want to eat the sweet I wanted to hold on to it, somebody gave me something, somebody was kind.[41]

These memories are tiny fragments of kindness and consideration. Their inclusion in the final moments of the play is important because of how these few statements enable survivors to remember, alongside their painful memories, a narrative of pleasure or humanity. This inclusion on Raftery's part is less about creating a "balanced" view of the institutions and more about acknowledging within the structure of the play an entirety of past experience and memory. To exclude these statements, though they are only a very small part of the report's material, would not allow survivors to narrate or remember a full and complex memory of their lives in the institutions. The trauma framework can be empowering in identifying a terrible experience that has a lasting impact on the victim. Yet it can also be an overpowering label, which engulfs the variations within an experience. Finally, of course, these "kind" memories do not narratively destabilize the remembrance of pain, but actually reinforce it, bringing into focus the otherwise relentlessness of abuse.

Collective Witnessing

The final statement of *No Escape* reads:

> **Witness (male) 13:** They all said "that couldn't have happened" but they can't say that to 5000 of us when we all have a similar story to tell.[42]

The citing of the thousands of other victims at the end of *No Escape* is a powerful reminder of absence—of what cannot be represented on stage, both because of the scale of victimization versus the limited scale of the theatre's stage (and the equally limited scale of the audience's capacity) and because of the loss of those victims to death, to emigration, and to silence. Yet despite this obvious absence, the claiming of solidarity is a key moment in the play for the creation of a collective that is more powerful than individual victims alone, or a singular victim standing synecdochically for the whole.

Within this brief statement, the witness acknowledges that previous attempts to tell his story met with disbelief, but that this response is no longer tenable in the face of *collective witnessing*. The historical attempt at bearing witness to abuse underlines the fact that the survivor-witnesses do not constitute new subjects, but constitute newly valued subject positions—newly valued, that is, by the audience. They were always there, but it is only now that they are being listened to. The correspondences between the five thousand memories—"a similar story"—suggests both the commonality of abuse within the system, and the sense that within this collective witnessing each memory corroborates another in a mutually supportive group narrative that has the ability, through combined memory capital, to change the memory narrative and social capital of the whole community ("they all"). The witness's description of his memory as a "story to tell" underlines the importance of performing that narrative to an audience. The role of the witness is obviously to give testimony, to tell the story. The role of the audience is to respond adequately to that performance. This is not, as we have seen, a straightforward invitation.

When the audience fails to believe the witness because the witness's testimony contradicts, or is proscribed by, the dominant power in the memory marketplace (i.e., the Catholic Church, the state), then that effective repression of witnessing is damaging for both the individual and the society, for as Paul Ricoeur puts it, "the circumscription of the narrative is thus placed in the service of the circumscription of the identity defining the community."[43] The audience's past failure to believe the stories of survivors was, itself, a further act of abuse, compounding the physical, sexual, and emotional abuses. As Ricoeur argues, "a devious form of forgetting is at work here, resulting from stripping the social actors of their original power to recount their actions themselves."[44] The purpose of *No Escape* is to combat the dispossession of the abused, to return to them the right and the power to tell their own stories and, in doing so, to build a new collective memory and a community of witnessing. And the purpose of the audience to *No Escape* as a theatrical event is to make up for the failures of previous audiences by according these acts of testimony with the respect and capital denied to them—despite their constant labor to be heard, seen, protected—by the dominant community for so many decades. This is, of course, an artificial process of latent recognition, given that the original abuse was actually visible ("Everyone knew") but nevertheless went unacknowledged ("They were Gods").

Spectatorship is constituted in particular ways within the theatre—the house lights are dimmed, the stage is raised, the audience is primed to attend to the performance. The experience of witnessing the play is thus very different from witnessing actual abuse; the documentary theatre form can only represent a formal version of past events, so that an audience for *No Escape*, performing as ethical listeners to the abuses being catalogued, can do so in a relatively passive and unchallenging way: it is perfectly possible to see the play with no sense of having to intervene, to speak up, or, indeed, to act. This is very different from the role of contemporary witnesses, such as Mrs. McCarthy or the cane-breaking shopkeeper, who had a much greater level of investment and risk attached to witnessing and acting ethically in response to the violence occurring within institutions. While it is commendable that documentary plays like *No Escape* make this historical violence accessible and knowable, whether it can produce a transfer of meaning through active spectatorship, or create what Alison Landsberg terms "prosthetic memory," is debatable.

Active Spectatorship: Belated Witnessing and the Risk of Shame

One of the reasons why active spectatorship failed for so long can be explained by using Jacques Rancière's term, the "intolerable image," which describes something that audiences find unbearably painful to look at or listen to. According to Rancière, when the audience is presented with something they cannot face, there is a shift from "the intolerable *in* the image to the intolerable *of* the image."[45] The image, in this case the image of children being abused by religious figures, becomes taboo and thus off limits. As I have suggested, the shift in attitudes to the "intolerable image" has been led by cultural and official representations and acknowledgements of the abuse. However, this is not to say that the intolerable has been rendered completely or easily palatable through this process. Rather, the intolerable image is sustained by Raftery, as in the lists of modes of punishment (and my students' reactions). The challenge to the audience is to find a capacity to tolerate the intolerable so that historical abuse can be recognized and acknowledged without lessening the severity of what happened via mitigation or historical distancing. This may contribute to what Landsberg terms the "alien nature of the past," necessary, she argues, to producing real historical knowledge: "The affective engagements that draw the viewer in must be coupled with other modes that assert the alien nature of the past, and the viewer's fundamental distance from it."[46]

The necessity for the audience, in turn, to critically reflect on their roles as witnesses to this play is underscored if we consider the major absence onstage—and in the list of the play's witnesses—of any representative of the *bystanders*; the communities that housed these institutions and that allowed children to be sent to them remain invisible. This absence raises the question of whether the audience stands in for these communities. Audiences may not even notice this as an absence, with the structure of the play as a binary opposition of the Department of Education and the religious congregations on the one hand and the survivors on the other. In this binary model, in large part, the community escapes responsibility and censure. One question for the audience, however, is whether the next duty of listening is speaking, whereby the audience gives their own testimony, and move from being secondary to being primary, remediating witnesses themselves.

I want to return here to the fact that the work of the Commission to Inquire into Child Abuse was stimulated by the state's belated acknowledgment and official apology in 1999 for the history of abuse. Salient features of the apology include the fact that it was not only on behalf of the government, but included all citizens in the apology for what was framed as a "collective failure." This apology led to real and measurable change, from the opportunity to give evidence to the commission, to compensation under the redress scheme. Yet the publication of the Ryan Report in 2009, and the award of compensation to the survivors of abuse, are also markers of closure, and this closure threatens to label this history "over," and the collective responsibility fulfilled.

The national shame felt by the exposure of this history is also expended. The apology, moreover, discursively creates a binary of "us" and "them," in the opposition between "the victims" and "our collective." As Sara Ahmed argues, the apology for national past wrongs functions to bond and assert the nation as a group, and at the same time it acknowledges that group's failings.[47] In theory, *No Escape* frees the survivor-witnesses from the shame they experienced as children and, later, as adults. The feelings of shame and anger produced in the theatre auditorium, then, are redirected at those culpable—primarily, in this production, at the religious and state spokespeople. The experience of the spectator may be to share in this shame, following the logic of the apology. (Other emotions, of course, may also be engaged, from anger to guilt to denial.) Shame, as Ahmed has formulated it, illustrates the potential danger in provoking an emotion that audiences want to rid themselves of, or to divest. Shame is an emotion that is highly individualized, despite its collective "national" quality in this example. While an individual feeling a painful or difficult emotion like shame is moved, the issue is what they are moved to do. One of the greatest limits on witnessing pain is that the nature of that witnessing can be "felt change" rather than actual change, and that feelings, particularly negative feelings like shame, are more likely to lead to inaction as the witness tries to repress or avoid the implications of the emotion.

Though the spectator to *No Escape* can feel changed, or more precisely feel a changed relationship to the particular history of institutional child abuse, it is more problematic to identify further outcomes, such as resistance to current and continuing abusive practices or callous structures of institutionalization, many of which can be identified in modern-day Ireland, from psychiatric institutions to direct provision centers for interning asylum seekers. We still lock away a lot of very vulnerable people, we are doing it every day, and we are ignoring it every day. And these are the conditions in which abuse flourishes. How can we better witness this new reality and not just past abuses? How can we move from consumption to witnessing?

The applause that comes at the end of *No Escape* acknowledges the work of the theatre makers in bringing the show to the public. Yet it may also function as a moment of closure, a way of making noise to assert the end of the show and the end of that history. We can clap, in the present moment, and thereby perform our empathy for the survivors and our distance and difference from those in the past (as well as those in the present) who failed as caregivers and as witnesses to "the victims." But that clapping, that release of noise, may also represent a cathartic absolution of shame, a ritual action that divests the individual of the feeling of shame, shares it among the group, and reasserts the power of the collective, within which the individual can remain anonymous. The collective sharing of shame is a lessening of the individual's burden, while the individual's incorporation into the group action of clapping dissociates both the individual and the group from the abuse they have witnessed, and thus from the shame, and from any attendant requirement to act.

We might therefore argue that the utopian possibility of *No Escape* is, first and foremost, the creation of a shared and inclusive—nonbinary—memory community in the theatre space. Secondary utopian possibilities include the opportunity for audiences to use their experience of spectatorship of the play, and the resulting understanding of the consequences of the total disempowerment of disenfranchised and vulnerable members of society, as a catalyst to build a more ethical present and future and to combat continuing structural callousness. This is, however, a distinctly limited opportunity given the play's representation of the "intolerable" and, as a result, its provocation of negative emotions such as shame.

This speaks also to the risk of the "facts" alluded to at the start of this chapter, the risk that audiences will not want to go to the theatre to confront crises or to engage with troubling histories. This may be why *No Escape* had a very limited run. The play ran for two weeks on the Abbey's Peacock stage (the studio space) in April 2010 as part of its "Darkest Corner" series of three plays, aimed at responding to the revelations of institutional abuse (which had been termed "Ireland's darkest corner"[48]). Though it was widely reviewed on radio and in the national newspapers,[49] the play's run was not extended, nor did it tour.[50] In contrast, in the 1960s, Richard Johnson's fiction play, *The Evidence I Shall Give*, represented the abuse of a young girl by nuns in an industrial school, but couched within a gentler courtroom drama. That play was hugely successful and returned for extended runs. Forty years later, the same market success did not manifest for *No Escape*, despite the more tolerant social context of its production. Aideen Howard, the Abbey's then-literary director, commented that the play did not have the performance run she thought it should have.[51] And yet Howard also commented that many more people claimed to have seen the play than box office receipts verify, suggesting that the play has a certain cultural capital, and that audiences who did not attend retrospectively want to claim attendance, perhaps because they feel that they should have attended (another permutation of shame?). *No Escape* was revived for a one-off staged reading in January 2014 at the Peacock,[52] and in 2015 was translated into Portuguese and performed as a staged reading by the Cia Ludens Company in Sao Paulo, Brazil (November 10, 2015). At this performance, audience members made connections to abuse scandals in Brazil and Chile. While having relatively limited direct market exposure and, judged financially, a low level of success in the marketplace, the play has both a national and an international reach, and impact on the memory marketplace that belies the number of actual performances and ticket sales.

Given that the past is a major formative factor in determining an individual's and a community's future identity, the revolution in understanding the past, brought about by the Ryan Report, should also invoke a similar shift in the future identity of Ireland and its treatment of the vulnerable. In many ways, however, the absence of the community from *No Escape*—and the primary assignation of guilt to the religious congregations—fails to tackle the structural social problems that created an environment that fostered, rather than hindered, an abusive childcare system, and continues to limit narratives relating to the abuse circulating in the marketplace. If docu-verbatim theatre is to have a real and lasting impact on the present and future, each audience member, and the audience as a collective, must take on the more active role of audience-witness in the present.

PART TWO

Marketplace Success: Laramie *and Telling the Story of Memory*

The Laramie Project, first produced in late 2000 as a reaction to the 1998 hate-crime murder of gay University of Wyoming student Matthew Shepard, has become one of the most performed plays in America, toured by Tectonic Theater Company and taken up by student and professional companies across the United States as "the examination of the American psyche at the end of the millennium."[53] Its ascendancy has been phenomenal—in 2010 the company's founder, Moisés Kaufman, attributed this striking market success to the fact that Shepard's death was "a watershed historical moment for our culture."[54] As Kaufman said: "We felt that Matthew Shepard would trigger a conversation and that if we were able to record that conversation we would be able to gather a document that talked about how the whole nation was speaking." As Kaufman introduces the play: "There are moments in history when a particular event brings the various ideologies and beliefs prevailing in a culture into sharp focus."[55] Positioning the play as a response to a watershed cultural moment chimes with *No Escape*'s representation of dramatically shifting capital within the marketplace, and Kaufman's use of the term "prevailing" further demonstrates his interest in how that marketplace functions, both locally and nationally. This interest informs *The Laramie Project* and its sequel *The Laramie Project: Ten Years Later*, both of which represent multiple voices and perspectives within a framework of interrogating prevailing views and, in the latter play, the ways in which remembrance culture is shaped in accordance with these prevailing views. As with *No Escape*, Tectonic use the collective social and memory capital of their interviewee subjects to project both onto the silent victim.

A confluence of events created the market conditions for *The Laramie Project*'s popularity: Shepard's death occurred at a time when America was increasingly seen as a post-AIDS society and, theatrically, *The Laramie Project* further capitalizes on the national and international success in the early 1990s of Tony Kushner's play *Angels in America*.[56] Having said that, the climate of tolerance is not so universalized that the play has not been controversial; Tectonic describes many occasions in which schools and communities have blocked student productions. In one case in Oklahoma a teacher was suspended for teaching the play; in this example, we can see that the reception of the play mirrors the social divides that the play seeks to stage.[57] However, the controversy has now become part of the play's market appeal, as one student said to me "It's kind of sexy," suggesting that notoriety, or the "cool" factor of the play, feeds into its market success. A final contributing factor in the high frequency of nonprofessional productions is its franchisability to schools and local drama groups looking for scripts suitable for large ensembles.

So What's It About? Now or Then? Shepard or Laramie?

As with *No Escape*, the Laramie plays show a high level of intervention and mediation and, likewise, in order to tell the story of memory and have it appeal to a wide audience, Tectonic uses the microcosm as a representative reflection of the larger picture.

Both of Tectonic's Laramie plays—in focusing on the community rather than on the individual at the center of the story, Matthew Shepard—render Shepard a symbol or an icon of victimhood. This is not necessarily a fixed symbol, but one that resonates differently for different memory communities and individuals, from Matthew's family, who grieve him as a lost son, to those who did not know him personally but campaign in his name for legislative recognition of hate crimes and discrimination. Additionally, Shepard functions as a negative symbol for those in Laramie (and nationally) who do not recognize his murder as a hate crime and wish the "incident" were forgotten. How Shepard's death is multiply remembered, interpreted, and symbolically reified into different kinds of capital are thus key aspects of both *The Laramie Project* and *The Laramie Project: Ten Years Later*.

Tectonic's decision to create a sequel was informed by the continued market success of *The Laramie Project* as well as the desire to chart the legacy of Shepard's death. The later play not only follows up on *The Laramie Project* in returning to many of the same issues but reframes them according to how they have changed over the course of a decade; *The Laramie Project: Ten Years Later*, then, both advertently and inadvertently, makes *The Laramie Project* a historical document that the more recent play responds to and, in some ways, restages. Having said that, similar to *No Escape*, *The Laramie Project* and *The Laramie Project: Ten Years Later* are set in a historical past (even at the first production of these plays they were already "past" the moment of their inspiration and creation), they are, like all theatre works, also always "present," given the perpetually regenerative power of theatre to make the past and present coterminous. In his work on performing history, Freddie Rokem argues that this is the paradox of history theatre, wherein "performing history" the play inevitably acknowledges the time lapse between the event, the reflection on the event, and the performance of that reflection, yet also tends "to bring all of these as close together as possible."⁵⁸ In this respect, *The Laramie Project: Ten Years Later* not only acknowledges but makes a feature of the temporal and cultural difference between "then" and "now," "us" and "them." The sense of coming after allows audiences, as in *No Escape*, to survey the marketplace anew and to consider how it is currently different. The break between the past and the present that is inevitable in docu-verbatim theatre is therefore an advantage in creating critical witnesses to painful memory.

Tectonic Theater began their research, primarily through interviews with the townspeople of Laramie, Wyoming, and other directly concerned figures, only four weeks after Shepard's murder. *The Laramie Project* thus has a double temporality—both immediate (four weeks is a very short space of time for a theatre piece to begin to emerge) and long-term, as the play took two years from its inception to performance. Tectonic also had to literally travel the distance to Laramie from its base in New York. The process of this play being created by outsiders to Laramie potentially grants the play an almost anthropological air, raising questions of outsider objectivity, identification, stereotyping, and cliché. The form of the play, like *No Escape*, makes its source material visible, including verbatim interview testimony and documents, media reports, and trial transcripts. And, again like *No Escape*, the construction process behind the narrative is highlighted, provoking us as audiences and scholars to consider this process and the choices that the company made in its material. However, since the vast majority of the oral interview archive Tectonic amassed is not publicly accessible, it is impossible to determine what was left out and what the relationships are between the material included and that which was excluded.

Indeed, the amount of source material is overwhelming. Tectonic made six visits to Laramie, gathering two hundred interviews (over four hundred hours in total), and requiring four writers to organize and edit the interview transcripts; even with this editing, the play has sixty-seven characters. Of course not all of these characters are significant, many have only a single contribution to the script. Nevertheless, this is a large number of characters for the actors to portray,⁵⁹ and for audiences to keep track of and relate to. As a result, the play has a few defined characters (including the Tectonic artists as "characters" themselves) who make repeated appearances, while other figures have one or two lines each, creating a background collage of memories and opinions. The silent witness throughout is Matthew Shepard.

It is necessary for Shepard to be silent as the Laramie plays are not about him as an individual but as a symbolic example of hate crime in America (in the same way that survivor-witnesses in *No Escape* are anonymous). The consistently salient point of both plays is that the occurrence of Shepard's death in Laramie reveals the underlying (as well as the overt) homophobia within the community, challenging Laramie's view of itself as having a strong and tolerant value system. Moisés Kaufman's desire that this single murder in one town become the catalyst for a national conversation about homophobia and gay rights indicates the play's foundational principle of a universalized message, designed to intervene in the rights discourse, what Allen Feldman calls "a curative trajectory."⁶⁰ This trajectory precludes the play from dwelling on Shepard as a living person; Shepard's life and death, the course of the criminal case, and the reaction of the community, are thereby all transformed into symbolic capital and the "usable past" (and, arguably, the usable present).

The Usable Past

The idea of use, or utility, is key to understanding how *The Laramie Project* functions to mediate memory and the past. Usability is raised early on in the play by two of Laramie's residents, Marge Murray and Alison Mears. Murray describes Laramie as an ideal place to live due to its rural setting: the relative underpopulation of the area meant that "I could run around the house in my altogethers, do the housework while the kids were in school."⁶¹ Greg Pierotti, the Tectonic company member conducting the interview, queries Murray's term: "I just want to make sure I got the expression right: 'in your altogethers'?"⁶² This contrast between Murray's rural colloquialism and Pierotti's delicate urban sensibilities is singled out by Jill Dolan as creating a binary of rural/urban in the play, thereby exposing the company's condescending attitude to the community's "country ways."⁶³ So here, again, we see how the social power imbalance affects access to, and voice within, the memory marketplace. Dolan's critique is salutary, yet it overlooks Murray's use of the past tense and her evocation of nostalgia for how Laramie used to be. In addition to characterizing Murray and Laramie as charming or quaint, Murray's nostalgic testimony is knowing—and it is hence used here to show how the idea of an innocent, almost prelapsarian

Laramie is now viewed as romantically archaic, by *both* Pierotti *and* Murray, in the post-Shepard era.

Murray's friend, Alison Mears, follows Pierotti's query with her own retort: "Now how's he gonna use that in his play?"[64] Mears is thus fully aware of their testimony as usable material and that much of what they say has little theatrical capital. Moreover, they are both aware that Pierotti-as-interviewer is not a transparent conduit but rather a playwright who will "use" what he wants out of the material they give him. Mears's comment overvalues Pierotti's labor, while undervaluing Murray's colloquial culture. In identifying Pierotti's agenda in this scene and questioning her friend, Mears also suggests that she as a witness will shape her own testimony, self-scripting in order to provide what she sees as usable material, prejudging her own capital. Though Dolan is right to identify the "uneven distribution of social and theatrical power,"[65] this is a power balance that both Mears and Murray are well aware of. Murray is quoted near the end of the play: "To show it's not the hell hole of the earth would be nice, but that is up to how you portray us."[66] Though in the earlier "altogethers" scene Murray may seem naively trusting, she is revealed later as fully cognizant of the power dialectic between performance and representation. Including Murray's reference to her "altogethers" and Pierotti's slightly prudish querying of the phrase is also evidence of Tectonic's awareness of that same relationship, and, like *No Escape*, an exemplary moment of making the construction of the play—the interview format—visible, so that audiences may see the process in action and, to an extent, judge for themselves. Throughout both plays, Tectonic maintains this highly self-aware methodology, for example using the term "character" to denote real people, so that the art—and labor—of theatre is constantly made visible.

The residents of Laramie, like Murray and Mears, are also highly aware of the different uses to which narrative can be put, as shown by the remarks of one of the sergeants who worked on the Shepard murder:

> **Sergeant Hing**: Now, when the incident happened with that boy a lot of press people came here. And one time some of them followed me out to the crime scene. And uh, well, it was a beautiful day . . . and the sky was that blue . . . it's just gorgeous . . . And they were just—nothing but the story. I didn't feel judged, I felt that they were stupid. They're, they're missing the point—they're just missing the whole point.[67]

Here, Sergeant Hing's awareness of "the story" casts his labeling of the murder as an "incident," and his ensuing description of the gorgeous sky, as a deliberate attempt to shift the focus away from the brutality of Shepard's death (perhaps surprising given the sergeant's public position as a law enforcement officer). Since the play maintains the focus on Shepard's death and its aftermath, Hing's testimony is used to indicate what Tectonic views as the problematic narrative construction of Shepard's death as a one-off happening rather than a social crisis. The sergeant's reaction thus exemplifies the conflict in the discussion of Shepard's murder (in these two plays and elsewhere) over its narrative importance, at either the center or the margins of the community.

Shepard's death is central to two sides of the Laramie, and wider, community—those who are horrified by the homophobic motivation of his killers (Aaron McKinney and Russell Henderson), and those who refuse to condemn the killers because homosexuality is viewed as sinful in itself. *The Laramie Project* is, in some ways, a tug-of-war between these two sides, and in the end the triumph of love and hope in actively resisting the depiction of Shepard's death as inevitable.

The conflict over how to frame Shepard's death is even more central to *The Laramie Project: Ten Years Later*, a play that shows how, over time, the narrativization of the murder in the memory marketplace changes as individual and social memory are subject to new and different pressures or demands, from reclaiming the landscape of Laramie as a site of beauty, to defining Shepard's legacy through the campaign for anti-hate-crime legislation. *The Laramie Project: Ten Years Later* sets out to revisit Laramie (combining testimony from previous and new witnesses) in order to chart the social and cultural change a decade after Shepard's death. The changes Tectonic encounters illustrate the shifting status of different group's memory capital, and the ongoing labor (across the theatre, news, and media industries) required to maintain, or gain, status.

Temporal Distance and Moving On

If *The Laramie Project* questions how a community reacts to a homophobic murder, then *The Laramie Project: Ten Years Later* questions how a community writes its own history. The answer is that it depends on which memory community you belong to. In Laramie, broadly speaking, two memory communities exist, one of which actively remembers Matthew Shepard's murder as a hate crime, and one of which downplays or denies the murder as a hate crime and uses this renarrativizing of the past as a way of moving on from the stigmatizing perception of Laramie as a homophobic community. Both memory communities view Shepard's death as a traumatic event that demands progress in the present, but how that progress is imagined and enacted takes different forms, from the campaigns, for example, for equal partner benefits at the University of Wyoming (Shepard's alma mater), to the perception that the trauma is best dealt with by "putting this behind us."[68]

The two main narratives that *The Laramie Project: Ten Years Later* identifies are that Shepard's murder was either a hate crime or a drug robbery gone wrong. This latter narrative is traced to the 2004 episode of the television program *20/20* (ABC Network), which refuted the hate-crime label and identified drugs as the culprit. This has been a major factor in mediating this particular memory, as Professor Catherine Connolly states, "Over time, that *20/20* piece has made a tremendous negative impact on how Matthew Shepard's murder is perceived,"[69] because, as Dave O'Malley (the original investigating officer) says, ABC is "a major, respected news source." Though PBS did a show to rebut ABC's version, O'Malley questions its market impact: "How many people watch PBS and how many watch *20/20*?"[70] ABC's dominance of the television market translates into greater capital and thus power in the memory marketplace; audience-consumers (or, seen from a more sympathetic perspective, audience-witnesses) reinforce this greater capital because ABC presents a narrative to which they can more easily subscribe.

Competing Witnesses

The *Laramie Boomerang*'s editorial, titled "Our View: Laramie Is a Community Not a 'Project,'" suggests that the restructuring of the narrative of the motivation for Shepard's killing enables the Laramie community to avoid the stigma of being perceived as homophobic.[71] As witness Jeffrey Lockwood says in the scene "Boomerang #3," "The Matthew Shepard murder flies in the face of who we are, the story we've told ourselves, and so you've either got to radically adjust your story or you've got to throw out the data. And so far what we've done is throw out the data."[72] The effect of this rejection of "data" is the marginalization of Shepard's murder in the dominant community narrative, an example of what Professor Beth Loffreda positions as "we all agree to lie."[73] To explain why and how this has taken place, later in the scene Tectonic performs their interview with professor of folklore, John Dorst. This is the only time in either play that the testimony given does not relate directly to the murder or its aftermath, but is a form of expert testimony on the processes of knowing the past. Dorst is introduced twice, first by Leigh Fondakowski ("We spoke to John Dorst, a folklorist at the University of Wyoming."), and in the next line by Greg Pierotti ("So as a folklorist, can you tell us how this change in the story occurred here in Laramie?") In response, Dorst says: "As a folklorist, I can tell you that there's a desire for communities to own and control their history. And when that gets taken away, a 'reaction formation' occurs."[74] Dorst's professional expertise is noted three times, which, combined with his use of academic terminology, underlines his social capital and thus the value of what he says. The irony of Dorst's testimony of course is that the same desire to "control" is manifest in both the Laramie community's retelling actions and in Tectonic's; using Dorst's folkloric framework, we might read *The Laramie Project: Ten Years Later* as Tectonic's "reaction formation."

Though Tectonic's huge success with *The Laramie Project* ensures that their own retelling has a cultural impact, *The Laramie Project: Ten Years Later* also demonstrates that Tectonic's impact in the Laramie marketplace is limited to those that already agree with their premise, that Shepard's death was a hate crime. Power in the memory marketplace is thus dependent on the ideological agendas of different memory communities with distinct memory formations, which are in direct competition with each other. Though Tectonic may have capital, and thus power and influence, within the national theatrical memory marketplace, this does not, as the second play effectively shows, translate to capital within the local memory marketplace, which is dominated by a consensus that Shepard's death was caused by a material problem (drugs) rather than a cultural problem (homophobia). This consensus (or agreed "lie") empowers the community to "write its own history" within a framework that shifts the blame away from the town's values and toward a more easily identifiable and externalized problem, and also to erase the association of Laramie with shame. As Reggie Fluty (investigating officer) says in regard to this shame: "It's hard when you're very ashamed of yourself to stand up and say, 'Yeah, we screwed up.' Instead we start making excuses, and pointing the blame at somebody else or others—we do that as individuals, we do that as a community, we do that as a nation. And that's what I think we've done."[75] As discussed above in relation to *No Escape*, the production of shame is not conducive to ethical or active witnessing. This shameful antiresponsibility reaction provides a depressing postscript to the promise of ethical witnessing (as defined by Tectonic, at least) that is the curative trajectory of the first Laramie play.

Witnessing Forgetting

The outcome of positioning the story within a drugs framework is the concomitant marginalization of Shepard's memory within the Laramie memory marketplace. When Tectonic member Greg Pierotti returns to the University of Wyoming campus, he discovers that most of the students he asks are unclear of who Shepard was and have no real sense of why Shepard died, though many of them vaguely attribute it to drugs. This displacement of Shepard's memory from the university is underlined by the location of his memorial bench in "a remote corner" of the campus.[76] Its official unveiling by the Shepard family and university authorities is characterized by one witness, Laramie resident and equal-rights campaigner Zackie Salmon, saying "I just felt there was a certain forgetfulness in the air that morning... because we've worked, worked, worked, worked, worked to get domestic partner benefits here on campus, and we still don't have that."[77] Salmon identifies remembering with the pursuit of change, and views the memorial bench as a signifier of how memorials can function as substitutes for an active, ethical memory culture. In some ways, this suggests that Salmon sees memory culture in terms of social legacy rather than as actual memory in and of itself, that is, not in remembering Matthew Shepard the individual, but remembering Matthew Shepard by acting in the present for change in his name and for a cause with which he has become synonymous.[78] Salmon's conspicuous repetition of "worked" illustrates the labor required in order to translate memory capital into social and political change.

The opposite memory formation is to position Shepard's death as a painful event from which to move on. As one witness says, "it's time to let the boy go," while Deb Thomsen, editor of the *Laramie Boomerang*, says, "You know, we're trying to put this behind us, and keep going. You have brutality and you deal with it, and you move on."[79] Both of these witnesses, however, also express the view that the murder was not a hate crime. The play thus links an explicit desire to move on from the traumatic details of the murder with a deliberate repression of the reasons for the murder. Thomsen claims to express the dominant views of the community; the *Boomerang* editorial explains that the paper had requests for less coverage of the anniversary and in some cases that subscribers had requested their delivery be suspended during the week of the anniversary.[80] This willed amnesia or avoidance is in contrast to other Laramie residents, such as Jonas Slonaker, whose letter to the editor, remembering Shepard, is not published by the *Boomerang*. Slonaker is a subordinate operator within the memory marketplace, whereas Thomsen, who reflects but also presumably influences public opinion as the paper's editor, is framed as a dangerously successful memory entrepreneur.

It is not unreasonable for a community to want to define itself in terms other than the site of "brutality," to deal with it, and move on. It is also not unreasonable for a local newspaper to suggest that a community is more complex than a single "project" can suggest. The unfortunate aspect is that in the play these appeals are mainly expressed defensively by those intent on denial so that Tectonic constructs moving on, in itself a healthy desire for individuals and communities after painful events, as a conservative desire or a form of cover-up.

Additionally, the *Boomerang* editorial asserting that Shepard's death was "a robbery gone very wrong" is placed in the second half of Act 1, after testimony from a range of witnesses, including two police officers, that the murder was motivated by hate and that both perpetrators were clean of drugs, so that the view that the crime was not motivated by homophobia is undermined before the editorial is read.[81] As in *No Escape*, though the audience can of course identify with the *Boomerang* editorial view, the structure of the play makes this identification difficult. This is not to say that I agree with the newspaper's editorial, rather to illustrate how documentary sources are manipulated by Tectonic to give a competitive edge, through enhanced memory capital, to those with less social capital.

Tectonic's reactive bias in gatekeeping is discernible in the theatrical attention they grant to Jonas Slonaker. After the *Boomerang* refuses to print his letter calling for the community to more actively mark the tenth anniversary, he displays his distress: "I drove out to the prairie and screamed until my throat hurt. It really broke my spirit when they refused to print my letter."[82] *The Laramie Project: Ten Years Later* enables Slonaker's voice to be heard uncensored, temporarily lending him more social capital than he has outside the play, and rebalancing the access that different groups have to the marketplace.

Sites of Memory: "It's Just a Place"

In *The Laramie Project*, company member Greg Pierotti says of his 1998 visit to the fence, the site of Shepard's attack: "I broke down the minute I touched it. I feel such a strong kinship with this young man."[83] Pierotti reads the fence as a highly emotive and meaningful site, implying that the fence stands as a productive node in a complex social and memory marketplace. This reading obviously contrasts with Sergeant Hing's earlier characterization of the site as defined predominantly by its natural beauty and not its social history. This conflict, between the interpolation of this location as a general landscape or as a specific site of memory, is complicated by the later removal of the fence itself, because, as former Police Officer Reggie Fluty states, "The owner didn't want people coming out onto his property to see it."[84]

Without the fence as a marker, it is difficult for people, particularly outsiders, to visit the site; company member Stephen Belber comments: "It seems like all the visible markers of Matthew's death are gone."[85] If the docu-verbatim play relies on "the facts" to give its testimonies weight, then the removal of the fence, one of the core "facts" of the Shepard murder, potentially weakens the play's connection to the landscape of the real and demonstrates the concomitant strengthening of perspectives such as Sergeant Hing's, denying the landscape as a site of memory. Indeed, even for locals the site—without the fence—becomes less important as a memorial space. Slonaker says, "I remembered where the place was and I would still go back, and it's... yeah. The fence is gone. Ten years later and the fence is gone.... And ten years of snow and rain have washed through there. I mean it's just a place, in the end I guess. And I decided not to go anymore. I had to let it go."[86] Slonaker's decision to cease this particular act of commemorative performance resonates with the active forgetting of other witnesses, but with none of the negativity associated with denying the hate crime. However, this cessation also seems forced on Slonaker by the absence of the fence or of any permanent memorial of the crime. This absence provokes questions as to the function of memorials, their purpose and utility within a culture and for a memory community. Zackie Salmon also questions the point of memorials when she says, "A bench to Matthew Shepard is nice—but a university's values are reflected in its policies."[87]

Marge Murray, however, takes issue with the absence of a memorial: "Well, there were two things, though, that I really hated. Tearing that fence down and not puttin' up some kind of... something to say 'This is where it happened. Straighten up, Laramie.'"[88] Murray makes an explicit link between a site of memory and positive change, to the extent that a memorial has the power to demand change (or at least has the power to chastise). The absence of a memorial at the fence signifies the absence of change, so that the nonmemorial, in *The Laramie Project: Ten Years Later*, is interpreted by the active memory community as a marker of the dominant community's resistance to the meaning of Shepard's death and their struggle to effect change within either the memory or social marketplaces. The bench memorializing Shepard on the University of Wyoming campus and Murray's regret about the fence site also suggest another dimension of the marketplace—that in the case of physical memorials, the ownership of the land is a major factor in the types and spatial presence of remembrance culture; yet another reminder that economic capital affects memory capital.

Slonaker's comment on the erosion of the site also suggests the vulnerability of physical signs of memory, in contrast to the resilience of his own personal memory. This is also expressed by Dave O'Malley, for whom the Shepard murder is a defining event, yet who only owns a single photograph of the fence site. Though often it is personal memory that is seen as ephemeral or fragile, the contrast between the memory communities demonstrates that the meanings that are attached by individuals and groups to past events determine the trajectory of memory, which is always an act of adapting and readapting to the present, whether it fades or intensifies. And so were there a permanent memorial at the fence site, or had O'Malley taken scores of photographs, Shepard would not necessarily be any more clearly or actively remembered by those not already inclined to do so. Memory capital is not determined by materiality. In Marge Murray's view the absence of a permanent memorial is not about remembrance per se, but how forgetting enables the community to look away from its own past and its responsibilities to acknowledge that past.

Certainly *The Laramie Project: Ten Years Later* emphasises the tearing down of the fence as a communal loss, a result of competition in the marketplace. It's worth noting, however, Tectonic's manipulation of their own data in order to create this emphasis. In an earlier version of the script, Tectonic included a scene called "Two Guys at the Strip Mall" in which two guys (one a Laramie resident, one a visitor) discuss going out to visit the former fence site. Though this scene is not included in the final version of the script (published in 2014), it is included in the "Audience Guide to the Epilogue," still available online. Originally, this was the fourth scene of the play:

> **Guy 2:** They took the fence down.
> **Greg Pierotti:** They took it down?
> **Guy 2:** Oh yeah.
> **Greg Pierotti:** Really? The fence . . . where Matt Shepard was killed?
> **Guy 2:** Definitely. It's gone. For a while now.
> **Greg Pierotti:** Why did they take it down?
> **Guy 2:** The owners didn't want people coming on their property. People still do, though, even though it's gone. They got "no trespassing" signs all over the place out there.
> **Greg Pierotti:** So, why'd you bring him out there then?
> **Guy 2:** Because that's what we're famous for.[89]

I have quoted this exchange at length because I'm interested in its absence from the final published text and the concomitant reorganization of scenes. In this exchange with Pierotti, Guy 2 casually appropriates the fence not as a site of memory but as a signifier of fame, a different kind of cultural capital. This matches the play's characterization of the dominant community's misremembering of Shepard's death. Yet it contradicts Belber's statement that "all the visible markers of Matthew's death are gone." The "no trespassing" signs now represent a kind of antimemorial, supporting a successful performance of dark memory tourism.

An obvious reason for the deletion of this scene from the published text is that it repeats material. In the published text's third scene, "Reggie and Marge," Marge Murray informs Greg Pierotti that the fence has been taken down:

> **Greg Pierotti:** They took the fence down?
> **Marge Murray:** Yeah, they did.
> **Reggie Fluty:** The owner didn't want people coming out onto his property to see it—there's "no trespassing" signs all over there now.[90]

Obviously Tectonic does not want to include two scenes with such similar subject matter and expressions; the inclusion of Murray and Fluty (in place of Guy 1 and Guy 2 in "Two Guys") is an opportunity to revisit two sympathetic characters from the earlier play.[91] However, since Pierotti features as the interviewer in both scenes, in one of these his expression of surprise cannot be genuine. In gathering oral history, interviewers inevitably play roles, and it is no great shock to learn that Pierotti acts in a way that facilitates further discussion from his interviewees, though it does seem disingenuous. However, this deletion (or substitution) suggests that Tectonic has remediated their own work in order to more closely define the parameters of *The Laramie Project: Ten Years Later* so that the play emphasizes active forgetting rather than the kind of remembering, and capital, visible in "Two Guys."

Misremembering? Who Is Still Not Being Heard in the Docu-verbatim Marketplace?

The form of both Tectonic plays is self-reflexive, highlighting the role of the theatre company in interviewing and mediating material and projecting the process as transparent. Yet what is left out of a narrative will always trouble the attempt at representing the whole story, and may even undermine the idea that Tectonic is trying to represent the whole story at all. Shepard's killers get relatively little attention. For example, there is no discussion, or interviews with or about, the two young Latino men attacked by Henderson and McKinney after they had attacked Shepard. Tectonic never includes any detail on this later assault, though at one point Dr. Cantway, the ER doctor who treated Shepard, testifies in *The Laramie Project* that he also treated McKinney for injuries sustained in another fight. Tectonic either excerpted the details of the fight or chose not to ask about it, and because of this it would be easy to watch the play and be completely unaware of this sequence of events or the racial dimension of this later fight. Additionally, as critic Jennifer Peterson points out, there is altogether much less representation in *The Laramie Project* of poor, rural, ethnically diverse, or conservative residents of Laramie than there is of professionals, university students, and professors:[92] "Given the exclusion of segments of the Laramie population, the 'microcosm' presented is somewhat limited, in terms of both Laramie and the larger nation it is supposed to stand in for."[93] These exclusions are not accidental, as argued above. Kaufman had a clear agenda in taking the Tectonic company to Laramie and the resultant focus of both *The Laramie Project* and *The Laramie Project: Ten Years Later* on homophobic violence, both implicit and explicit, is a deliberately aimed corrective to the "various ideologies and beliefs prevailing in [the] culture"[94] of Laramie and, more broadly, the nation. Moreover, by foregrounding stakeholders with higher social capital, Kauffman must have known he had a better chance of creating higher-value memory capital for Shepard (and the play) in the stratified memory marketplace. Yet, equally, this choice opens up both plays to the charge that their exclusivity of focus makes them guilty of throwing some of the data out and performing an act of misremembering. At the beginning of this chapter, I argued that docu-verbatim tends to represent the disenfranchised. Tectonic's focus on gay and lesbian university professors, whose jobs give them status in the marketplace, shows that social vulnerability is not necessarily coterminous with low economic capital. But as Peterson's point highlights, in focusing on individuals who are socially marginalized by their sexuality, Tectonic ignores other forms of disenfranchisement with the consequence of silencing those with lower social capital.

Some of the exclusions of *The Laramie Project* are balanced out by *The Laramie Project: Ten Years Later*, which includes firsthand interviews with the two perpetrators, Russell Henderson and Aaron McKinney (as opposed to their indirect testimony via police transcripts in *The Laramie Project*). In contrast to an unrepentant McKinney, Henderson is deeply regretful of his role in Shepard's death and reflective on the social and cultural dimensions of the crime. Henderson also reflects on the event in the context of his own life and his mother's death (some months after Shepard):

> My mom was killed. Which was, obviously, different circumstances, and a different level of attention... My mom was killed in Laramie; she was raped, and then the guy just left her on the side of the road. She tried to make it back into town, but she froze to death.[95]

Strikingly, Henderson recognizes the "different level of attention" that his mother's death provoked in the media, though the similarities with Shepard's death are also arresting: a crime motivated by sexual aggression, and death caused by abandonment in a hostile environment. Henderson's mother's brutal death challenges the idea that Laramie was generally exempt from violent crime and that Shepard's death was, as a result, completely exceptional. The lack of attention to this woman's death is shocking, and resonates with Kaufman's comments on Shepard's murder as an exceptional watershed: "There are so many murders but we haven't heard about them so I think there are many things we're still not ready to hear ... so we still have worthy and unworthy victims."[96]

In my earlier discussion, I suggested that *The Laramie Project* derived some of its popularity from Shepard's classification, in the post-AIDS era of 1998, as a "worthy victim" (a pre-echo of Judith Butler's "grievable" victim). Russell Henderson's mother, in contrast, is not the subject of this or any other play, and, in Kaufman's terms, she is thus socially constructed as an "unworthy victim" without either social or memory capital. Though her death is included in *The Laramie Project: Ten Years Later*, this brief mention constitutes only a very minor acknowledgment of the other sex- and hate-crime victims in Laramie and in the United States, and in particular of gender-based violence as a national crisis on a larger scale (in terms of numbers) than homophobic violence.[97]

I don't want to suggest that there should be a hierarchy of victimhood, quite the opposite; reviving my earlier point, made in relation to *No Escape* and the importance in that play of collective witnessing generated by a collective experience of violence, I would suggest that in the Laramie plays Tectonic could broaden their focus to create a multidirectional tapestry of memory. Though in both plays there is a sense of collective witnessing on the part of those campaigning for equal rights, there is only ever one victim, Shepard, where, as Henderson's testimony implies, there could be—there are—more. From this angle, the very iconicity and singularity of Shepard's death, and Tectonic's decision to focus solely on it, which has been such a powerful force for audience engagement through the story's accessibility and universalizability, key factors in market success, also unfortunately works against the formation of a collective of victims of violence—the idea that Shepard and Henderson's mother might have something in common and that, through that commonality, both social justice and social memory might apply to and encompass them both equally. Tectonic's use of a plot strategy that focuses almost exclusively on Shepard's death as a homophobic hate crime necessitates (from their perspective) the exclusion in both of the Laramie plays of class, race, and gender as causative factors in violence toward vulnerable men and women. Though conforming to this plot actively furthers Tectonic's equal rights agenda and memory capital for Shepard, this strategy also contributes to supporting the binary of worthy/unworthy victims, and maintains the low market status for others.

In Tectonic's suggestion that Shepard is an exemplary or singular victim, for whom empathy can thus be felt, we can see that the social and memory marketplaces are both competitive and hierarchical. If social attitudes do not recognize the event as significantly traumatic in the first place on a societal, as opposed to individual, level, then the response to the event in the memory marketplace is equally dismissive. Shepard as a symbol stands synecdochically for all victims of hate crime, which can empower campaigners in his name (who are bolstered by a strong and clear symbol), but this synecdochical function also means that his history occludes the histories of other victims and fails to raise up victims with different histories, identities, and capital.

Legacies: The Effects of Mnemonic Labor

The Laramie Project: Ten Years Later moves on from the need for a physical memorial by emphasizing the enactment of memory via legislation. Catherine Connolly, who, in the wake of Shepard's death, became the first openly gay member of the Wyoming legislature, acknowledges both the need for and limitation of legislation as a solution to cultural crises: "One shouldn't be naïve—we certainly know from any social movement that we still have racism, we still have sexism, those haven't gone away."[98] This reference contextualizes homophobia and the campaign for equal rights more broadly, and acknowledges the disparity between the top-down and government-led political and social culture on the one hand and the operation of the sociocultural sphere. This disparity can work two ways, in that certain communities can perform cultural values, such as equality and mutual respect, long before government legislation changes to reflect those values as civil rights, but equally it suggests that civil rights as enshrined in legislation are not necessarily performed by all communities within the state/nation. Legal capital is not coterminous with social capital. Just as there are different memory communities with distinct and often conflicted dominant memory narratives, it is axiomatic that there will be different social communities that are governed by often conflicting social mores, attitudes, and rules; all of which translate in *The Laramie Project: Ten Years Later* into the conflict over how to remember Matthew Shepard's death.

The final section of the play dramatizes the struggle to achieve equality in legislation. First, in the scene "Language of Delay," Zackie Salmon reports that the University of Wyoming granted all employees equal partner benefits (though these are postdated to when it is "fiscally feasible").[99] Following this, in the "Defense of Marriage" scene Connolly narrates the battle to defeat homophobic legislation in the Wyoming House when the House votes on a bill "defining marriage in Wyoming as being exclusively between a man and a woman."¹⁰⁰ The bill fails because of some of the representatives having or knowing gay relatives and friends and wanting to ensure their future rights. This experience is also, however, combined with the legislature's investment in Wyoming's history as a progressive state. This latter point is a kind of performance of memory, for when the representatives vote they are remembering that Wyoming "is the State of Esther Hobart Morris, first female Justice of the Peace in the United States, and Nellie Tayloe Ross, first woman to serve as a governor of any U.S. state."¹⁰¹ This positive framing of a liberal tradition illustrates that, combined with attitudinal shifts in the present, memory capital has the power to create change for the future. The idea of memory as a powerful force of change, introduced early in the play by Marge Murray, is echoed by Judy Shepard, Matthew's mother, whose campaigning labor is a way of "keeping his story alive."¹⁰² This is not a campaign without opposition, however. During the legislative debates, one congresswoman calls the labeling of Shepard's death as a hate crime "a hoax"¹⁰³—an accusation that is both personally and politically hurtful, and demonstrative of the reach and impact of cultural narratives (ABC's 20/20 program in particular) within the political marketplace. Notwithstanding this, the narrative of mnemonic labor leading to positive social change is confirmed in the penultimate scene when the Narrator declares that on October 28, 2009, President Barack Obama signed the Matthew Shepard and James Byrd Jr. Hate Crimes Preventions Act into law.¹⁰⁴

Closure

The signing of the act provides an uplifting conclusion to both plays and counteracts some of the negativity associated with the misremembering of Shepard's death within the local community. Shepard's legacy is properly enshrined in ethically and future-oriented legislation, despite conservative and bigoted resistance to it. Yet despite the importance of this fact and its legacy for the future, its inclusion means that in *The Laramie Project: Ten Years Later*, Tectonic creates a relatively closed narrative in response to the rupture caused by Shepard's murder and its aftermath, and by the backlash against the hate-crime label. The ending in particular illustrates what Amanda Stuart-Fisher critiques as a tendency in verbatim theatre to emphasize closure and thus to limit audiences' witnessing in turn.¹⁰⁵

The Laramie Project: Ten Years Later ends with a reflection on the effect of ten years and the company's attempts to tell the story:

> **Narrator:** We're leaving Laramie for the last time. And I find myself thinking about how this story will be told.

...

Romaine Patterson: I guess over the years . . . I've kind of defined Matthew in two ways. There's Matt who I knew and the good friend that I had, and then there's Matthew Shepard [. . .] this iconic hate crime that has happened in our history, and Matthew Shepard is not necessarily about Matt, it's about a community's reaction, it is about the media that followed . . . I had to . . . hold on to who Matt was to me personally, but also to recognize the importance of Matthew Shepard, and that story, and how it was told and will continue to be told throughout the years.
(*Romaine gets up and leaves the stage. A light on the empty chair. Black out.*)[106]

It's unclear here whether the Narrator is referring to how Tectonic will tell the story or how Laramie and the nation will. This is a final acknowledgment of the multiplicity of memory, implicit throughout the play in the polyphonic testimony, much of which is contradictory or conflicting. The "story" will continue to be told and retold, as memory is continuous and evolving—and its shape is dependent on which memory community narrates the story and the shifting nature of both social and memory capital.

Tectonic decides to give the last word of this version of the story to Romaine Patterson, one of Shepard's close friends; her words allow them to acknowledge the absence of "Matt" as a character, and to recognize not only the mediating role of theatre and Tectonic in "how this story will be told" but also to recognize the utility of "Matthew Shepard" as an iconic symbol (and symbolic capital). For both the Narrator (as an embodiment of Tectonic) and Romaine the story will inevitably evolve beyond either of their control, including of course how the plays' audiences will remember what they have seen, or recount it to friends, or write about it for school and college. The remediation of the play is thus a more amorphous performance of telling and retelling, structured by each audience member's own priorities, personal and political plots, than can be contained or reflected by either the original play or its epilogue.

THE WITNESS AS IDEAL REMEMBERING SUBJECT

To conclude this chapter I want to pick up on a line that I quoted earlier from *The Laramie Project: Ten Years Later*: "We agree to lie."

In thinking about Beth Loffreda's comment, which describes the community's misremembering of Shepard's death as a drug-motivated robbery as a form of consensus, I have begun to consider the opposite implied possibility—the idea that "we" could all "agree" to tell the truth. I think this is the wished-for trajectory of docu-verbatim plays. The ultimate goal of this form of theatre is the constitution or production of an ideal remembering subject in the form of a witness. The ideal remembering subject (along the lines of the citizen consumer) is able to act as a critical witness to documentary pasts and verbatim testimony, to weigh that testimony, and to respond not only empathetically but also intellectually and civically. However, this ideal remembering subject is simultaneously acknowledged not to exist, as both plays demonstrate the competitive nature of memory capital, the lack of proportional rewards for mnemonic labor by those with low social capital, the negative effects of shame, and the ways in which spectators consistently fail to transform from consumers into witnesses—for example, by ignoring evidence of child abuse in *No Escape* and preferring an easier explanation for Shepard's death in the *Laramie* plays.

Yet, as I suggested in the introduction, theatre (and theatre critics) are loathe to give up on the utopian potential of collective witnessing. To illustrate one possible incarnation of this ideal audience we can consider the example of Jedadiah Shultz in *The Laramie Project*. Schultz is interviewed by Tectonic on more than one occasion—in his first interview he is tolerant of gay people but says he does not agree with their "lifestyle." In his later interview, however, Schultz expresses disgust at his earlier views and that "I ever said that stuff about homosexuals, you know. How did I ever let that stuff make me think that you were different from me?"[107] In the intervening time between the two interviews, Schultz had played the role of Prior in *Angels in America* in a production at the University of Wyoming, an experience that pushed him to become "personally involved in the Matthew Shepard thing."[108] Following this university production, Schultz got in contact with Tectonic to revise his testimony, so that the record would be corrected. Schultz's radical shift in attitude toward gay people's moral standing—and thus social capital—is driven by his involvement in theatre and, though it is as an actor not an audience member that he came to change, the underlying point here is that through active participation in culture, social attitudes can shift, and, as Schultz puts it, he can see Shepard in "proportion."[109] Though this is an individual example, I think it is indicative of how Tectonic views the transformational and political power of theatre to work on its audience. Out of this process of exchange, an engaged, active, witnessing audience to a piece of theatre can become, like Schultz, more enlightened and hence eager to act in the present to effect positive change.

The implicit ambition within docu-verbatim work for these plays to be received by an ideal audience-witness is more than the observation that for the playwrights it is self-evidently important to remember the violence done to individuals in the past. Rather, it suggests that the utility of the past and the docu-verbatim theatre form is in creating a future in which audiences remember in particular ways and use this memory capital as a basis for further mnemonic labor that will positively affect the social as well as memory marketplaces. To this end, for example, the Abbey hosted postshow discussions after performances of *No Escape*, and, in 2016 a whole symposium titled "Theatre of Memory" as a way of engaging with audiences over questions of ethical remembrance and witnessing. Likewise, Tectonic supports their work with educational materials and an online discussion forum as a way of continuing to guide audience responses.[110] However, as Connolly states in *The Laramie Project: Ten Years Later*, top-down "guidance" does not automatically translate into ethical action, just as the ideal audience-witness may not be realizable.[111]

Furthermore, inevitably, we can't all agree to any one version of the past, no matter how strong the narrative, not least because whether the play is hugely successful, like *The Laramie Project*, or is very limited in its production history, like *No Escape*, no single show can play to an entire market or demographic, and even if we were to imagine that it could (in the case, for example, of other major "shows" like presidential inaugurations or international sporting events), audiences will always take different sides, influenced by their alignment with different social identities, groups, and their relative social capital.

Within docu-verbatim as a genre, there is a diversity of form that reflects the diversity of memories being presented, from the personal to the political, and from affirmation to denial, a diversity that insists on the practice of memory as multiple and heterogeneous. A play is neither fixed nor unchanging because of the dynamics of performance, and equally its meaning and interpretation will change because of the combined dynamics of audience reaction and discourses of memory. No matter how strong or singular the story being told onstage, audiences will always engage in their own social, cultural, and memorial practices. I am critical of the way in which docu-verbatim plays often attempt to insist on a single hegemonic story of memory. Yet this will always be impossible because of the heterogeneity of audiences who decide what story matters to them. Though, for example, *The Laramie Project: Ten Years Later* tries to give an audience some kind of closure through the announcement of Obama's signing of the hate-crimes legislation, the audience's response is often more radically open and diverse (and may shift in unforeseen ways depending on the current political and social contexts). In this discussion of the audience, it is also worth noting that this is merely the audience in attendance at the play—the broader issue is that there is an even larger audience not in attendance, whether that nonattendance is an active choice or not. The audience to any show is thus always limited and bounded, a group constituted by the selection of a show, a date, a ticket price, as well as by how they react to the narrative performed onstage.

The inevitable distance between the ideal and the real, the witness and the consumer, the ethical and the actual, however, undercuts the theatrical ambition to produce an ideal remembering spectator, the audience-witness, and to cocreate meaning and memory capital with that audience of witnesses. As this chapter on docu-verbatim shows, often this distance is heightened by the very mediation strategies that theatre makers use to make the intolerable tolerable. And in the opposite case, where a play maintains the intolerability of the subject, the risk is that audiences will not cope with, or will stay away from, a show that demands too much.

Despite these limitations, theatre consistently performs the utopian hope that to involve the audience in the practice of memory is a good thing in and of itself, and that it can have ethical results, even if the only direct impact is a change in the individual and social memory banks of some audience members. And though I have identified problems of shame and selectivity, which compound other more banal limits such as aversion to risk, lethargy, and being overwhelmed by trauma, I am not arguing that docu-verbatim shows foreclose the possibility of taking responsibility. Rather, my argument is that, as Ahmed argues, an expression of feeling is often perceived as being "sufficient." Applause, or indeed filling in an anonymous comment card or "liking" a post on social media, are taken by consumer audiences to be actions that are "sufficient" "to finish the action" of enfranchising the disenfranchised.[112] Instead, the message of docu-verbatim shows is that continued social and mnemonic labor is required if the transformation of the social and memory capital of the formerly powerless in the marketplace is to be more than temporary.

NOTES

1. Roberta Sassatelli, "Virtue, Responsibility and Consumer Choice: Framing Critical Consumerism," in *Consuming Cultures, Global Perspectives*, ed. John Brewer and Frank Trentmann (Oxford: Berg, 2006), 219.

2. See Ann Cvetkovich, *An Archive of Feelings: Trauma, Sexuality and Lesbian Public Culture* (Durham, NC: Duke University Press, 2003).

3. Sassatelli, "Virtue, Responsibility and Consumer Choice," 221.

4. The term docu-verbatim theatre is a blended one, recognizing that the boundaries between documentary (archival and document based) and verbatim (testimony based) are blurry, and that each form borrows from the other. This is a term I use throughout the book as an acknowledgment that most productions

partake of both documentary and verbatim approaches. The productions discussed in this chapter, for instance, range from the tribunal format to auto-performance, and though each could be broadly categorized as what Carol Martin has called "theatre of the real" (see Carol Martin, *Theatre of the Real* [Houndmills, UK: Palgrave, 2013] and Carol Martin, "Bodies of Evidence," *The Drama Review* 50, no. 3 [2006]: 8–15) they each borrow from different forms: there is testimony within the tribunal, there are documents included in the verbatim, the auto-performed narratives are scripted. Because of this blurriness, and the unifying "brand" of authenticity, audiences do not distinguish between these different forms of theatre of the real. For my purposes in this book, it is useful to maintain the term "docu-verbatim" as the origin of the production, and it is important to the argument that these shows are anchored in clearly acknowledged sources, rather than an amorphous "real."

5. Cvetkovich, *An Archive of Feelings*, 7.

6. Alison Forsyth and Chris Megson, introduction to *Get Real: Documentary Theatre Past and Present* (Houndmills: Palgrave, 2009), 1.

7. Carol Martin, *Theatre of the Real*, 14.

8. The term "witness" was explored in some depth in the introduction; an outline is presented here: Dori Laub defines witnessing as having three levels, from the firsthand witness of subjective experience to secondhand witnesses to others' subjective experience to thirdhand witnesses who observe the testifying process. Laub argues for the importance of testifying and witnessing in the wake of painful experience, and the importance of being an "authentic witness" by recognizing the truth of the experience being testified to. Without all three levels of witnessing functioning authentically, Laub argues, there is a "collapse of witnessing" whereby the experience and its subjective pain is not recognized. Ashuri and Pinchevski, likewise, view witnessing as a complex field in which there are three zones: (1) the eyewitness, (2) the mediator, and (3) the audience. This tripartite schema of witnessing demonstrates that successful witnessing involves the event being seen by one person, who then testifies about their experience to a second person (who did not experience the event), and that second person chooses how to mediate that testimony for the third form of witness, the audience. This is a complex performance, as the information about the event must go through two stages in order to be communicated to the audience. It is also a perpetuating performance, in which the audience can themselves become witnesses and further mediate the testimony to another person, creating new audiences in turn.

9. David Hare, *Via Dolorosa* (London: Faber and Faber, 1998), 38. Hare's play is a documentary monologue based on his experiences of visiting Israel and Palestine.

10. As Liz Hoggard wrote of the Tricycle, critics see the "tribunal" plays as "more revealing than any news report," and the appeal of this is testified to by

the sold-out runs and Broadway transfers of these plays. See "Out of Crises, a Drama," https://www.theguardian.com/stage/2005/mar/27/theatre.

11. See the discussion of the distinctions made between primary and secondary witnesses in Caroline Wake, "Towards a Taxonomy of Spectatorial Witness in Theatre and Performance Studies," in *Visions and Revisions*, ed. Caroline Wake and Bryoni Tresize (Copenhagen: Museum Tusculaneum Press, 2013), 33–56.

12. Carol Martin, *Theatre of the Real*, 5.

13. Brian Friel, John Andrews, and Kevin Barry, "Translations and a Paper Landscape: Between Fiction and History," *The Crane Bag* 7, no. 2 (1983): 118–24.

14. Caroline Wake, review of *Get Real*, *Performance Paradigm* 7 (2011), http://www.performanceparadigm.net/wp-content/uploads/2011/07/review-get-real-documentary-theatre-past-and-present.pdf.

15. See the success of the film *Spotlight* (2015), directed by Tom McCarthy, as a recent example of this. Indeed, the plot of *Spotlight* follows the journalists covering the story of clerical abuse in Boston as they become increasingly convinced by allegations of abuse and disillusioned with toeing the line advocated by Boston's social elite/status quo, led by the archbishop.

16. Official state apology delivered by Taoiseach Bertie Ahern, May 11, 1999, https://www.rte.ie/archives/2019/0430/1046590-apology-to-victims-of-institutional-child-abuse/.

17. For a discussion of this process, and the role of theatre, film, and television in shifting marketplace attitudes, see Emilie Pine, *The Politics of Irish Memory* (Houndmills, UK: Palgrave, 2010), 18–51.

18. Aideen Howard, November 2014, in *Ways of Representing the Past: Documentary Theatre in Ireland and Brazil* event at UCD, podcast, http://irishmemorystudies.com/index.php/memory-cloud/.

19. Ahern's apology was read aloud at government buildings on May 11, 1999, just hours before the final episode of *States of Fear* was due to be broadcast. The apology begins: "On behalf of the State and of all the citizens of the State, the Government wishes to make a sincere and long overdue apology to the victims of childhood abuse for our collective failure to intervene, to detect their pain, to come to their rescue."

20. Catriona Crowe and Padraig Ó Morain, review of *No Escape* on *Arena with Sean Rocks*, RTÉ Radio One, April 15, 2010, http://www.rte.ie/radio1/arena/programmes/2010/0415/352096-arena-thursday-15th-april-2010/.

21. Mary Raftery, *No Escape*, unpublished script courtesy of Abbey Theatre and the Raftery Estate (2010), 14–16.

22. Raftery, *No Escape*, 34.

23. Raftery, *No Escape*, 50.

24. Raftery, *No Escape*, 51.

25. Raftery, *No Escape*, 50.

26. Raftery, *No Escape*, 23–24.

27. As Rosanne Kennedy argues in relation to Australian public remorse for the Stolen Generations, a large part of the campaign to elicit individual and collective apologies was about educating the public audience on how to respond with compassion, and to extend "the compassion that a previous generation withheld." Rosanne Kennedy, "An Australian Archive of Feelings," *Australian Feminist Studies* 26, no. 69 (2011): 257–79, see esp. 265.

28. Raftery, *No Escape*, 7.

29. Raftery, *No Escape*, 6.

30. John Banville, "When Irish Eyes Were Shut," *New York Times*, May 27, 2009, 7.

31. We might make a link between the Irish context and the Boston context—as the film *Spotlight* (2015, dir. Tom McCarthy) shows, allegations of abuse made to the *Boston Globe* in previous years had been significantly underreported, implicitly because of a failure to believe the allegations and the concomitant high status and regard of the *Globe* for the Boston Catholic Archdiocese.

32. Raftery, *No Escape*, 37.

33. Paul Connerton, *How Societies Remember* (Cambridge: Cambridge University Press, 1989), 19.

34. Connerton, *How Societies Remember*, 19.

35. Raftery, *No Escape*, 9.

36. Raftery, *No Escape*, 9.

37. Raftery, *No Escape*, 10.

38. Raftery, *No Escape*, 53.

39. Raftery, *No Escape*, 54.

40. Raftery, *No Escape*, 55, brackets and ellipses in original.

41. Raftery, *No Escape*, 54.

42. Raftery, *No Escape*, 55.

43. Paul Ricoeur, *Memory, History, Forgetting*, trans. Kathleen Blamey and David Pellauer (Chicago: University of Chicago Press, 2004), 85.

44. Ricoeur, *Memory, History, Forgetting*, 448.

45. Jacques Rancière, *The Emancipated Spectator*, trans. Gregory Elliott (London: Verso, 2009), 84.

46. Alison Landsberg, *Engaging the Past: Mass Culture and the Production of Historical Knowledge* (New York: Columbia University Press, 2015), 10.

47. Sara Ahmed, *The Cultural Politics of Emotion* (Edinburgh: Edinburgh University Press, 2004), 102.

48. Taoiseach Brian Cowen, speech to the Dáil, June 11, 2009. Quoted in "Shining a Light into the State's Darkest Corner," *Irish Independent*, June 12, 2009.

49. See in particular Fintan O'Toole's review "A Form of Theatre Permitting No Escape from Reality," *Irish Times*, April 24, 2010; Emilie Pine, "Powerful Theatre, Morally Essential," *Irish Theatre Magazine*, May 2, 2010.

50. A production was hoped for the UK, given that many institutional survivors settled in the UK as emigrants, but finances were not available.

51. Aideen Howard, "Ways of Representing the Past," talk at symposium on documentary theatre in Ireland and Brazil, November 2014, podcast, http://irishmemorystudies.com/index.php/memory-cloud/#doc.

52. This reading was part of the Abbey's "Theatre of Memory" symposium, January 2014.

53. Mike Kuchwara, Associated Press, accessed October 1, 2015, https://www.tectonictheaterproject.org/?avada_portfolio=laramie&portfolioCats=4.

54. "Laramie Project *Ten Years Later*," Washington Arena Stage, November 20, 2010, hosted by Metro Weekly. Debate participants included Kaufman, members of Tectonic, US assistant attorney general for civil rights Tom Perez, and SMYAL executive director Andrew Barnett: https://www.youtube.com/watch?v=FdbOPUy_cz4.

55. Moises Kaufman, "*The Laramie Project*" and "*The Laramie Project: Ten Years Later*" (London: Bantam, 2014), ix.

56. *Angels in America* is an important intertext within *The Laramie Project*, as student Jedadiah Shultz performs in *Angels* and, through this experience, positively transforms his attitude about homosexuality. The play also resonates, of course, with Tectonic's aim to create a nationally important history play.

57. Emily Douglas, "Take Action! Oklahoma Teacher Forced to Resign for Teaching 'Laramie Project,'" Rewire.com, March 13, 2009, http://rhrealitycheck.org/article/2009/03/13/take-action-oklahoma-teacher-forced-resign-for-teaching-laramie-project/.

58. Freddi Rokem, *Performing History: Theatrical Representations of the Past in Contemporary Theatre* (Iowa City: University of Iowa Press, 2000), 19.

59. This feature of the play may also contribute to its popularity with school and nonprofessional productions, given the opportunities for a large ensemble cast.

60. Allen Feldman, "Memory Theaters, Virtual Witnessing and the Trauma Aesthetic," *Biography* 27, no. 1 (2004): 163–202, see esp. 165.

61. Kaufman, *The Laramie Project*, 13.

62. Kaufman, *The Laramie Project*, 13.

63. Jill Dolan, *Utopia in Performance* (Ann Arbor: University of Michigan Press, 2005), 117.

64. Kaufman, *The Laramie Project*, 13.

65. Dolan, *Utopia in Performance*, 114.

66. Kaufman, *The Laramie Project*, 98.

67. Kaufman, *The Laramie Project*, 6.
68. Kaufman, *The Laramie Project*, 122.
69. Kaufman, *The Laramie Project*, 135.
70. Kaufman, *The Laramie Project*, 135.
71. Kaufman, *The Laramie Project*, 139–40.
72. Kaufman, *The Laramie Project*, 143.
73. Kaufman, *The Laramie Project*, 147.
74. Kaufman, *The Laramie Project*, 144.
75. Kaufman, *The Laramie Project*, 143.
76. Kaufman, *The Laramie Project*, 126.
77. Kaufman, *The Laramie Project*, 127.
78. Though Shepard was, of course, a student and not a staff member, and single, not in a partnership.
79. Kaufman, *The Laramie Project*, 122.
80. Kaufman, *The Laramie Project*, 139.
81. Kaufman, *The Laramie Project*, 122.
82. Kaufman, *The Laramie Project*, 143.
83. Kaufman, *The Laramie Project*, 32.
84. Kaufman, *The Laramie Project*, 118–19.
85. Kaufman, *The Laramie Project*, 141.
86. Kaufman, *The Laramie Project*, 186.
87. Kaufman, *The Laramie Project*, 129.
88. Kaufman, *The Laramie Project*, 118.
89. The order of the scenes is also changed—for example, at the premiere, "Reggie and Marge" is the sixth scene or "moment," in the published text, this interview is the third scene. There are other deletions from Act 1: "Smarter Than That" and "Romaine Patterson," and insertions "Nikki Elder." Act 2 is unchanged in content and order (perhaps because its focus on legislative change and the interviews with Shepard's killers, and Judy Shepard, have a stronger narrative follow-through. In Act 1, in contrast, there is a greater sense that the scenes are malleable and can be reordered to create a different impression.).
90. Kaufman, *The Laramie Project*, 118–19.
91. The published text also represents a significant reorganization of material, as the "Reggie and Marge" scene is listed as the sixth scene or "moment" in the original script, thereby shifting the emphasis away from the casual attitude of "Strip Mall" to Murray's outrage at "Tearing That Fence Down."
92. Jennifer Peterson, *Murder, the Media, and the Politics of Public Feelings: Remembering Matthew Shepard and James Byrd Jr.* (Bloomington: Indiana University Press, 2011), 56. Peterson's work is one of several published books on the subject of Shepard's death, and *The Laramie Project* and *The Laramie Project: Ten Years Later* are just two works of a relatively large number of publications on the murder.

93. Peterson, *Murder, the Media, and the Politics of Public Feelings*, 56.
94. Kaufman, *The Laramie Project*, ix
95. Kaufman, *The Laramie Project*, 158.
96. "Laramie Project *Ten Years Later*," *Metro Weekly Debate*, November 20, 2010.
97. This moment echoes the earlier play when Sherry Johnson, the wife of a highway patrolman, complains that a patrolman was killed by a dangerous driver at the same time as Shepard died, but that there was no coverage of that death. In this case, there is less sense of worthy versus unworthy in social terms, and a greater sense that the patrolman's death was not media-worthy. Kaufman, *The Laramie Project*, 62.
98. Kaufman, *The Laramie Project*, 160.
99. Kaufman, *The Laramie Project*, 162.
100. Kaufman, *The Laramie Project*, 163.
101. Kaufman, *The Laramie Project*, 166
102. Kaufman, *The Laramie Project*, 183, 185.
103. Kaufman, *The Laramie Project*, 184.
104. Kaufman, *The Laramie Project*, 185. Notice the date: it is after the ten-year anniversary and, indeed, it is almost a month after *The Laramie Project: Ten Years Later* had its premiere, so the Narrator's statement was added to a later version of the script. The act had, however, passed the House by the time of the plays' premiere and was expected to be signed into law. What's also striking is the absence of any explanation of who James Byrd Jr. is and why his name is also on the bill, another striking example of the primacy of Shepard in Tectonic's shaping of this national story.
105. Amanda Stuart-Fisher "Trauma, Authenticity and the Limits of the Verbatim," *Performance Research* 16, no. 1 (2011): 112–22; see pages 116 and 118 in particular.
106. Kaufman, *The Laramie Project*, 187.
107. Kaufman, *The Laramie Project*, 96.
108. Kaufman, *The Laramie Project*, 95.
109. Kaufman, *The Laramie Project*, 96.
110. See Tectonic's commitment to education through the Moment Work Institute, details available at: https://www.tectonictheaterproject.org/#TMWI.
111. Kaufman, *The Laramie Project*, 160.
112. Ahmed, 119–20. As Ahmed puts it, "What is shameful is passed over through the enactment of shame."

TWO

THE WITNESS AS COMMODITY
Autoperforming Memory

IF DOCU-VERBATIM THEATRE DERIVES SOME of its cultural capital and emotional impact from the idea that these are "real" stories with an origin in real lives, then autoperformance, in which the performer is not an actor with a script, but actually a firsthand witness who narrates their own story, further ups the ante. Autoperformance theatre seems designed, in fact, to capture consumer attention with its combination of high emotion, novelty, and accessibility; and while it is not a mainstream brand, autoperformance has strong consumer appeal for a particular market segment keen to buy into bottom-up stories by previously "unheard" witnesses (though the market segmentation that supports the development of this brand also has its drawbacks). Autoperformance carries the risk of alienating audiences by presenting difficult stories and witnesses, but the risk is lessened through production strategies that encourage identification and empathy; indeed we might even argue that painful memory, far from being off-putting, is used to sell difficult witnesses to the audience. Though low in social capital, these witnesses—who tell stories of extreme violence and suffering—are high in emotional capital. Autoperformance would, then, seem to be an ideal forum for using one form of capital—emotional—to raise the levels of other forms of capital, from social to cultural. Yet this does not happen automatically or without effort, indeed these plays rely on the immaterial labor of real victims, a labor that is repeated night after night. Moreover, while there are clearly significant dividends for the performers, not least of which is the sense of being heard and witnessed, there are also social and financial dividends for the theatrical gatekeepers, from financial profit to the cultural capital accrued by being seen to invest in victimized communities. The privatization of suffering and the market-commodification of both the victim's and the audience's catharsis are thus serious risks for shows that depend on empathy as both an engagement and marketing tool, what I call the empathy-paradox. To elucidate these issues, this chapter focuses on two plays that use autoperformance to dramatize the event and aftermath of sexual violence against women: *I Once Knew a Girl*, directed by Teya Sepinuck (Theater of Witness & The Playhouse, Derry, 2010), and *Nirbhaya*, directed by Yael Farber (Farber and Ensemble, Edinburgh Festival, 2013). In these shows, the individual is integral to selling the story to the audience, but this relentless focus on the individual threatens to play into what Michal Givoni has termed the hazard of "unwittingly creat[ing] anchors for a neoliberal policy that transfers responsibility to private individuals in matters pertaining to both global and social injustice."[1]

A Conflict?

It is quite something to feel as if you are being directly spoken to by someone who is describing how, as a child, they were raped. In my own experience as an audience member at autoperformance testimonial plays, two distinct features of this form have surfaced. First, it feels as if there is a greater urgency on the part of the performer to relate the story and, second, I have felt a strong sense that the performer and the performance are *entangled*. Because of these two features, I have emerged from seeing these productions with something of a conflict between my emotional reaction—which is to feel an enormous level of empathy for the people whose stories I have witnessed—and an alternative reaction, which is to feel actually slightly alienated and disempowered by the process of witnessing these shows. Of course these stories are moving, and it is a reminder to me (and the audience more widely, I presume) of our shared humanity that I/we are so moved in reaction to stories of acute hardship. The gravity of the memories and stories being shared requires a reciprocal gravity in the audience. Yet while it is humbling to witness these individuals, and to see the capacity of the audience to be moved by their stories, it remains to be asked whether the catharsis of tears and feelings are sufficient responses.

When I say that I have felt disempowered as a spectator of autoperformance testimony, it is because, for me, the tension between consuming and witnessing such performances is immobilizing. I simply don't know what to do after the show, as if the enormity of the feelings projected by the show, and felt by the audience (of which I am part), prevents the translation of consumption into action. As Marianne Hirsch provocatively asks, "How can we allow the knowledge of past atrocity to touch us without paralyzing us? What aesthetic strategies might galvanize memory in the interest of activist engagement for justice and social change?"[2]

My discussion here focuses on two testimonial ensemble works, featuring the stories of women who have suffered violence, in two seemingly different contexts—Northern Ireland and India—that are, in fact, unified by the transnational reality of violence against women. The first production, Sepinuck's *I Once Knew a Girl*, is stimulated by the desire to tell women's stories of the Troubles in Northern Ireland and to reveal some of their experiences and the legacies of violence. The second production, *Nirbhaya*, was provoked by the murder and gang rape of Jyoti Singh Pandey in Delhi in 2012. Under the direction of the productions' writer-directors, Teya Sepinuck and Yael Farber, respectively, twelve women's stories are presented on stage in plays that call for active witnessing by the audience. Both of these productions are deliberately bottom-up, as Sepinuck puts it, using theatre to give "voice to those that are invisible in society."[3] In this they follow a tradition of feminist autobiographical theatre that, as Deirdre Heddon explains, since the 1970s has translated personal material "into live performance" as an act of "consciousness raising" focused "specifically on women's experiences."[4] While the shows' feminist agendas clearly establish these works as political interventions, at the same time they also serve as branding in a competitive marketplace (*Nirbhaya* premiered, for instance, at the Edinburgh Fringe Festival). Together with the brand advantage of prestigious international directors, the shows have significant market appeal. *Nirbhaya*, in particular, has been internationally successful, touring widely and garnering a high degree of media attention. Like the "starving man" (as discussed in chap. 1), there is a market for stories of abuse and rape. The double-bind here, however, is that such consciousness-raising is in tension with the emotional impact of the shows, which threatens to paralyze us.

VERBATIM AS SOCIALLY HEALING: *I ONCE KNEW A GIRL*

I Once Knew a Girl includes six monologues, each of them distinct but with recurring central features. None of the performers is a professional actor and each narrates her own story. This format follows the Theater of Witness program that Sepinuck developed for using theatre to deal with conflict and to promote social healing; the subtitle of the program is "where art and social justice meet." Having worked in Poland and with prison communities in the United States,[5] Sepinuck was funded by the Derry Playhouse, Londonderry

City Council, and an EU Peace III grant (2012–14) to work with the Derry Playhouse and Holywell Trust in Derry/Londonderry city to produce a cycle of verbatim plays dealing with the legacy of the Troubles conflict.[6] *I Once Knew a Girl* is, then, one of four testimonial shows, which were all produced in Derry/Londonderry and that toured Northern Ireland; the play is not typical of Theater of Witness's catalog, however, in that it is exclusively devoted to women's stories. Given that the show focuses on the trauma of the Northern Irish conflict, one of the risks of bearing witness is the emotional impact of "stories of suffering" on the audience. To that end, counselors are present at all shows, and every show is followed by a postshow forum to ensure maximum support as well as full participation. The goal for Theater of Witness is to "put a face and heart to societal issues of suffering" with the added purpose of "peace building and inspiration," aims that clearly overlap with those of the public funding bodies hoping to use these shows to intervene in the cultural and social marketplaces and demonstrate the positive impact of socially minded gatekeeping.[7]

Being representative is clearly important to Sepinuck, in order to reach as wide an audience as possible, and to balance the depiction of experiences of the Troubles. Each of the women featured in *I Once Knew a Girl* has been chosen for being representative of some aspect of the community affected by the Troubles, including both victims and perpetrators of violence, and political representation from both the unionist and nationalist communities. The women are:

- Catherine, who grew up in a unionist home and who now stands at the barricades to keep the peace.
- Anne, a former member of the paramilitary Irish Republican Army (IRA).
- Therese, who was burned out of her home and then suffered childhood sexual abuse.
- Maria, who was abused and raped and subsequently became a member of the new PSNI (police service of Northern Ireland). Maria could not appear in the live shows because, as a Catholic member of the police force, she is a terrorist target.
- Ruth, who grew up in an evangelical family and who struggles with the dual impact of the Troubles and her religious upbringing.
- Kathleen, whose husband was killed by the IRA.

I want to concentrate my discussion here on Anne, the former IRA combatant; Kathleen, the victim of paramilitary violence; and Therese, the woman abused as a child. These three stories depict key elements of the kinds of painful experiences that *I Once Knew a Girl* presents, and the ways in which empathy works to create a particular kind of witnessing.

As in all verbatim theatre, the primary material is carefully crafted. The script had a long gestation as Sepinuck worked with the women over several months, individually and as a group, to collect their stories. Sepinuck then scripted the stories herself and presented them back to the women, who perform them alone onstage. The performance style is a mixture of direct address and physical reenactment of particular gestures and scenarios (such as crouching to avoid violence, or climbing stairs toward an abuser). Since the participants are not professional actors, they can at times have difficulty learning and delivering their lines or an obvious artificiality in their movements. This is partly because of a lack of performance training and also, presumably, nerves at presenting their personal stories to an audience of strangers. The emotional difficulty of the material is also obviously a factor as recounting memories of abuse, violence, and loss can be incredibly stressful for the women who, though they are performing from a script, do not have the distance that an actor would bring to the role.

Protagonists as Victims

The second monologue that the audience witnesses is Anne's, who has been involved in the conflict in various ways during the Troubles. Sepinuck's dramaturgical strategies for presenting Anne illustrate the possibilities—and pressures—of theatre made in a transitional-justice context of overlapping identities of perpetrator and victim, subject and witness.

Anne begins by recounting that her uncle, her mother's brother, was killed on January 30, 1972, known as Bloody Sunday, when she was three years old. The Bloody Sunday reference will be clear to a Northern Irish audience, a day on which fourteen civilians were shot dead by the British army following a civil rights march in Derry. The army alleged that the people they shot were armed and dangerous, a verdict upheld by the Widgery Report, a contemporary inquiry, but subsequently exposed as untrue by the publication of the long-running (1998–2010) Saville Report. In June 2010 David Cameron, then British prime minister, apologized unreservedly for the "unjustified and unjustifiable" events and deaths of Bloody Sunday, saying, "It was wrong."[8] As Cameron's apology was delivered just a few months before the premiere of *I Once Knew a Girl*, this is an important context—the unjustifiable actions of the British army—against which Anne relates her personal link to Bloody Sunday, as well as allowing Anne to embed her story in the longer history of

Northern Ireland and the struggle for civil rights. As she says, "After that everything was about the Troubles. *Everything*."⁹

Anne grew up being victimized: "One morning they arrested my daddy and took him away. Another morning they arrested my mother and took her away.... The Brits and the Police had us terrorised and over the years we knew loads of people who had been killed or taken away by the Brits and Police." Anne also says that the "Provos could do no wrong"; they were "our saviours and protectors."¹⁰ In this narrative, the traditional forces of stability—the state and police (which are, for Anne, synonymous)—were the victimizers, while the paramilitary force, the Provisional IRA, were protectors. This reversal and the ensuing feeling of victimization led Anne to, justifiably in her view, join the "Provos." As a quartermaster, Anne was responsible for moving guns but never fired a gun herself. This is a crucial distinction for her, as she says that it "was never in me to go so far down that road." However, Anne later reflects that killing isn't "really in any of us" and that, as quartermaster, she was actually "directly involved in the deaths of people in this war. That's hard to take." Thus, despite recounting her enthusiasm and "rush" at joining the paramilitaries, Anne also acknowledges the impact of her actions.

Sepinuck structures these two parts of Anne's narrative very carefully. Beginning with the experience of victimization under the "Brits." Anne's move toward the IRA seems inevitable and understandable. When she is ordered by the IRA leadership to take part in an ambush, she is deeply uncomfortable but goes along with the order. This obedience mirrors her compliance when she is subjected to sexual harassment within the IRA: "It wasn't something that I wanted but I didn't know how to say no." The night of the ambush Anne experiences a brain hemorrhage, an act that she reads as a divine intervention that enables her to leave the IRA.

Following this change in her life, Anne moves to the Republic of Ireland, goes to university, gets married, and has a child. Her husband, however, becomes violent. As she says: "The first time he hit me, I didn't hit him back. The second time he hit me, I managed to land him on the ground. I remember thinking, Jesus Anne if you kick him you'll really hurt him. I kicked him anyway. I thought, I used to be in the Provos, I don't have to take this." Here, again, the Provos act as a kind of protector as Anne draws on that experience as self-defense—yet she goes further than defense and becomes the aggressor. The audience reaction to Anne's action is interesting: the night I saw the production, and on the DVD recording, some audience members laughed at the line "I kicked him anyway." This, to me, suggests audience support for Anne and a sympathetic view of her as a battered woman, whose actions are justified by being hit first. If this were a man's narrative, even if he had been the victim of domestic abuse, I very much doubt that the audience would have laughed at a man saying "I kicked her anyway." And, likewise, had this violence been played out on stage, rather than being narrated by a calm woman speaking directly to the audience about her past experience, the reaction may also have been different, tending instead toward a chilling recognition of the impact of violence. Narration is thus key as a performance strategy that enables sufficient critical distance for the subject (Anne) and the audience in order for both to witness the message that Anne and Sepinuck want to project of empowerment and moving on.

Sepinuck ensures that Anne is a figure who, despite her extreme experience of being in a paramilitary organization, is relatable because of her parallel encounters with sexual and domestic violence. Anne also links her experience to those of other women in Northern Ireland: "I was finding out that more and more men back in Derry were being violent with their women.... It's the damage of war on culture that doesn't get talked about here." Anne breaks a taboo silence surrounding domestic violence, linking her experience to that of others, so that she becomes representative of "more and more ... women." By kicking her husband, Anne implicitly stands up for all battered women in Derry/Londonderry and Northern Ireland, acting as a voice for their concerns in a culture that is heavily male-dominated, and in which women struggle to achieve independent social and cultural capital. Indeed, Anne's narrative, as the voice of a female ex-combatant, is highly unusual in a culture that rarely prioritizes women, and in which the Troubles are represented as an almost exclusively male-oriented experience and legacy (in which women have low social capital, though as this show proves, high emotional capital). As Lisa Fitzpatrick argues, "Sexual and domestic violence is often minimized or marginalized in representations and narratives of the Northern Irish conflict, where the focus is on the 'masculine' construction of nation and nationalisms, with the security forces or paramilitaries cast as heroes."[11] All of these factors in Anne's narrative—victimization, breaking a taboo, finding a voice and a power for women—are crucial to her reception at this point by the audience. Though it is impossible to generalize and say that every member of the audience is likely to be sympathetic to Anne, for reasons that have to do with her association with violence, nonetheless based on audience reactions recorded on the DVD (and my subjective memory) it would seem that Anne was sympathetically received.

Anne's acknowledgement that she was "directly involved in the deaths of people in this war" comes only after she has described her experience of domestic violence. This acknowledgement is a very necessary reflection on and conclusion to the earlier part of her narrative and her naive assertion that she never fired a gun. Following this admission, Anne ends her reflection on her past by commenting on her current life: "I need to learn to forgive myself. The biggest job that I have now is to be the best mother that I can to my son.... Because after all we're all just ordinary people. We just live in extraordinary circumstances." This conclusion casts Anne in a traditional gender role as mother and establishes her ambitions to excel at this actively nurturing job. This, obviously, represents a massive shift in the narrative away from the violence of the past (paramilitary, sexual, and domestic) to the stable and supportive present. The final lines on ordinariness and extraordinary circumstances distance Anne from past violence (and her support for the IRA) and display instead a fateful view of how people react to extraordinary circumstances. Though Anne's witness testimony includes many taboo and challenging experiences, ones that she is incredibly open about sharing, they are nevertheless tempered in very careful ways so as to be amenable and accessible to a post–Good Friday Peace Agreement audience. Sepinuck's message here is designed to be consumed sympathetically by a local Northern Irish audience, very many of whom will have lived through the same "extraordinary circumstances."[12]

Sexual Violence and the Power of Listening

Anne's story is followed by Therese, who is also a victim of Troubles violence. After being intimidated out of their home as Catholics living in a Protestant area and because her father was a Republican, Therese's family was housed in a series of safe houses, and she continued to suffer routine discrimination and harassment because of her religious status. Therese left school at eleven to "run the house" and was sexually solicited by her uncle and, later, while visiting her grandmother's house, abused by her cousin, who "told me not to tell anybody." Therese's story is an incredibly moving recollection by someone who has suffered repeated abuse and victimization. Her conclusion is worth quoting in full:

> I once knew a girl who got pregnant at seventeen but married in white. Whose first born was born premature the night Patsy O'Hara died. Whose daughter died at six weeks old, who was a girl who grieved forever. I once knew a girl whose marriage was haunted by her history of sexual abuse, who suffered depression and isolation, but couldn't tell why. Who divorced then met a man who beat and abused her, whose daughter watched while he tortured her with violence physical, verbal and more. I once knew a girl who became silent, ashamed, who believed the abuse and thought herself stupid, who never spoke up and lived in fear, abandoned by hope. But I once knew a

girl who grew into her strength, who learned to say no, and claimed back her life, who never stopped imagining... and got help and support and found out she wasn't alone. I am that girl, Therese Parker McCann. A woman of strength.

Therese's narrative conclusion is highly stylized, with the repetition of "I once knew a girl," a phrase that depicts a sense of frozen adolescence as Therese is stuck at the point at which she was told "not to tell anybody" about her pain. This silence leads to more pain, and so Therese's narrative and self-naming as a "woman of strength" represents a deliberate counter to that, particularly given the highly public nature of this testimonial forum. The necessity of this counter narrative is urgent; as Fitzpatrick writes, "These 'disappeared' stories of sexual and domestic violence offer a glimpse of an aspect of Northern Irish conflict that is rarely visible, rarely discussed, and only occasionally staged."[13]

In an interview, Therese says that the process of telling her story to Sepinuck, the group of women, and then an audience was a vital step in her recovery as she was listened to, without interruption, "for the first time."[14] This gives us an insight into the positive effects of successfully being witnessed as Therese reaches an audience she would not normally have access to and, moreover, with whose supportive listening she can finally quash the injunction not to tell anyone about her experience of childhood abuse. In writing about the process of making Theater of Witness productions, Sepinuck cites Therese's story as one example where she "took liberties," writing words that she did not say herself but that seemed to fit her story.[15] Therese was happy with this, and so this interventionist form of mediation was integral to the positive experience of witnessing and being witnessed. Yet this intervention also questions the veracity of the verbatim show, particularly given the power of autoperformance. Though it is relatively minor as manipulations go, and though there is obviously always some expectation on the part of the audience that the show they are seeing will be molded and shaped as a dramatic piece, this form of mediation is nonetheless slightly dissonant, a dissonance that is particularly striking when you notice someone stumbling over their "lines."

The experience of sexual violence is fracturing—but in performing the story, it becomes (depressingly) unifying. During Therese's monologue, she is flanked by Anne and Kathleen, who both contribute their own narratives of sexual abuse. After Therese has talked about being abused by her cousin when a young girl, Kathleen emerges on stage and says, "I thought I was Daddy's special little girl, but it was all lies. I was much too young for my secret." Anne joins in: "I've been raped more than once but I never told anybody because compared to all the violence of the Troubles I thought it was insignificant, but it wasn't. It happens to too many of us." Kathleen finishes this mini-section, asking, "Who knows what goes on behind closed doors. Who's going to believe you anyway?" The multivocal nature of this small segment of the show provides solidarity for Therese and, as in Raftery's *No Escape*, a sense of collective witnessing that reinforces the credibility and capital of all three testimonies of sexual abuse. Anne is, ostensibly, far more assertive than Therese, yet she still "told nobody" of her rape, illustrating the extent of voicelessness felt by women subjected to sexual violence, and thus also illustrating the process of the verbatim play as a coming into voice. Kathleen's question, "Who's going to believe you anyway?" anticipates any disbelief that this jointly voiced testimony might encounter in the audience, and, combined with Anne's suggestion that in comparison to the "violence of the Troubles" the privatized, domestic sexual abuse of women was "insignificant," critiques the belief gap that often blocks the process of witnessing victims.

Peace-Building: Reconciling Perpetrators and Victims

By the point of Kathleen's final monologue, the audience has listened to a range of stories (including Catherine, Maria, and Ruth), all of which express painful memories about different forms of violence. Kathleen speaks last, presumably because Sepinuck wanted to use her reconciliatory experience to conclude the show, and because many of the audience would already be familiar with aspects of her story from news sources, as her husband, Patrick (Patsy) Gillespie, was killed by the IRA in 1990 when he was forced to drive a van loaded with explosives to the army base where he worked, where it was detonated by a remote control, killing Patsy and five British soldiers.

Kathleen recounts the story of Patsy's abduction and murder in a manner that is both factual and deeply moving, and then she turns to talking about the impact and legacy of his death. After his murder, Kathleen received many letters of support from around the world; the other women in the cast read out excerpts from these letters, including one of support from Australia, saying, "I have never written to anyone like this but we wanted to let you know that there are people worldwide who feel for you and focus their love on you . . . one day there will be peace . . . our father's family was killed in the Treblinka concentration camp in 1934." Again, multidirectional solidarity (rather than competition) is key here as Sepinuck uses these links between Northern Ireland and the international community to show the common experience of violence and the collective witnessing power of victims and survivors. The international recognition of Kathleen as a survivor demonstrates that she has already successfully testified and been witnessed; this monologue nevertheless represents a different form of witnessing as Kathleen, though mediated by Sepinuck's script and the context of the show, can finally address an audience directly rather than being excerpted by journalists. Kathleen uses this opportunity to recount the story of how she was visited by Patsy's ghost, a visit that gave her some peace. She talks of how she wanted to write "murdered by the IRA" on his gravestone but that she resisted this impulse, and that, later, joining a peace and reconciliation program brought her "back to sanity."

During Kathleen's monologue, the other women are seated on stage, and Anne is right behind Kathleen. The capacity of the show (and it is not accidental but part of its raison d'être) to include the memories and stories of a victim *and* a perpetrator, Kathleen and Anne, puts pressure on the audience to reciprocally respond. Audiences will have multiple and varying reactions, but the presentation of the women, and the narrative trajectory of the show, strongly encourages them, first of all, to see the women as victims, and second of all, to buy into the message of reconciliation. Anne's is the most difficult narrative to reconcile, given her role as a perpetrator of violence. However, the emphasis on Anne's experience as a victim, her retrospective reevaluation of her responsibility for violence, and her repositioning of herself as a mother do much to offset her otherwise negative position as a perpetrator, translating her into what Luke Moffett calls "a complex victim."[16]

Making the Witness Tolerable

Anne's testimony is not the first time that the Theater of Witness project in Derry/Londonderry had staged the story of a perpetrator: in Sepinuck's first Northern Irish production, *We Carried Your Secrets* (2009), one of the witnesses, James, was a former member of the UDA (Ulster Defence Army, a Loyalist paramilitary organization). Sepinuck has written of her awareness that James's story would be "a hard sell" to an audience, and so before the audience learns of his UDA background, he relates the story of how as a child he was unable to save his friend from drowning, a failure that has always haunted him. As Sepinuck says, "I knew that hearing the story would humanize James for the audience before they heard about his involvement in the UDA."[17] The presentation of both Anne and James as traumatized themselves during childhood, before the audience realizes they are responsible for violence done to others, is an important insight into how these stories of remembrance are constructed in order to be successfully consumed and witnessed in the memory marketplace.

To observe that Sepinuck deliberately uses the experience of trauma as a dramaturgical tool is not to deny that perpetrators can also be victims—but to highlight the use of victimhood in the framing and "selling" of ex-combatants.

It's also the case that while I identify Anne as the perpetrator, other audience members might not. And, indeed, that other audience members might identify Maria, a serving police officer, as a perpetrator or upholder of a violent regime. Indeed, Maria gives her testimony by video, rather than being live onstage, because of the risk of death threats (Catholic members of the PSNI can be targets of violence). Her absence underlines the literal danger of autoperformance.

The salient identification here is not which individual is "guilty," but how memory projects such as Theater of Witness address a history of violence, translating painful memory into useful memory. As I've already suggested, in this instance in order to be a successful witness in the memory marketplace, the perpetrator has to be "humanized" via victimhood. Theater of Witness is not unique in emphasizing loss as an important, and sympathetic, component in a complex view of the perpetrator; in *The Laramie Project: Ten Years Later*, Russell Henderson is likewise humanized by his admission of guilt at his complicity in Matthew Shepard's murder and by his mention of his mother's murder. Indeed, we can also identify the defining and influential role of these humanizing strategies in noting their absence from other docu-verbatim plays, in particular tribunal plays, in which (as in *No Escape*) the lack of admissions of responsibility, or any dimension of victimhood, makes it *impossible* to identify with the perpetrators. While audiences may derive some satisfaction in exercising moral judgements against perpetrators, the sympathetic victim is a far more rewarding object of the audience's emotional labor.

Without the framing device of victimhood, the perpetrator, to return to Rancière's term, is an "intolerable image."[18] Sepinuck is thus vital as a mediator in ensuring the witness is witnessed, by making figures like Anne "tolerable." The inclusion of painful, and pitiful, elements in the depiction of the perpetrator highlights the role of sympathy for the pain of the other as the primary mode, perhaps even a foundational requirement, by which that recognition can happen. Observing this requirement means that we also have to observe that if the objective of a memory play is to provoke empathetic witnessing, then certain memories are more useful than others—and noticeably it is painful memory that becomes the common denominator, as if unhappiness, which is not, a là Tolstoy, unique but universal, is what unites us all. Painful memory, which provokes empathy, then is vital in the process of presenting "difficult" witnesses, circumnavigating questions of political identification and using familiarizing strategies to boost both consumption and witnessing.

Identification—familiarity—is a precondition for sympathetic (and thus profitable) consumption. The opposite process is one of alienation. To avoid this latter sensation, Sepinuck combines the unfamiliar—a female combatant, a victim of child sexual abuse—with the familiar. If you want to know what it feels like to be an audience member at one of these productions, well, you might also ask—how does it feel to grow up in a family and feel like you don't belong? How has your life turned out differently from how you expected? How does it feel to lose a loved one? How does it feel to be sexually harassed or raped? How does it feel to live in a situation of constant conflict? How does it feel to be a mother? The relatability of the women is underlined by their repetition of the phrase "I once knew a girl" and the recurring use of the term "ordinary," both of which help to establish the women as a nonthreatening presence. This production, like so much other docu-verbatim theatre, trades on the tension between the familiar (the common experience of family life, for example) and the defamiliarizing (the less common experience of direct paramilitary violence, or rape) to create a spectacle that is both accessible and novel, while also being nonthreatening, three key components for market success.

BREAKING THE SILENCE: *NIRBHAYA*

Nirbhaya, like *I Once Knew a Girl*, is unified by a concern for, and a focus on, women's memories of violence. And, again, director Yael Farber presents these memories through direct address and an appeal to the audience's empathetic sensibilities. Farber combines this with the enactment of one story—the gang rape and killing of Jyoti Singh Pandey (given the pseudonym "Nirbhaya," meaning "fearless one," by the media) on a Delhi bus in 2012. Pandey's death stimulated mass protests across India (and internationally) and provoked actor Poorna Jagannathan to contact Farber to ask her to make a piece of drama in response. Like Shepard's relationship to Tectonic's *Laramie* plays, then, Pandey is the absent presence—a catalyst and symbol at the heart of the work; yet unlike Tectonic's approach, Farber casts an actress to represent Pandey onstage and the cast narrates and enacts her rape, killing, and death ritual. Alongside this enactment, five other women present their own stories of sexual violence (some of these women were already professional actors); the women are: Sapna Bhavnani, Priyanka Bose, Poorna Jagannathan, Sneha Jawale, and Rukhsar Kabir.[19] The cast is completed by one male actor (Ankur Vikal) who portrays all the male roles in the play. Like Sepinuck, Farber worked with the women to listen to and then script their stories, turning a series of individual testimonies into a collective witnessing of rape culture.

As with other testimonial plays based on people who have experienced victimization, most of the women refer to never having been able to tell their stories before this production. Crucially Pandey's death served to inspire them to step forward to tell their stories. The reasons for their former silence included not being believed by family and not wishing to bring shame on their family. As Poorna says, "To tell our parents, court rooms, teachers, the police—is to risk not being believed. Or accused of having invited this upon myself. We tell our children not to shame us. And so their small bodies carry us all."[20] When Priyanka's abuse was seen by an adult, it was ignored: "My father's mother is combing her hair one afternoon. She sees him rubbing himself on me.... And turns away. I am—after all—only a girl."[21] The experience of harassment is not limited to the family but is omnipresent: "On the buses ... I am groped daily. At the park a grown man slides his tongue in my mouth."[22] These experiences combine to make the experience of being female in these contexts absolutely toxic. And the feeling of toxicity is not limited to India: Sapna Bhavnani was raped by a gang on New Year's Eve in Chicago, but didn't report the rape to the police because she thought they would never take her seriously.

Sneha Jawale's narrative is a particularly difficult story to listen to (in a show that is consistently challenging), as she describes how her husband's family, demanding more dowry payments, attempted to kill her in a "dowry attack" in which they poured kerosene over her and set her on fire. Sneha survived and describes how she continued to live with her husband and their young son until, after some time, her husband abducted her son, and she never saw either of them again. Sneha, who is not a professional actor, visibly bears the scars of the kerosene and audibly bears the scars of her pain at losing her son. She speaks in vernacular and is "translated" by another cast member, who stands behind her relaying her story in English. Sneha talks in interviews about her need to be in the show, despite the emotional difficulty of relating her story every night, in order to prevent any more attacks happening to other women and in a quest to find her son.[23] In her separation from her son, Sneha's pain is ongoing and cannot be resolved in a therapeutic manner. Though each of the women is relating a memory, their pain crystallized by the process of looking back, the belated nature of their witnessing should not suggest that the pain is safely located in the past.

The Absent Witness

Though the women relate their stories in direct-address style, there is also a considerable amount of stagecraft and onstage action, including the ensemble standing in for the crowds on the bus and enacting particular scenarios. This creates a greater sense of watching a drama unfold, rather than the primary focus on delivering testimony that audiences encounter in other docu-verbatim and autoperformance testimonial work. This is also the only way that Jyoti's story can be enacted, as her voice is the underlying absence of the work. This enactment and its direction is harrowing, as the audience not only hears about the brutal violence done to Jyoti, but also watches as the cast enacts the attack, including a moment where one of the metal bars of the bus set is taken apart and used to symbolically rape the prone body of the already violently abused young woman.

This horrific moment is followed by the actors performing the ensuing scene, in which Pandey's friend attempted for over two hours to get help for her from bystanders who simply continued to pass them by. There is an inbuilt critique, then, not only of the perpetrators, but of a bystander society that fails to witness violence, in this case because of the disdain for women and a caste-like fear of the taboo of touching someone "dirty." Following these scenes, Pandey, who has been costumed in white throughout (while the other performers wear black) is bathed by the women, wrapped in a fresh white cotton sari, then carried shoulder-height. Pandey then rises from her deathbed and sings, indeed she sings throughout the show, particularly at moments in the narration of others' experience of violence and during the narration of her own death. The dramaturgy thus contributes to a feeling of transcendence, as if Pandey's spirit exists after death (which one might say it does, considering this play as a form of legacy), underlined by what one review called actress Japjit Kaur's embodiment of Pandey as "unearthly serenity."[24] Indeed, this is called for in Farber's script, which describes Pandey as "an ethereal figure dressed in iridescent white" and an "other-worldly presence" singing "in a pure, haunting voice."[25] The supernatural atmosphere that attaches to Pandey as a character obviously raises the question as to how the absent witness can be represented. The white costuming and "pure" performance style distinguish Pandey as different from the other women and acknowledge her symbolic power after death; yet in setting her apart these devices also suggest her transcendence of the problems of this world. Pandey becomes angelic, and while this may be uplifting in contrast to the brutality of the rest of the show, it also risks leavening the horror of her death.[26] As reviewer Lyn Gardner writes, "The show too often hides behind a wafty, soft-lit aesthetic... [that] veers dangerously close to well-meaning theatrical misery-memoir."[27]

CAN WE HAVE TOO MUCH EMPATHY?

My ambivalent reaction to the representation of "Nirbhaya," the "fearless one," as an angel figure, is part of a more consistent questioning of the effect of affect, by which I mean the question as to whether audience empathy represents "feeling change" rather than "acting change." Sepinuck's and Farber's work is marked by different styles of direction, yet both result in an emotionally charged production that generates an equal emotion in audiences, an example of what Ridout and Schneider have called "the affect factory."[28]

As I sat in different auditoriums watching *I Once Knew a Girl* and *Nirbhaya*, I saw the same reactions around me at both, as audience members audibly and visibly cried in response to the sadness of the stories they heard. It seems to me that the shows inevitably produce this reaction; and though Sepinuck is wary of traumatizing the audience, with counselors available after the show, for instance, the Theater of Witness actually trades on the effect of trauma narratives on an audience to deliver the sense of "redemption" promised in their mission statement. This mission, overt in Theater of Witness's political manifesto and implicit in Farber's "pure" representation of Pandey, limits the possibilities and the spaces for critical thought—evoking only sympathy and/or empathy from the audience. Karine Shaefer writes that "What a witness-producing performer wants to happen to the spectator, then, is that someone who is essentially an onlooker could be so affected by an experience that it becomes a challenge."[29] Yet, as Schaefer points out, "In testimonial drama there is less room for the audience to find their own interpretation of the event. Essentially, the characters are undertaking the interpretive work for them."[30] Likewise, Amanda Stuart-Fisher argues that docu-verbatim theatre is all too often satisfied with representing painful events as "just bad," without disclosing "any insight into the politics of these situations or what motivates someone to commit themselves to act in this way."[31] Though in *Nirbhaya* there is some reflection on the link between social disenfranchisement and the drunken aggression that drove the lethal gang rape of Pandey, the over-riding focus on the women's subjectivity excludes any consideration of the motivation of the perpetrators of sexual violence. Without such a consideration, it is difficult to position these productions as interventions in a rape culture.

I don't want to suggest that the audience's performance of humanity at these two shows is the wrong response or that vulnerability should not be part of our discourse. But rather that we need to question how vulnerability is being staged and to what purpose. Of course, in my impressions of the audience,

I am assuming a certain level of emotional consensus, while being aware that an apparently shared reaction may well be diverse, to quote Sara Ahmed, "emotions in their intensity involve miscommunication, such that even when we feel we have the same feeling, we don't necessarily have the same relation to the feeling."[32] There are many feelings that may be equally intended (or masked) by a seemingly uniform reaction like crying—such as anger, despair, pain. Tears might either be an empathetic mirroring of the pain displayed and performed onstage or be a sign of some other, more personal grief (or both, and more). Tears may also represent a final catharsis for the audience, allowing each person to express a reaction to the show through crying and then to move on. Alternatively, tears may be a signal of deep disturbance, a disturbance that leads to enacting change outside the theatre. Without a sociological approach, it would be difficult to diagnose this reaction more fully—I want to raise these possibilities, however, as one way of suggesting that tears may look like an active reaction, but that they may just be a sign of a too-easy empathy.

How Can We Be Expected to Do This (Mnemonic) Work?

Through the emphasis on empathy, both *I Once Knew a Girl* and *Nirbhaya* use the emotional capital of the female performers in order to capture audience attention and raise the social capital of the women in the show and, in theory, of other women like them. The theatre, in this reading, becomes a forum for collective emotional and social witnessing. Alison Landsberg's idea of prosthetic memory suggests a model of memory that might be useful here—where the memory of the "other" or "not-I" is projected onstage and internalized by the "self" of the audience member.[33] In theory then, these stories, through their public performance and the audience's affective reaction, become part of "our" social memory, thereby "traveling," to adapt Astrid Erll's term, from the individual to the collective, from the "I" to the "we," enabling the audience to become incorporated in social memory.[34] That collective or social form of memory impresses itself on the individual, thereby distributing ownership of memory across the audience community in the intense and shared space of the auditorium. Co-ownership is thus figured as shared responsibility (the ethical goal of the audience-as-witness). The effect of this empathetic witnessing is doubly therapeutic, healing the divisions between "other" and "self," as each member of cast and audience-as-community are reimagined and collectively defined as witnesses to an unjust past.[35]

But is therapeutic value the same as witnessing? Theater of Witness audience feedback suggests both dimensions. While one commenter said, "I feel a lot of movement in my heart right now—sadness and celebration. Thank you for creating a thing of such great and delicate beauty out of such sadness and survival. And for everything, ladies, thank you," another noted the impact of presenting women as "resilient and powerful."[36] And while the majority of the comments collected by Theater of Witness focus on the "heartrending" nature of the work, some gesture toward how empathy can produce a desire for change: "Very moving. Powerful. Makes me want to make a difference." Despite my wariness, then, some comments suggest empathy and change are not mutually exclusive.

Empathy may also produce new performances of witnessing, unanticipated by the market gatekeepers. Farber notes how during *Nirbhaya*'s initial run, people wanted to meet the cast to talk to them.[37] This is a marker of its success: Tim Etchells argues that the definition of successful witnessing is when the docu-verbatim play produces spectators who can't stop talking about the show afterward.[38] As a result, cast members are now present after shows interacting with audience members, many of whom share previously untold stories of violence. These postshow interactions suggest that the radically open vulnerability of autoperformance is a potentially empowering performance that, in turn, creates further performances combining both witnessing and testifying.

Without labor—and often difficult labor—witnessing cannot happen. In *I Once Knew a Girl*, Kathleen talks of the restorative-justice work she has done with ex-combatants:

> I remember the first time they suggested that I meet with ex-combatants, it was horrific. I got terrible flashbacks. How could I sit in the same room as ex-IRA men or people like that? How could I listen to them and talk to them? I actually got up and walked out of the room. But then I started to think to myself, if I'm somebody who wants peace, and I can assure you I am, then I have to be prepared to mix with these people, talk to them, listen to their stories. And if I can't do this, how can I expect other people in Northern Ireland to do this work?

Kathleen's testimony highlights the necessary immaterial labor—often performed by women and victims—to move toward reconciliation. This labor requires personal sacrifice in order to generate larger social dividends. While Kathleen's is an extreme case—her husband was murdered by "people like that"—she does not let the audience off the hook, but in her expectation issues an instruction to the audience of the necessity of *work*. Through overt testimony such as this, and also by using nonprofessional performers, autoperformed testimonial theatre not only conveys a message about the ethical duty to witness, but also makes visible the otherwise invisible immaterial labor required by such tasks.

Labor is also acknowledged in *Nirbhaya*, which demonstrates that silence, though a kind of labor itself, erodes social capital, disempowering victims in the hierarchical marketplace. As Poorna puts it, by staying silent, the victims of sexual violence maintain a code of shame that protects the abusers and further weakens the vulnerable: "I am her. She is me. And I know. My silence all these years . . . is part of what that dark night brought."[39] Yet by sharing stories of past suffering, memory can also be future-oriented: "Breaking the silence we break the cycle of violence."[40] But "breaking" takes work, and is only possible through the collectivization of social capital, as Jagannathan goes on to make clear: "Each person is responsible for changing, and for unravelling, the fabric of this rape culture that we live in" (this statement is not in the play but made during a television interview, suggesting the power of media in disseminating this message).[41] Farber also acknowledges the work required to counteract the shame of victimization and ensuing silence: "I want to break the silence. It's a modest, but incredibly powerful, gesture. Sexual violence creates a response of shame in the victim, and so you go silent. And when you just go, 'I claim this as an event that happened in my life, but I will not claim the shame or the loss of honour,' then it begins to dismantle that system."[42]

Acknowledging the labor of change is vital and an important corollary to empathy. However, the shows' relentless focus on the individual and the lack of structural analysis (for example, in *Nirbhaya* there is no explanation that marital rape is not a crime in India) make it difficult to separate the message of collective change from the individualized stories that the audience consumes. The mode of delivery—direct address—while highlighting the labor of the performer, threatens to act as a hindrance to the message. Indeed, as Rosanne Kennedy and Gillian Whitlock argue, this is one of the pathologizing effects of the trauma framework, which focuses "on the individual effects of traumatic experience rather than social structures and collective experiences, and . . . position[s] sufferers as victims rather than survivors."[43] Individuals, of course, can lead social change, and the theatre makers are also fully aware of the need for collective action; but the concentration on the individual voice and the dramaturgy of trauma, which are built-in to autoperformance testimonial theatre that stages pain and vulnerability, create an individualized audience-witness who may feel empathy for the victim, or experience a connection relating to their own experience of sexual violence, but who is also encouraged to feel change (consume) rather than enact change (act).

These limits were one of the reasons why Sapna Bhavnani, one of the *Nirbhaya* cast members, left the show in 2015. Bhavnani felt that the play, despite its international success, was a "niche" experience that was not reaching a wide enough audience—the market segmentation that enabled *Nirbhaya*'s success, appealing to consumers of the verbatim "brand," pushed Bhavnani to leave. She also argues that, "Reliving the process every day onstage was not healing at all. And it was making me more a victim of my circumstance. It didn't show me as who I am. Not as the woman I am today."[44] The emphasis on painful memories—she described being gang raped—was too past-oriented for Bhavnani, who now works to set up nursery schools and women's centers in villages in India. Bhavnani's concern that these memories only reflect one part of her experience is another illustration of the tensions caused by a mission to expose that drives these testimonial dramas, so that they isolate and focus on these memories as single and defining experiences, and don't integrate the stories into either the context of the women's lives or the still larger context of social life in general.

Market Segmentation

The single focus on one type of experience—and one type of victim—alongside Bhavnani's view of the play format as "niche," also troubles the hope that these kinds of plays might lead to wider social change beyond making people feel sad or angry. The exclusive focus in both *Nirbhaya* and *I Once Knew a Girl* allows the shows to become a safe space for the women whose stories are being shared, and for those in the audience who identify with what is being shared onstage. The focus also signals that these women's voices represent sufficient cultural capital to be center stage and to occupy the whole of a production, a deliberate counter to the usual marginalization of women's stories within a male-dominated mainstream culture. Yet the productions' identification of these women's stories as *distinct* from the mainstream risks segmenting the memory marketplace. Market segmentation works to create distinct markets or audiences for particular demographics. In one sense this is productive because segmentation helps to expand the market, so that, for example, a play reflecting the stories of one particular social group attracts that group to the theatre on the promise that this audience will be specifically catered to. The same is true here, yet when that market segment is "women," that is, technically half the population, it's risky to suggest that this is a particular collective that needs to be disconnected from the mainstream audience. This is not to adopt a patronizing "inclusive" agenda and the tokenism that can create, but rather to suggest that the mainstream memory marketplace itself be revolutionized so that it becomes a safe space for narratives of women's experiences of violence. Though *Nirbhaya* was a hit at the Edinburgh festival and has toured the UK, India, and Canada, and Theater of Witness played to sold-out audiences in Northern Ireland and New York, this does not make them mainstream. Just as violent histories such as the Holocaust are relevant for non-Jewish audiences, narratives of rape should be considered as central to, not a segment of, the wider memory marketplace.

Funding Feeling Not Change

Theater of Witness (which produced four shows in Northern Ireland in total) is a theatre enterprise funded on the basis of market segmentation—in this case targeting an audience seeking reconciliation after the Troubles. Funding is from a range of sources, but primarily from an EU Peace III grant program, which aims to "reconcile communities and contribute towards a shared society for everyone." *I Once Knew a Girl* certainly delivers on the program's first three priorities:

1. To build positive relations at the local level
2. To acknowledge the past
3. To create shared public spaces

But I would question whether it can ever deliver on the fourth:

4. To develop key institutional capacity for a shared society.[45]

Sepinuck's dramaturgy works to reconcile victims and perpetrators through a common emphasis on pain and empathy; yet the unity created by Theater of Witness shows during the moment of the production and its immediate aftermath as the audience remediates its meaning, is itself vulnerable, not least because of the absence of political unity outside the theatre—as suggested by the repeated breakdown of a power-sharing government in Northern Ireland and the continuation of sectarian violence, both in terms of actual physical violence and the cultural violence of a sectarian school system. Of course I recognize that hearts are broken by conflict, but so are social systems. As with *Nirbhaya*, the problem here is that the cultural marketplace is flooded with (and funded to sustain) empathetic narratives that focus on an economy of feeling change, which, however social, are largely about the individual relationship created via painful memory between the "other" and the "self" (or about healing divisions within the self), rather than changing the processes of othering that lead to violence and inequality in the public sphere. Stef Craps has thus urged the need to move beyond accounts of individual trauma to attend to the wider contexts: "Refusing to move from the individual psyche to the social situation can only have damaging consequences. A narrow focus on individual psychology ignores and leaves unquestioned the conditions that enabled the traumatic abuse. Indeed, the individualization of social suffering encourages the idea that recovery from the traumas affecting the members of marginalized groups is basically a matter of the individual gaining linguistic control over his or her pain."[46] In highlighting voice above all, social justice testimonial plays become, to paraphrase Lauren Berlant, "a technology of amelioration" not a solution.[47]

Financial viability is obviously a major concern for theatre companies doing verbatim work—without financial support from national theatres, government grants, and ticket sales (and in the case of *Nirbhaya*, crowdfunding), these shows would not be possible—and theatre is a much more expensive business than, say, social media, as a way of giving voice to the marginalized and voiceless. The risk to any model of culture, however, that depends on generating money in order for it to exist, is that it is explicitly—or inadvertently—modeled on also generating particular outcomes and satisfaction ratings. In *Nirbhaya*'s marketing, for example, it is easy to see a distinct branding of the show as both a compelling piece of theatre and a trauma product that will satisfy the consumer. Posters, social media posts, and YouTube trailers declare the show to be "one of the most powerful pieces of theatre you'll ever see," "one of the most powerful and urgent pieces of human rights theatre ever made," and make a feature of the five-star reviews, sold-out shows in London, New York, and India, and awards from Amnesty International, *The Scotsman*, and the *Herald Angel*.[48] This kind of marketing is successful and enables the play to reach a citizen consumer audience who, arguably, approaches seeing the show not as simply entertainment but as a socially important and responsible act itself. Yet these promotional strategies by the company, and the theatres that host the touring show, also rely on offering audiences an opportunity to consume someone else's pain in a prestige format, and to thus not only be moved by the performance of pain, but to share in the high cultural capital of the show, validating the audience in turn as "powerful" and "urgent" audience-consumers.

The Audience as Consumer: The Empathy Paradox

The docu-verbatim play functions as a particular mode of memory transmission that relies on "the facts," direct address, and empathy to create a sense of collective witnessing among a new "remembering community."[49] Within this mode of exchange, memory additionally functions as a product that the audience consumes—in the case of all the docu-verbatim plays discussed so far, that memory product could be labeled "painful memory." Five-star reviews, sold-out shows, commissions from the National Theatre, international tours, and funding from the European Union all contribute to endorsing that product, and demonstrating that certain kinds of, or approaches to, memory are sanctioned and thus perform successfully in the memory marketplace.

Docu-verbatim theatre additionally mediates "the facts" in such a way as to offer audiences the opportunity to form an opinion (or buy a position) on the morality of the past. Viewed this way, these plays are both a working through, and a packaging of, memory. Audiences who go to these shows and find them powerful of course have an equal opportunity to respond with action as well as empathy. Yet the emphasis on suffering, emotion, and, in the case of autoperformance, on the individual, risks privatizing that suffering. Moreover, the retrospective gaze of memory plays, and the nature of theatre to rehearse exactly the same story every night, further risk suggesting that suffering is fated and inescapable, thereby generating sympathy not provoking change.

The empathy paradox troubles successful marketplace performances of pain, because while audiences are encouraged to feel, that emphasis on feeling may prevent change. The trauma paradox is usually taken to be the struggle of the original witness to overcome the silencing of trauma, and to make trauma speak. This struggle is further complicated by Theodor Adorno's warning of the danger of the aesthetic transfiguration of the horror of the victim.[50] Docu-verbatim shows address both of these paradoxes. Yet in doing so they create another: the empathy paradox whereby the transmission of trauma from the stage to the audience may silence that audience because of the empathetic pain that group now feels. The same mechanism affects audiences who feel shame (as discussed in chap. 1). These are such strong emotional reactions that further actions become either limited, or indeed eclipsed, by the initial emotion provoked by the show, so that empathy is both an immediate and enduring response.

The feeling-experience of empathy, and in particular, the expression of grief, through tears or anger during and after the performance, connotes the audience's recognition of the horror of the victim. This feeling-experience, in offering validation to the onstage witness, also offers catharsis to the audience member. This catharsis, combined with the feel-good nature of docu-verbatim due to the form's association with social justice, creates a context in which the audience member can identify their empathy and expressions of grief as the discharge of their social responsibility, to the victim and to the past. This is particularly the case in shows that move toward a form of closure, performing reconciliation on stage, or transcending painful reality, so that the work of ethical witnessing is presented as already having been done (both interpretively and practically). Jen Harvie's point on participatory theatre is relevant here as she argues that theatre shows appear to offer opportunities for engagement but may actually effectively limit "how much agency they actually divest to their audiences."[51] For an audience, the feel-good factor of being part of a communal experience of witnessing is combined with the feel-good factor of participating in the social justice actions—doing the work—assumed to be synonymous with such witnessing, thereby generating significant cultural capital. This combination leads audiences to read their attendance at the theatre as an expression of agentic labor, and to use their consumption of this memory product to define themselves and their actions, analogous to the way that, for example, Fair Trade consumption operates. This consumption *looks* like ethical spectatorship, but that appearance masks the fact that very little has actually changed. Indeed, as Harvie suggests, far from leading to social change, theatre shows may "operate insidiously as a distraction, offering pleasantly diverting opportunities for social engagement and equality but ones which can only ever be temporary and limited, and which cannot remotely begin to compensate for the larger" social problems.[52]

It is true that the performance of memory can reach a range of audiences and, in forming a community, however temporary, can create a vision of what social cohesion might look like. When cast members perform that cohesion onstage, there is further potential for multidirectional memory. Yet Bhavnani's comment that *Nirbhaya* is a "niche" product should also alert us to the fact that memory plays cannot be assumed to generate universal social goods such as peace and reconciliation, particularly given the lack of connection between these individual theatre works and the actual infrastructures of power (even if linked to them by funding strands). As Roger Simon argues, it is questionable whether consumption of memories of painful suffering leads audiences to perceive those experiences as "part of ongoing relations of power and privilege, the legacy of which I participate in and I am called to transform."[53]

I am torn on this issue because I want to believe in the ability of theatre to speak to a large audience and for theatres to operate as spaces of profound feeling and thinking. However, the "extreme close-up" version of theatre that concentrates on individual painful memory seems to offer that opportunity for profundity, but at such a singular level as to be hampered from translating into action outside the theatre. This is particularly the case under the empathy paradox, whereby performances of painful memory encourage identificatory rather than disruptive responses, a process that disables critical thought. Combined with the positioning of art as a consumer product, this disabling maintains the gap between the auditorium and the world, the audience member and the activist.

To note that docu-verbatim theatre is not always a catalyst for direct action on social change perhaps makes me too harsh a critic, and creates an unreasonable expectation that social justice is the responsibility of theatre. And who am I to say that audiences are wrong to cry, or that directors are wrong to want people to cry? It's not because I hate feelings, or because I don't think that theatre has a responsibility to stage vulnerability—quite the opposite. A broken woman onstage can be a powerful symbol. But I suggest that when that performance becomes a trend or product then it becomes dangerous. Women (and other "damaged" groups) onstage become experts at being hurt and the past becomes framed exclusively as a space of trauma that can only be witnessed emotionally. This is particularly the case for autoperformance, which mobilizes the victims themselves—yes, this gives the victims a platform, a voice, and cultural memory capital within the marketplace. But it also compels them to repeat their painful experience for the benefit of an audience who can then, quite easily and with little risk, consume that experience, empathize with it, and appropriate it, in a process that commodifies the victims' pain.

The commodification of pain is not, by any means, unique to theatre—rather, my argument here is that while docu-verbatim theatre may look like a new product in a cultural marketplace that is eager for "the facts," in reality docu-verbatim as a mode tends toward the individuation of trauma that is typical of current culture, both high-brow and popular, a mode in which pain is identified with the present body of the individual. That individual is highly articulate (even the nonactors) and trained to appeal to the audience. They are not unlikeable subjects, on the contrary, though the stories they narrate demonstrate painful othering, the actor-subject herself is sympathetic and, to use Judith Butler's term, "grievable."[54] If the agenda of these shows is to break the silence, then they fully achieve their agenda. If, however, we expect theatre that represents abuses of human rights to go further than simply providing a voice and limited memory capital for these experiences, then we need to reconsider.

To point out these limits is to begin a conversation that goes beyond critiquing theatre and toward asking larger questions about whether one citizen needs to feel another's pain in order to grant that person respect and equal civil rights. This is problematic because if empathy is the tool we, as a society and a culture, consistently use to create connection and social solidarity, then it weakens the assumption that equality and safety for society's most vulnerable members is the remit of well-funded social welfare agencies and robust and active legislation. While audiences may feel empathy for the individual witness onstage, this does not necessarily challenge the structural callousness that so often underlies the individual case, nor does it challenge the lack of empathy available to "unlikeable" subjects.

The good intentions of both theatre makers and audiences are valuable; but they are small gestures indeed in the neoliberal context in which these shows operate and, arguably, that they exploit in order to be successful. This context is influential in the positioning of the audience as an individualized consumer of a public theatre production in which memory is actually privatized through a practice of performing identity-based affiliation through empathy. And, finally, in the context of recent moves to the political right in many of the countries in which these shows were first performed, it is also salutary to remember that definitions of ethical memory, witnessing, and action are entirely relative and that the engaging of audience sentiments through powerful calls on their emotions can operate not only conservatively, but can create hate and social division as much as healing.

NOTES

1. Michal Givoni, *The Care of the Witness* (Cambridge: Cambridge University Press, 2016), 25.
2. Marianne Hirsch, "Connective Histories in Vulnerable Times," *PMLA* 129, no. 3 (2014): 330–48, see esp. 334.
3. Teya Sepinuck, *Theatre of Witness: Finding the Medicine in Stories of Suffering* (London: Jessica Kingsley, 2013), 14.
4. Deirdre Heddon, *Autobiography and Performance* (Basingstoke: Palgrave, 2018), 21.
5. Sepinuck's current project focuses on stories linked to the US police department.
6. I use the joint name Derry/Londonderry because the city's name varies depending on political affiliation, and it is necessary to include both nomenclatures.

7. See Theater of Witness, "About Theater of Witness," accessed October 14, 2019, http://www.theaterofwitness.org/about.

8. BBC News, "Bloody Sunday: PM David Cameron's Full Statement," June 15, 2010, http://www.bbc.com/news/10322295. The apology was delivered just four months before the production of *I Once Knew a Girl.*

9. All quotations are taken from the DVD recording of *I Once Knew a Girl,* directed and produced by Margo Harkin, Besom Productions, 2010. For a copy of the DVD, please contact the Derry Playhouse Theatre, info@derryplayhouse.co.uk.

10. The "Provos" are the Provisional IRA.

11. Lisa Fitzpatrick, *Rape on the Contemporary Stage* (London: Palgrave, 2018), 173.

12. *I Once Knew a Girl* interviews, dir. Margo Harkin, 2013. https://vimeo.com/57846616.

13. Lisa Fitzpatrick, "Gender and Affect in Testimonial Performance: The Example of *I Once Knew a Girl*," *Irish University Review* 45, no. 1 (2015): 126–40, see esp. 137.

14. *I Once Knew a Girl* interviews. In fact, this process is so successful for Therese that she appears in a second production, *Sanctuary,* in 2013.

15. Sepinuck, *Theatre of Witness,* 180.

16. Luke Moffett, "Reparations for 'Guilty Victims': Navigating Complex Identities of Victim-Perpetrators in Reparation Mechanisms," *International Journal of Transitional Justice* 10 (2016): 146–67, see esp. 146.

17. Sepinuck, *Theatre of Witness,* 171.

18. Jacques Rancière, *The Emancipated Spectator,* trans. Gregory Elliott (London: Verso, 2009), 84.

19. This was the cast line-up for the show that I saw. In some performances, the cast includes Pamela Sinha and does not include Sapna Bhavnani.

20. Poorna Jagannathan's testimony in Yael Farber, *Nirbhaya* (unpublished script, courtesy of the company), 24.

21. Priyanka Bose's testimony in Farber, *Nirbhaya,* 35.

22. Priyanka Bose's testimony in Farber, *Nirbhaya,* 37.

23. "'Fearless' Play Voices Outrage over Delhi Gang Rape," November 14, 2014, https://www.youtube.com/watch?v=vO7ijsqDLjo.

24. Ben Brantley, "Review: 'Nirbhaya,' a Lamentation and a Rallying Cry for Indian Women," *New York Times,* April 27, 2015, http://www.nytimes.com/2015/04/28/theater/review-nirbhaya-a-lamentation-and-a-rallying-cry-for-indian-women.html?_r=0.

25. Farber, *Nirbhaya,* 2, 4.

26. Fitzpatrick identifies this moment as raising "questions about the exploitation of an individual's tragic death," *Rape on the Contemporary Stage,* 235.

27. Lyn Gardner, "Nirbhaya—Edinburgh Festival 2013 Review," *The Guardian,* August 5, 2013, https://www.theguardian.com/stage/2013/aug/05/edinburgh-festival-2013-nirbhaya-review.

28. Nicholas Ridout and Rebecca Schneider, "Precarity and Performance: An Introduction," *The Drama Review* 56, no. 4 (2012): 5–9, see esp. 6.

29. Karine Schaefer, "The Spectator as Witness? *Binlids* as Case Study," *Studies in Theatre and Performance* 23, no. 1 (2003): 5–20, see esp. 6.

30. Schaefer, "The Spectator as Witness?" 17.

31. Amanda Stuart Fisher, "Trauma, Authenticity and the Limits of Verbatim," *Performance Research* 16, no. 1 (2011): 112–22, see esp. 113.

32. Sarah Ahmed, *The Cultural Politics of Emotion* (Edinburgh: Edinburgh University Press, 2004), 10.

33. See Alison Landsberg, *Prosthetic Memory* (New York: Columbia University Press, 2004), 25–48.

34. See Astrid Erll, "Travelling Memory," *Parallax* 17, no. 4 (2011): 4–18.

35. For a discussion of some of these same issues in the context of South Africa, see Stephanie Marlin-Curiel, "The Long Road to Healing: From the TRC to TfD," *Theatre Research International* 3 (2002): 275–88.

36. Theater of Witness, "Audience Reflections," *I Once Knew a Girl*, 2010. Obviously, this feedback has to be treated carefully as it is gathered by the Theater of Witness itself (on anonymous comment cards) in the immediate wake of the show, when reactions are likely to be both vivid and impulsive.

37. Laura Barnett, "Edinburgh Festival 2013: Yael Farber, Interview," *The Telegraph*, August 14, 2013, http://www.telegraph.co.uk/culture/theatre/edinburgh-festival/10242915/Edinburgh-Festival-2013-Yael-Farber-interview.html.

38. Tim Etchells, *Certain Fragments* (London: Routledge, 1999), 18.

39. Poorna Jagannathan's testimony in Farber, *Nirbhaya*, 21.

40. "Poorna Jagannathan: Breaking the Cycle of Violence," March 23, 2015, https://www.youtube.com/watch?v=X4-QUVcTFOk.

41. "Nirbhaya the Play: A Powerful Story of Authenticity & Experience," March 2, 2016, https://www.youtube.com/watch?v=Eka1nQKCiKY.

42. Barnett, "Edinburgh Festival 2013."

43. Rosanne Kennedy and Gillian Whitlock, "Witnessing, Trauma and Social Suffering: Feminist Perspectives," *Australian Feminist Studies* 26, no. 69 (2011): 251–55, see esp. 251.

44. "Why I Am Speaking about My Gang Rape," *NDTV*, July 9, 2015, http://www.ndtv.com/india-news/why-i-am-speaking-about-my-gang-rape-by-sapna-bhavnani-779850.

45. Special European Union Programmes Body, *EU Programme for Peace and Reconciliation in Northern Ireland and the Border Region of Ireland 2007–13: Operational Programme* (Belfast: SEUPB, 2007). For a general overview of the Peace IV programme, see https://www.seupb.eu/piv-overview (accessed January 2, 2020).

46. See Stef Craps, "Wor(l)ds of Grief: Traumatic Memory and Literary Witnessing in Cross-Cultural Perspective," *Textual Practice* 24, no. 1 (2010): 51–68, see esp. 55.

47. Lauren Berlant, "Introduction: Compassion (and Withholding)," in *Compassion: The Culture and Politics of an Emotion*, ed. Lauren Berlant (Abingdon, UK: Routledge, 2004), 2.

48. For an example, see https://www.youtube.com/watch?v=l6jh1hWokuU.

49. Sara Jones, *The Media of Testimony* (Basingstoke, UK: Palgrave, 2014), 187.

50. Theodor W. Adorno, "Commitment," in *Can One Live after Auschwitz: A Philosophical Reader*, ed. Rolf Tiedemann, trans. Rodney Livingston, et al. (Stanford, CA: Stanford University Press, 2003), 240–58.

51. Jen Harvie, *Fair Play: Art, Performance and Neoliberalism* (Houndmills, UK: Palgrave, 2013), 3.

52. Harvie, *Fair Play*, 3.

53. Roger I. Simon, "The Touch of the Past: The Pedagogical Significance of a Transactional Sphere of Public Memory," in *Revolutionary Pedagogies: Cultural Politics, Education, and Discourse of Theory*, ed. Peter Trifonas (London: Routledge, 2002), 61–80.

54. Judith Butler, *Precarious Life: The Power of Mourning and Violence* (New York: Verso Books, 2004).

THREE

THE COMMISSIONED WITNESS, THEATRE, AND TRUTH

WHAT DO WE EXPECT OF the witness? To tell the truth? To tell us their truth? To give us what is known already, in their voice, from their mouth? To give us something we didn't know? Who do we expect the witness to be? The victim? The perpetrator? How do we expect them to be? Nervous? Confident? Protesting? Do we expect the witness to be a *person* or a *story*? And how do our expectations shape how the witness behaves, how the witness is received, how the witness is treated? How is witnessing produced? How is witnessing consumed? How is witnessing commodified? And how can that process of commodification be resisted? This chapter considers these questions in the context of the marketplace, specifically in relation to the effect of emotional labor on the fluctuating value of victims' and perpetrators' social capital.

In recent decades there has been an increasing number of "truth commissions," which, as framed by the South African Truth and Reconciliation Commission (TRC), aim to "restore the human and civil dignity of victims by granting them an opportunity to relate their own accounts of the violations of which they are the victims."[1] Public truth commissions literally give witnesses a stage or platform and an audience. In so doing, like the genre of docu-verbatim theatre, truth commissions involve labor-intensive performances of production, dissemination, and consumption. These performances explicitly demand that both producers and consumers act ethically.

But this stage is not available to all. There are, quite simply, too many witnesses, too many victims, too many survivors. There is a problem of abundance, or an imbalance, in the market—characterized by an excess of emotional labor and capital and a scarcity of cultural and social capital. Truth commissions are thus highly selective, adjudicating the different market values of particular witnesses. In the case of the South African TRC, less than ten percent of the twenty-one thousand survivor-witnesses who made statements were selected to give public testimony as part of the public TRC hearings.[2] As identified in chapter 1, in relation to *No Escape* and the Irish child-abuse commission, there is a tense relationship between the need for collective witnessing by survivors in order to illustrate the widespread nature of trauma, and the audience's need for a synecdochical witness to stand in for the many. Perhaps—and it may seem an oxymoron—by having fewer witnesses, the audience can better perceive the larger picture. This is as true for theatre as it is for truth commissions.

By selecting and thus lifting up particular witnesses, commissions and theatre makers have the capacity to—temporarily—rebalance power hierarchies. As Catherine M. Cole writes of the South African TRC, many of the witnesses were the most "lowly in society";[3] these are not witnesses with social capital, who are usually given time or attention in the memory marketplace, but those who require an intervention by more powerful gatekeepers in the market. The TRC's process was about "restoring the human and civil dignity of victims," but also about ameliorating structural power relations.[4] I say ameliorate, of course, because while this model of ethical production and consumption of witnessing obviously emerges from civic and political activist roots, its top-down nature and emphasis on catharsis and being heard, rather than on social transformation, not only limits its effectiveness but also risks producing a spectacle of witnessing and commodifying the pain of the victim-witness.

This chapter considers not the TRCs themselves, but how theatre mediates the experience and expectations of TRCs and the processes of witnessing. Through analysis of three key plays, I argue that theatre can acknowledge the risks of witnessing to a truth commission—false confessions, temporary catharsis, and commodification—while also using creative strategies to limit or foreclose those risks. As Brenda Werth writes of Argentinian witness plays, "theatre both complements and contests legal and political performances."[5] The first play for consideration—*Ubu and the Truth Commission* (1997) by Jane Taylor and the Handspring Puppet Company—is a response to the South African TRC. Though the play is the most experimental of the three discussed in this chapter, it is also the most literally linked to a truth commission, representing what Caroline Wake has termed the need for culture "to respond to the inquiry as well as to the incident itself."[6] The second play—*Death and the Maiden* (1990) by Ariel Dorfman—is set in Chile, exclusively in a private home and can best be read as an alternative and, crucially, *private* truth commission. The third play—*Claudia* (2016) by La Conquesta del Pol Sud and Claudia

Poblete Hlaczik—exists in the vacuum created by the absence of a national truth commission in Argentina and, like Dorfman's play, creates an alternative theatrical space for engaging with a difficult past. All three plays probe the relationship between the survivor and the perpetrator. Perhaps most profoundly, however, the three plays share a concern with the process of defining the truth itself and the shifting roles of both survivor- and perpetrator-witnesses within processes of production and consumption.

The theatre makers' choices relating to who is given space to testify illustrate varied responses to the process of truth commissions in attending to, and weighing, both sides of the conflict. In *Ubu*, the dramaturgy combines human actors and puppets—and, possibly against expectation, the play's perpetrators are depicted by human actors, while survivor-witnesses are depicted by puppets. In *Death and the Maiden*, Dorfman creates a scenario in which a victim of the regime comes into direct contact with a perpetrator, indeed, with the man who victimized her. *Claudia* combines autoperformance with video to depict multiple victims of the regime and to show the offstage spaces of torture used during the dictatorship, but the figure of the perpetrator is missing. Unlike the autoperformance plays discussed in chapter 2, in both *Death and the Maiden* and *Claudia* the theatre makers use different strategies to avoid the trend of "confining victims, particularly women, to the role of narrator of pain and suffering."[7] These three different approaches demonstrate alternate ways of prioritizing and highlighting the voices and presences of victims and perpetrators, and simultaneously show how the struggle for capital is devolved from the institution/state to the individual.

In *Ubu*, though it might be expected that empathy would attach to the human actors, in fact the quiet simplicity (hugely helped by direction and production features such as the lighting design) and the deep sense of personal loss expressed by the puppets engages much more empathy for the victims. Yet the perpetrator, Pa Ubu, is nevertheless given far more stage time than his victims, and he dominates the play as a result. In *Death and the Maiden*, Dorfman carefully establishes empathy for the victim, Paulina, early on, and then brings this into tension when the man who may, or may not, be her torturer appears. This man's reasonable and affable demeanor make him an unlikely perpetrator and strongly contrasts with the obvious and rambunctious violence of a figure like Pa Ubu, yet it is also this *reasonableness* that makes him such a chilling perpetrator. In *Claudia* the real-life victim herself testifies about her childhood, the killing of her biological parents by the dictatorship, and her realization that her life had been a lie. *Claudia*'s autoperformance docu-verbatim style leaves no room for the presence of the perpetrators (her illegally adoptive parents), who are only inferred through reported speech and photographs. Of the three performance styles, as with the autoperformance shows in chapter 2, the latter is the most obvious engagement of audience empathy for the victim and the clearest choice to prioritize her subjectivity.

In many ways these three plays are unalike: where *Ubu* gives physical preeminence to the perpetrator, *Death and the Maiden* and *Claudia* prioritize the voice of the survivor of violence; *Death and the Maiden* includes the perpetrator's voice, *Claudia* does not. The plays are also formally very different and, in spanning three decades and three continents, emerge from very different theatrical and social justice contexts. However, there is a unity of purpose here too—all three enact an awareness that the empathy that attaches to the victim-witness has to be negotiated carefully, and in their formal experiments illustrate a concern with exploring how the victim and the perpetrator actually give testimony. All three plays center on the process of staging a truth commission, in whatever form, and demonstrate the power of the commission in harnessing the emotional capital of victims' memories. All three plays also make visible not only the differentials between the victim and the perpetrator, but the structural power relations themselves, highlighting how the abuses of the past are always shaped by those with social and political capital.

Finally, all three plays ultimately present the idea that memory is a dangerous commodity. The productions question how that commodity is valued—for example, what is the social capital generated by credible (or not) testimony, and how is that capital determined by the changing political context—and outline how value and cost are defined differently by the individual, the family, and the society. The interest of the media in particular memory groups and their narratives is shown to be a key driver of how the marketplace narrative changes and also a fickle indicator of power. As Hackett and Rolston argue, a "disappointment for many victims testifying to the TRC was the discovery that their testimonies often became in effect commodities, paraded in news broadcasts, CDs etc."[8] Indeed, ultimately, all three plays demonstrate that memory, though potentially subversive and dangerous, is an unreliable foundation for achieving social power because of how easily memory can be commodified by the status quo. Though the cultural and social capital of the survivor-witness in the memory marketplace may rise at times of transition and/or peace and reconciliation, these plays reveal the bestowal of social and cultural capital on victims to be a *borrowed power*. Moreover, no matter how much personal empowerment survivors may achieve through giving testimony, their needs are always dwarfed by the larger needs of society and the demands of the marketplace for order. In other words, the disenfranchised witness, who owns the dangerous commodity of memory, can be granted a temporary space to speak, but ultimately order must be reasserted for the market to keep functioning. And how is that order imposed? Simply put, the status quo reasserts itself; this action is normalized by the audience, whose consumer power and presence demands both catharsis and closure. And what then? The victim-witness becomes voiceless once more, the perpetrator either accepts or, in two cases, largely escapes punishment, and the status quo of the memory marketplace resumes. These plays thus represent pointed responses to the closing-down of the marketplace for victims and survivors, highlighting, as Yvette Hutchison argues, theatre as a space within which to contest consensualizing narratives.[9]

UBU AND THE TRUTH COMMISSION: THE PERPETRATOR-WITNESS

Jane Taylor's script for *Ubu and the Truth Commission* combines a fictional premise (the central characters are modeled on Alfred Jarry's *Ubu Roi* [1896]) with verbatim testimony from the victims of apartheid as delivered at the TRC.[10] As already mentioned, the play is an explicit reaction to the real-life South African Truth and Reconciliation Commission, albeit staged in a nonrealist, avant-garde form, articulating the moment of the downfall of the apartheid system. The play's central characters are Pa and Ma Ubu, cartoonlike figures who rant and rave about their fall from grace as formerly successful agents of apartheid. The Ubus are the only two characters played by human actors; the remaining characters are portrayed by puppets, devised by Handspring Puppet Company and animated with screen drawings and captions by William Kentridge. These different dramatic elements cohere into a satiric and farcical representation of the aftermath and legacies of apartheid violence, and in the play's evocation of the real-life truth commission suggests that not a little of its action—in particular the testimony of perpetrators—was equally farcical.

The play's central plot depicts Ma Ubu's suspicions that her husband Pa is having a series of affairs due to his nightly absences from home. The dramatic irony is that the audience knows that Pa's excursions are in fact violent forays to torture and murder black South Africans, and that when he returns home to shower, he is washing off not evidence of sexual promiscuity but the blood of his victims. In these violent actions, Pa is helped by the three-headed puppet dog Brutus and advised by the puppet crocodile Niles. While Brutus represents the physical violence of the regime, reminiscent of the hounds of hell, Niles is the wily advisor, who is not directly implicated in the violence but acts as Pa's secret-keeper.

The contrast between Pa's sidekicks is manifest in their reactions to the advent of the TRC and the change in regime: Brutus's three heads are unrepentant, but Niles advises Pa to confess in order to be granted amnesty. Pa initially refuses to do so, but eventually realizes that a confession, and the betrayal and sacrifice of Brutus, are necessary to ensure his own safety. During this time, Ma discovers Pa's real actions, transforming him in her eyes from an unfaithful husband to a hero. It is chilling to see Ma so happy and so boastful of her husband's prowess and hypermasculinity as she declares, "I had no idea Pa was so important! All along, I thought he was betraying me and here he was, hard at work, protecting me from the Swart Gevaar. (*Wipes her eyes sentimentally. . . .*)"[11]

Watching Ma and Pa Ubu onstage is like spectating at a cruel and warped circus. However, there are brief pauses in the play's manic action as Taylor and Handspring create spaces for other kinds of experience. This is particularly powerful when puppet-witnesses appear onstage and quietly deliver testimony about their suffering under apartheid, often related to their experience of watching their children die or of having to identify their bodies. These moments of painful reflection act as counterpoints of sincerity and courage to Pa and Ma's hyperactive insincerity and moral cowardice. Indeed, the epitome of Pa's and Ma's moral blindness (and deafness) is represented by their ignorance of the victims—though they all occupy the stage at the same time, Pa and Ma act as if they hear and see nothing throughout the victim testimonies. As a result, the puppets are only witnessed by the audience, increasing the sense of an intimate or exclusive empathic connection between the audience and the survivors (this distances the audience from the consumption of the Ubus onstage, encouraging the audience to identify instead as citizen-consumers). Formally, too, the total division between Pa and Ma and the survivor-witnesses replicates the sense in which apartheid created two separate worlds, in which the elite were culturally deaf and blind to the suffering of black South Africans. However, the dramaturgical separation also creates a sense in which it is impossible for these testimonies to break through this divide; even in the context of the TRC, the "agents of the state" will not, and seemingly cannot, listen or attend to the experiences of victims. A final aspect of this is that though Pa and Ma are played by human actors, their humanity seems absent—they are caricatures, representing what Richard Crownshaw has identified as the problematic "othering of the perpetrator"[12]—making reconciliation impossible from the outset.[13]

Perhaps because of this continuing division, there is an absence of healing in the play. Indeed, the play ends relatively inconclusively, as if unsure of to what conclusion it can bring the Ubus. Though Brutus is executed for his lack of remorse at his crimes, Pa and Ma, along with Niles, are simply exiled. This relatively benign punishment is depicted like the "Owl and Pussycat" nursery rhyme, as the pair sail off into the sunset in a small boat, with Niles swimming behind. While the exilic journey suggests their new social isolation, it also implies that they have survived fairly unscathed. And despite their exile, in the final scene Pa and Ma declare their desire for "A new beginning / A bright future." Their optimism transforms their punishment into a voyage, sailing off into the sunset.[14] This is underlined by Kentridge's animation of a giant eye transmogrifying into a setting sun on the watery horizon.[15] The scrutiny of the TRC has turned into a "bright future" indeed, as Taylor et al. satirize the prioritizing of restorative justice over deep analysis or punishment.[16]

DEATH AND THE MAIDEN: THE SURVIVOR AS AN ACTIVE WITNESS

If *Ubu* is skeptical about the effectiveness of the truth commission to create actual social healing, Dorfman addresses the power dynamics of the commission from a different angle. Dorfman bases his fictional witnessing play on the real-life Rettig Commission in Chile, which, in 1990, was empowered by the new regime to investigate "the most serious human rights violations" during the military dictatorship (1973–90).[17] This commission, however, exists entirely offstage and, in a way, its existence is irrelevant to Paulina, the onstage victim. As with the Rettig Commission, the commission in *Death and the Maiden* will only hear the cases of relatives of victims who were killed during the dictatorship—Paulina's survival, ironically, rules her out.

This kind of selectivity, based on the perceived severity of victimization, is an understandable decision by a commission that needs, in a transitional phase, to demonstrate the most extreme cases in order to defend and justify its existence. However, it also creates a hierarchy of victims. Moreover, given that the experience of victimization was greatly exacerbated by the conditions of silence—the silence at the heart of the cases of the "disappeared," and the silence of survival, which made it necessary for victims to never speak of their experiences of victimization—the continued silencing of great numbers of victims by a commission that purports to exist to end the conditions of silencing is a painful and cutting irony.[18] In *Death and the Maiden*, the exclusion of Paulina from giving testimony thus continues her condition of silence and her disempowerment in the marketplace. By necessity, therefore, the action of the play must take place in the private sphere of the home, as the only space in which Paulina has social capital and where she is entitled to witness her own memories.

Paulina first appears as a nervous woman. Decades following her kidnapping and torture by the dictator's regime, she has the semblance of a recovery but has not healed. Part of this is, Dorfman implies, because she has never been able to articulate her story of suffering. And part of it is because she has never received justice—without the identification of the perpetrators responsible for the crimes against her, she lives in perpetual fear of their return and her repeated victimization. This is complicated by the fact that Paulina is married to Gerardo Escobar, a high-profile lawyer, whose identity she protected during her kidnapping. By not uttering Gerardo's name during her interrogation and torture, Paulina has kept him safe and ensured his current successful social and professional position. This act of bravery goes largely unacknowledged by Gerardo, who has just been named as a member of the new regime's truth commission. Gerardo's role requires that his wife have a public profile also, and her continued experience of trauma and sense of injustice makes this difficult. And though Gerardo will hear testimony from those who lost members of their family during the dictatorship, at home he seems more interested in repressing his wife's memories.

Despite these problems, Paulina lives an affluent and apparently safe life (illustrating how economic capital does not always correspond to social capital), but this semblance shatters when Gerardo is accompanied to their beach house late one night by Doctor Miranda, who has rescued Gerardo from the side of the road after his car tire was punctured. Hearing the stranger's voice as he talks to Gerardo, Paulina is instantly convinced that Doctor Miranda is one of the men who tortured her. Though initially a timid and fearful woman, Paulina undergoes a seemingly radical transformation and takes action—she kidnaps Doctor Miranda, holding him hostage until she extracts a full confession from him. The play, in effect, illustrates how Paulina not only transforms her nature, becoming active and powerful, but how she transforms her home into a private stage for a truth commission.

Paulina's negotiation for power begins even before Miranda's appearance, when she forces her husband to be truthful with her. Gerardo has already agreed to serve on the President's Investigation Commission, but when he arrives home he makes a show of asking Paulina for her consent, knowing that his work on the commission could upset her. Paulina, though initially reluctant, grants Gerardo what he wants, declaring "Find out what happened. Find out everything. Promise me that you'll find everything."[19] Paulina resists Gerardo's simple enthusiasm for the commission, however, by forcing him to acknowledge that the commission he will serve is "limited" by only having power to hear testimony and to "denounce" the crimes. With no legal power invested in the commission itself, any consequences for the perpetrators will have to be decided on by the "judges," men who, as Paulina says "never intervened to save one life in seventeen years."[20]

Paulina's disturbance at the obstacles to justice for what she suffered causes her to start laughing hysterically, which Gerardo interprets as a signal of her being a "silly girl."[21] But the audience, particularly given the ensuing standoff with Doctor Miranda, is more likely to interpret Paulina's laughter as a signal of an underlying disquiet with the systems of justice, a disquiet that Paulina can only express through hysteria.

Gerardo, who is alarmed by the violence of Paulina's emotions, and the potential for her recurring trauma to destabilize his career, takes Paulina in his arms and holds her till she *"calms down."*[22] Gerardo's actions, and his condescending attitude to Paulina from the beginning, indicate his paternalistic attitude toward his wife. They also indicate that Paulina has little opportunity of being objectively witnessed by those closest to her—obviously, a spouse is not the most objective witness to begin with, but Gerardo's dismissal of Paulina's concerns as those of "a silly girl" frames her as an unreliable witness, rather than as a distressed (and rightfully so) survivor. As a spectator, at this point, I begin to question how dismissive Gerardo will be of the other women who will inevitably cry as part of their testimony to the commission. The more immediate question, however, is what options are available to Paulina, given that she cannot testify publicly (to the commission) or privately (to her husband).

The overlap of Gerardo as husband and as member of the truth commission compromises both roles, so that he is neither the sympathetic supporter, nor the objective investigator. This clash comes to the fore with the introduction of Doctor Miranda, who returns late the same night to the Escobar house when he hears the announcement of Gerardo's role in the President's Investigation Commission on the radio. Miranda declares his return is motivated by a desire to congratulate Gerardo, but suspicious critics may identify an ulterior motive as he asks leading questions of Gerardo regarding the scope of the commission to publish the names of perpetrators.[23] Read in light of what later transpires—Paulina's accusation that Miranda tortured her during her kidnapping—Miranda's return to the Escobar house looks distinctly like a mission to extract information as to whether he is "safe" or not.

Unbeknownst to the men, as they discuss the limits on the commission—and the anonymization of the perpetrators—they have an audience in Paulina, who listens to their conversation from the terrace outside the living room. This act of eavesdropping leads to the rest of the play's action: when Gerardo insists that Miranda should stay the night in their guest room, this gives Paulina the access she needs to take Miranda hostage. When, in the morning, Gerardo demands to know why Paulina has tied and bound Miranda to a chair, she tells him that she recognized Miranda's voice as that of "the doctor who played Schubert" while he tortured her.[24] This recognition justifies Paulina in staging her own, alternative truth commission, threatening to hold Miranda (or kill him) unless he confesses. In this parallel commission, Paulina appoints Gerardo to act as Miranda's "counsel," mimicking the forms of an actual court and the protection of the perpetrator. Though Gerardo claims he believes Paulina, it is clear that he both detests her actions, sees her as an unreliable witness, and finds it hard to cast someone with as much social capital as Miranda in the role of perpetrator.

Whereas in the first scene, Paulina's actions and language were hesitant or hysterical, in the role of captor she becomes confident, determined, and strong. There is a hint here that in her cruelty to Miranda, in particular her aping of the language she remembers being used by her captors, and her threat to shoot him, Paulina is herself enacting the role of perpetrator (another kind of complex victim?). As Paulina says, she has spent years thinking of "Doing to them, systematically, minute by minute, instrument by instrument, what they did to me."[25] This scenario illustrates several issues: that victims are lastingly shaped by experiences of terror; that the search for revenge can corrupt the victim so that they become mirrors of the original perpetrators (though it should be noted that Paulina does not beat, rape, or otherwise torture Miranda); and, finally, that the confrontation with the perpetrator that the victim may wish for, is not the calm and orderly process of the commission but something more direct and visceral.

Gerardo, a stalwart of the socially approved approach, is horrified by Paulina's actions and taken aback by her command of the situation, saying "Oh my baby, my baby. You're—unrecognisable."[26] Gerardo advocates for a "reasonable" approach and complains that Paulina is indeed mimicking the behavior of the military junta, saying "We can't use their methods. We're different."[27] In response, Paulina appoints Gerardo as Miranda's "defense" and leaves him alone with his "client." Gerardo then attempts to wrest control back from Paulina by betraying her trust. Acting as counsel to Miranda, Gerardo asks Paulina to recount her memories of her ordeal, which he then relays to Miranda so that the prisoner can accede to Paulina's demands for a confession. Gerardo wants to resolve the situation and ensure Miranda's survival. He also clearly buys Miranda's story that he is innocent. Again, this questions not only Gerardo's loyalty to his wife, but his suitability for the commission.

Yet Gerardo's act of betrayal only strengthens Paulina's position. Paulina anticipates that Gerardo will act as a double agent and deliberately includes mistakes in her story of kidnapping and torture. When Miranda unconsciously corrects these mistakes, the proof of his involvement seems confirmed. Miranda's substitution of correct names and other details for Paulina's deliberate mistakes corroborates her allegations and, for this audience member anyhow, determines him as guilty. Of course, this is not a watertight case—the possibility always exists that Miranda is innocent of Paulina's allegations; if he is, then his kidnapping and possible death at the end of the play transforms him into one more victim of the regime.

Paulina's description of her experience to her husband in this new context is, somewhat strangely, the first time that Paulina has told Gerardo the details of her incarceration. Though he was the person she fled to on her release, and on the first night of her return she shared some of her story, she has never given him the full story before. This might be suggestive of the lack of intimacy and trust within their relationship, but it also indicates the powerful legacies of silence. During her captivity, Paulina "did not breathe" Gerardo's name, keeping him safe. Paulina's self-censorship of her narrative of her ordeal implies her continued desire to protect him from the trauma.[28]

In staging her own, alternative truth commission, and thereby creating and claiming her own space to testify to her memories, Paulina illustrates the necessity and central importance for survivor-witnesses to be heard in a forum not otherwise possible in the family or everyday society. As Paulina says to Gerardo, "I can speak—it's been years since I murmured even a word, I haven't opened my mouth to even whisper a breath of what I'm thinking, years living in terror of my own... but I'm not dead, I thought I was but I'm not and I can speak, damn it—so for God's sake let me have my say."[29] Yet the qualification of this statement is that Paulina's testimony is never heard directly. The audience hears snippets via her conversations with Gerardo, and through Miranda's confession, but there is no moment when Paulina performs her witness story. And so, in the end, Paulina's story remains private, told only to Gerardo. In one sense this is another frustration of Paulina's voice, as the audience never gets to act as witness to her memories. Yet in another sense, the occlusion of Paulina's "minute-by-minute" experience forms a protective barrier around her, denying the audience's voyeuristic interest in the gory details and refusing the process of commodification that so often engulfs victims. In establishing Paulina not as the witness who can be bidden to speak by a commissioner but as the commissioner herself, Dorfman puts her in control of the process (as director and active listener), a more empowering position than that of witness (speaker) because it means that her emotional labor is not the end product being consumed by audiences.

When Gerardo shares Paulina's version of the story with Miranda, he attempts to coach the doctor into acting as a ventriloquist-witness. As far as Gerardo is concerned, Miranda is giving a false confession. From the audience's perspective, it is unclear whether Miranda goes along with this because he is guilty or because of what Caroline Wake terms "culpable deception."[30] This form of deception is, like Pa Ubu, motivated by Miranda's recognition that in order to survive he must perform an acknowledgment of wrongdoing, even if he is innocent. Yet once Paulina has exposed the actual "truth" of Miranda's confession by revealing his correction of her deliberate mistakes, the false confession becomes a true confession, and Miranda becomes a genuine (if unintentional) perpetrator-witness.

Miranda's failure to control his confessional performance both validates Paulina's status as survivor-witness and underlines the importance of active listening. By being a witness to Miranda's confession, Paulina can potentially move on from her arrested position as silenced survivor, thereby revealing "listener" as an active, rather than passive, identity position with social capital (as well as refusing to commodify her own testimony). The limitations on this are, of course, still profound: Miranda is only recognized as a perpetrator in the private world of Paulina's home, Paulina's husband still acts as if she is hysterically dangerous, and there is no collective witnessing and thus no social healing. Paulina's sleight of memory, however, does illustrate that giving testimony is not the only avenue available to survivors and that there are significant advantages in taking on other subject positions.

CLAUDIA: THE VIRTUE OF TRIALS NOT TRCS

Claudia, an autoperformance, multimedia, docu-verbatim play by the company La Conquesta del Pol Sud and Claudia Poblete Hlaczik, is about the legacies of the Argentinian military dictatorship. It begins with a series of questions, recited by the two theatre makers, Carles Fernández Giua and Eugenio Swzarcer: "What are the limits to power?" "Do the citizens have tools to limit power?" "Is it possible to bargain with power?" "Is it possible to have a healthy society without judging the crimes of the past?" "What relation do we have to the generation before ours?" "What does history mean to each of us?" What is our relationship with the past?"[31] The video screens behind the two men show an animation of events from twentieth-century world history, contextualizing the story of the play within a century of conflict and change. The lighting then shifts to reveal a woman sitting at a sewing machine behind the video screens, who begins to tell the audience her story as the screen shows the title "1 Mercedes." At first she recounts how she didn't used to like sewing, but she enjoys the challenge of making patchwork quilts, perhaps because all her life she has been putting the pieces together. When the woman steps out from behind the screen she relates how, according to a "false" birth certificate, Mercedes Landa was born on June 13, 1978. This first section is the story of Mercedes, related in the third person, as she grew up in a military, upper middle-class home in Buenos Aires in the 1980s. Mercedes (known as Merceditas) was a fearful child, whose life was limited and controlled by her parents, to the extent that the films she watched were censored and the information she knew about her family, and the wider world, was even more drastically edited.

What kind of a witness is this woman? Audiences will perhaps know before the show begins that she is Claudia Poblete Hlaczik, the recovered daughter of two "desaparacidos" ("Disappeared"), José Poblete and Gertrudis Hlaczik. Claudia, as a baby, was taken from her parents when they were kidnapped by the Argentinian military and imprisoned in Olimpo, a detention center in Buenos Aires. The military claimed they would return the baby to her grandparents, but instead she was given to a military couple and raised as Merceditas Landa for twenty-two years, in ignorance of her real identity. In telling this story to the audience, Claudia relates all the sections pertaining to her life as "Merceditas" in the third person, an obvious distancing device of hindsight, which divides the present *knowing* witness from the former *unknowing* witness.

Though Merceditas had often wondered why her parents were older than those of her contemporaries, why the family took extended trips overseas, and who the men were who visited her father in his study, she never confronted the Landas about these issues. Merceditas comes across as a timid and introverted girl, whose intimations that there was something out of kilter with her family were only confirmed when her real family located her and a criminal investigation was launched. Merceditas is told she has to undergo a DNA test to determine her parentage. During this powerful scene, Carles, the director, voices the words of the legal team who ask her to take the test—when Merceditas asks if she can refuse, the reply is that it is "complicated because you, your body, yourself are the evidence of a possible crime."[32] The kind of witnessing that is being requested here has nothing to do with voice and everything to do with embodiment and how the body might speak in a way that contradicts, at that point, how Merceditas would verbally witness her life.

The witnessing voice comes later when Merceditas has to appear in court to testify in the case against her adopted parents (she testified for the defense). Again, Carles plays the role of interlocutor:

Court officer: State your name, please.
Claudia: I was prepared for a lot of questions. But sometimes the simplest questions, the most obvious ones, are the ones that I find most difficult to answer.
Court officer: State your name, please.
Claudia: Claudia Victoria Poblete Hlaczik.
Court officer: Your birth date.
Claudia: March 25th 1978.[33]

This is the moment that Merceditas becomes Claudia for the first time in the show, and the first time in her life. The video screens on stage begin to show archive footage of the courtroom erupting in a standing ovation with people clapping, cheering, and crying. Though Claudia's act of self-naming has a deep impact in the show, coming about three-quarters of the way through, the role of the footage in contextualizing this act is vital. The courtroom scene places Claudia as a key actor in a much larger struggle—the Poblete court case was definitive in changing Argentina's amnesty laws and defining the disappearances of parents and children as "crimes against humanity."[34] What one individual said when asked her name thus had a transformative effect on an entire country's history, and the knowledge of this imbues the show. Of course, at the same time, this is just one woman standing in front of us as an audience. And we, as the audience, are not necessarily invested in the larger picture but rather in consuming the detail of the transformation within her own life.

It is striking to watch Claudia deliver her performance throughout the show and to reflect that she seems very different from the overprotected, shy, and fearful Merceditas she has described for us. There is something in this implied change in manner and confidence that resonates with Paulina's transformation, as the survivor of trauma, who has lived for decades in the shadow of that trauma (knowingly and unknowingly) and who, through taking control, attains both agency and voice. In one way, while Merceditas was a witness within her life, Claudia is a witness *to* her life.

Unlike *Ubu* and *Death and the Maiden*, there is a justice within this play—the perpetrators are charged with the crime of the substitution of identity and found guilty. Yet unlike the other two plays, there is no truth and reconciliation because Argentina did not have a truth commission. Instead, the Poblete trial was a watershed moment when criminal trials for "crimes of humanity" committed during the dictatorship became possible. This play thus indicates the absence of a truth commission—and in enabling Claudia to give her full testimony, acts in lieu of a commission. But it also, in playing the footage of the criminal trial, indicates alternative routes to justice than the truth commission (even if this is on a far smaller scale than even the limited boundaries of a truth commission). Indeed, as multiple transitional-justice studies show, truth commissions are only one strategy in state-led reconciliation.[35] In evaluating twenty-five assessments of transitional-justice approaches, David Roman argues that public witnessing, as in a TRC, is only beneficial for selected participants: "Different victims have needs for different transitional justice measures [while] ... truth-sharing may produce both positive and negative effects."[36]

In the play, Claudia's testimony alternates with other scenes from the theatre company's trip to Argentina—video footage shows Eugenio, who is from Buenos Aires, leading his friend and colleague Carles on a guided tour of the city and country, during which they visit sites of memory associated with the disappeared and interview locals about their memories of the period. First up, the pair visit ESMA, the largest detention center in Buenos Aires. The day is very hot and the space is oppressive, physically and because of its history. Carles describes how most detainees were blindfolded, so that testimony about what the center was like is largely based on the sounds they remember. Carles then remarks that "at one point I had to go outside, to the fresh air" where he could hear the "sounds of the big city."[37] The video footage of the interiors of ESMA shift to depict the busy road and the train tracks that run past the grounds. Carles says, "I hear shouting, a roar, is there a rally?" But Eugenio corrects him that it is only the sounds of a nearby football match: "The stadium is just next to here, the one they built for the 1978 World Cup." It is salutary to think of this proximity—the temporal proximity of the World Cup to the disappearance of Claudia's parents, and the physical proximity of the city's social life. As in so many other cases of gross human rights abuses, ESMA was not invisible, to either the local or the global community.

Carles comments when he first visits ESMA that the center is fully signposted and that they take a guided tour—as he says, "It is an interpreted place."[38] Like many other sites, ESMA has become part of the heritage industry. Whether deliberately or not, Carles draws attention to this mediation of the past—not just in the case of ESMA as a site of memory but also to the acts of mediation in the play. The way that the three onstage witnesses choose to tell the story is an act of interpretation—this is such an obvious observation that it's barely worth articulating, except for how central it is to this performance, largely because of the way that the theatre makers themselves become characters. Both Carles and Eugenio describe their own family backgrounds, the video footage depicts their trip around Argentina, they explain how they met with the *Abuelas de Plaza de Mayo* (the Grandmothers of the Plaza de Mayo), and as they sit onstage, they describe what the trip to Argentina has meant to each of them. As theatre makers, they position themselves as internal witnesses, discovering the story gradually, as if they are interpreting it for themselves first and foremost, witnesses in the moment rather than in hindsight. Yet of course all these moments of discovery are in fact highly scripted and highly mediated. When Claudia remarks that "all of this is being studied and judged, all of this is written in books,"[39] the moment of live performance seems to stand in contrast to the linearly inscribed narrative of books, though it is equally studied and judged.

As in *Ubu and the Truth Commission*, *Claudia* has a range of witnesses. In addition to the three onstage "characters," there are a number of Argentineans who appear as interviewees on the video screen. Most of the interviews are conducted in Santa Lucia, a small town in the Tucamán Province, which was one of the last bastions of the revolution. In 1975, as the audience is told, Isabel Peron signed the "Extermination Decree" to kill all the subversives. The old sugar mill factory in the town was used as a site for the military to undertake these killings. The factory then became a detention center during the dictatorship. One of the Santa Lucia locals who is interviewed, Carlos Ferreira, worked as an ice-cream seller as a child and was trusted to enter the factory. When he was inside he saw people blindfolded and asked who they were but was told to forget what he saw, and so he did, he forgot it for many years. Ferreira then describes how he only understood years later that the factory was part of a national history, and that he "without realizing it, had been part of history."[40] This is reminiscent of the ESMA scene and the sense that there were countless witnesses to the history as it happened, but that the act of witnessing—in terms of the assignation of meaning to the events that have been seen—is in such contexts radically belated and possible only after the fact.

JUSTICE AND FORGIVENESS IN THE MARKET

One of the opening questions of *Claudia* asks, "Is it possible to have a healthy society without judging the crimes of the past?" As with the other questions that start the show, this is not directly answered, but implicitly addressed over the course of Claudia's maturing as a witness of her own life and, as a result, of her own society. By acknowledging the duality of her identity—as both Merceditas and Claudia, albeit with a strange third-person distance from

"Merceditas"—the show represents a complex reaction to "the crimes of the past." Justice is administered by the legal dimension—the DNA tests, the criminal charges, court case, and conviction—as well as through more personal negotiation—Claudia recounts the slow process of coming to terms with her new/old identity and of getting to know her new family. The show does not depict any confrontation between Claudia and her substitute/illegal parents—though Claudia articulates the extreme disorientation and shock of her new identity, and describes the fear of living alone for the first time as her "parents" have been arrested. She does not describe any conversation she had with them about their actions. She does refer, near the end of the play, to occasionally visiting them, so there is some contact between them but this is never fully clarified or discussed. The focus is maintained on the psyche of the individual witness and the internal emotional dynamics of dealing with the crimes committed under the dictatorship. Though Claudia's family reunion and the justice for her parents are facilitated by the legal machine of the state, "justice" has its own fallout (the destruction of Merceditas's life), and it is for the individual to work her way through the pain associated with both the legacy of the dictatorship and the actions of justice in the present. As a result, Claudia must be the one to undertake this work.

Whereas Claudia's sincerity is never in doubt, in *Ubu and the Truth Commission*, Taylor questions whether sincerity is possible within the processes by which justice is performed in the TRC. It is clear to the audience from the beginning of this play that Pa Ubu is a violent perpetrator, as he declares: "Once I was an agent of the state, and had agency and status. The country's money was in my safe-keeping, as I had blown up the safe and its keeper. I administered the funds to myself, to save the nation the burden of doing so. Now, after my years of loyal service, I find myself cast aside without thanks. My enemies are everywhere, and we therefore have to cover our back."[41] Much like Dorfman's play, Taylor sets *Ubu* at the juncture between regimes, as Pa Ubu transitions from being protected by, and protective of, the state's apartheid agenda, to the risky position of being exposed by the new administration—a total loss of social capital. And Taylor makes a brave and unusual move in placing an *unrepentant* perpetrator at the center of the play—Pa Ubu is not just unlikable, he's disgusting, beyond redemption, intent only on personal salvation, not social reconciliation.

The only redemption up for discussion in the play is a form of appeasement. Niles, the puppet-crocodile, advises Pa to make a full confession to the commission, not for the purposes of social healing, but so that he will be safe from his "enemies." Pa resists the amnesty offered by confession, however, and hedges his bets by concealing evidence of his crimes. Only when Ma Ubu discovers the evidence and goes "public," bragging about her husband's former power, is Pa forced into facing the commission. His confession is a model example of the genre and he rehearses it in advance: "There's one thing that I will have to live with until the day I die—it's the corpses that I have to drag with me to my grave, of the people I have killed. Remorse, I can assure you, a lot, a hell of a lot."[42]

Representing the murders he has committed as a burden, Pa also asserts that, "Our acts of violence are too awful for us to declare."[43] Indeed, the audience never hears, from Pa himself, descriptions of his crimes. Instead, when he gives his confession to the TRC, Taylor focuses on the framing of his actions:

> I stand before you with neither shame nor arrogance. I am not a monster. I am an honest citizen, and would never break the law. Like all of you, I eat, and sleep, and dream dreams. These vile stories, they sicken me. When I am told of what happened here, I cannot believe it. These things, they were done by those above me; those below me; those beside me. I too have been betrayed! I knew nothing.... I love my family. But their future was being stolen from them. Our destiny used to be in our own hands. Then the international conspiracies against us cut off our arms. Where could we go, we other Africans? Our children became the servants of servants, with their bowing, and bowing, and scraping, and it was left to our corpulent self to do the whipping, and stripping, and raping. Such loyalty is no longer fashionable.... But how is an army to survive if it will not reward in public what it knows is done in secret? ... Soldiering is not a selfish profession, as a true soldier is prepared to lay down his life for his fellow citizens and for his country. THIS IS MY COUNTRY. And I won't give it away without a damn good fight.... There's only one thing I will have to live with.[44]

What is this kind of testimony doing? We can identify four main functions: (1) the creation of distance, (2) the expansion of guilt to the wider group, (3) the claiming of victimhood for the perpetrator, and (4) the self-justification of crimes through a heroic, patriotic rhetoric.

Pa first declaims knowledge of the worst crimes, distancing himself from them with the phrase "when I am told." This performance of ignorance is only plausible because Pa has already shifted the blame to Brutus, planting evidence so that the three-headed dog (who does not testify to the TRC and so is not able to avail of amnesty) takes responsibility for the actual crimes. Pa then covers himself further by expanding that blame in all directions (above, below, beside) so that he represents the whole state apparatus as culpable. At the same time,

Pa declares himself betrayed, as he understands victimhood as capital. Pa's conceptualization of his own victimhood is pursued when he refers to "international conspiracies," and he represents himself as a soldier for a new group of oppressed Africans, the white supremacists.

Pa tries to identify himself as both exceptional—a soldier willing to make the extreme sacrifice of laying down his life for his country—and completely unexceptional in being "like all of you." Though he refers to his crimes ("the people I have killed," "raping"), he does so only after having established his heroic and patriotic loyalty, in a move that Bakiner argues is typical of the types of stories perpetrators tell, which are filled with "self-justifying tropes of heroism and sacrifice."[45] Pa's speech then concludes with a pledge of "remorse," but, given the rhetorical slipperiness of his testimony, this seems implausible. Throughout the second section of his speech, the microphones that Pa speaks into begin to move, operated by puppets who pull the microphone heads out of Pa's reach, "*taunting and mocking*" him with their refusal to stay still.[46] Ultimately, Pa's posturing illustrates how easily commodifiable and producible the identity of "remorseful perpetrator" is and thus how dangerous is the idea that social justice can be based on such performances.

The scripted and rehearsed nature of a perpetrator's confession does not necessarily undermine its veracity, but in this case, as Pa's only remorse is clearly about the regime change, Taylor questions the formalized expression of repentance to the truth commission. The commission's process depends on witnesses delivering testimony—the flaw, as with any testimonial-justice project, is that people can bear false witness. A question that arises is whether this flaw invalidates the process. Whereas in the case of the Poblete trial in Argentina, DNA evidence could be used to amplify the witness statements of the Poblete and Hlaczik families and prove the guilt of the perpetrators, in a process based purely on testimony, the verifiability of emotional claims, such as remorse, is much harder to judge.

Taylor highlights, through Pa's insincerity, the abuse of the amnesty system by unrepentant perpetrators who only play at, as if in a dangerous game, the mechanism of confession and absolution. When Niles first proposes confession as a solution to Pa's problems, Pa dismisses the suggestion:

> **Niles**: An inquiry is to be conducted by great and blameless men who measure what is done, and why, and how.
> **Pa Ubu**: And just what can these brilliant mathemunitions do?
> **Niles**: They can beyond all ambiguity indicate when a vile act had a political purpose.

Pa Ubu: And if they so resolve?
Niles: Then they can and must absolve. The righteous have to forgive the unrighteous.[47]

There is obvious sarcasm in Niles's phrase "great and blameless men," while the declaration that these men can decide "beyond all ambiguity" on the meaning of a person's actions is obviously, as the events of the play show, impossible. I'm most interested in the end of this excerpt of dialogue, where Niles asserts with confidence that "The righteous have to forgive the unrighteous." Niles delineates the roles on each side—the perpetrator must give "a full disclosure"[48] and in return he must be absolved.

Who gets to absolve? And is absolution different to forgiveness? Pa is given a form of absolution, which sends him into exile rather than prison. But this is different from forgiveness, which can only be given by the victim. Since the victim and the perpetrator in Taylor's script exist in completely separate (apartheid) dimensions, there is no moment in the play when the victim gives any kind of verdict on Pa. Nor do the judges appear onstage, so even their verdict seems enormously abstract. It is left, then, to the audience to engage with the play and to decide if Pa deserves absolution (at the risk of getting it horribly wrong, I'm going to hazard a guess that most audience members would not forgive Pa). The audience has the further capacity to decide on the moral benefits of the process or system of justice itself—to sit in judgement of the commission. The critical consumer is, in this instance, imbued by Taylor et al with greater insight than the TRC itself.

It is pertinent to consider here Paul Ricoeur's understanding of forgiveness as "a specific form of the revision of the past and, through it, of the specific narrative identities ... lifting the burden of guilt which paralyses the relations between individuals who are acting out and suffering their own history."[49] Pa Ubu attempts to take on a new narrative identity through his performance of remorse, but it is questionable whether either Pa Ubu or, in *Death and the Maiden*, Doctor Miranda, can be forgiven in Ricoeur's terms given their actual lack of remorse, thus continuing the "burden of guilt" and ensuing paralysis.

In both *Ubu* and *Death and the Maiden* the audience sees two unrepentant perpetrators, and witnesses their attempts to save their own skins via a system that is rigged to absolve those who confess and claim remorse, however insincere those claims may be. How the audience judges each of these perpetrators, however, may vary due to the ways that each witness is presented. In having access to Pa's unscripted private monologues, the audience has a privileged understanding of just how false his confession to the TRC is and can judge him clearly as a perpetrator. In *Death and the Maiden*, however, Miranda remains more enigmatic, and it is up to the audience to decide if the doctor's correction of Paulina's deliberate mistakes, and his love of Schubert, constitutes evidence of his guilt as a perpetrator. The audience may be unsure, in witnessing Miranda's confession, as to whether it is true or false. In not having incontrovertible evidence of either his guilt or his remorse, the audience—and Paulina—are inevitably conflicted over whether he should be punished (killed) or absolved/ forgiven (released).

Thus the question of forgiveness is very much at issue at the end of *Death and the Maiden*:

> **Paulina**: The truth Doctor. The truth and I'll let you go. Repent and I'll let you go....
>
> **Roberto [Doctor Miranda]**: No. I won't. Because even if I confess, you'll never be satisfied. You're going to kill me anyway.
>
> ...
>
> **Paulina**: And why does it always have to be people like me who have to sacrifice, why are we always the ones who have to make concessions when something has to be conceded, why always me who has to bite her tongue, why? Well, not this time. This time I am going to think about myself, about what I need. If only to do justice in just one case, just one. What do we lose? What do we lose by killing one of them? What do we lose? What do we lose?[50]

The survivor and the perpetrator are each entirely honest in this confrontation, perhaps for the first time, as they face questions about restorative versus retributive justice. Central to this honesty is the admission that confession and absolution are not enough, that they do not represent "justice" for the victim, but only the victims' repeated emotional, immaterial labor. In using the term "repent," Paulina invokes the idea that she will not just literally "let [Miranda] go" but that she will forgive him, so that she in turn can let go of what happened to her. However, Paulina then suggests that forgiveness would represent a renewed silencing of her as a witness ("why always me who has to bite her tongue?"), and voices a need for retribution rather than forgiveness. Though Paulina demands "the truth," it is much more than that which she requires.

It is unclear how Paulina will decide. Her repeated rhetorical question "What do we lose?" opens up a whole potential debate as to what is at stake—in one way, the victim receives justice by killing the perpetrator and claiming an eye for an eye. Yet Paulina doesn't phrase the question "What do *I* lose." Her use of "we" refers the audience back to Gerardo's earlier accusation that Paulina is using "their methods"[51] and what this means. By killing Miranda, Paulina would achieve something for herself as an individual and perhaps symbolically for other victims, but in undermining both legal and civil processes, she not only enacts the same kind of injustice as the dictator's regime but retrospectively validates de facto power as a course of action. The answer to the question, as Niles asserts in *Ubu and the Truth Commission*, is that the victim has no choice if they want to maintain the code of justice—the "righteous have to forgive the unrighteous."

This is where the understanding of memory operating as a commodity in a marketplace becomes highly relevant—as confessions, apologies (both categorical on behalf of the state and interpersonal, between survivor and perpetrator), and acts of forgiveness are transacted in order to determine an agreed-upon version of the past that both sides can live with. Within this dynamic, perpetrators and victims are not so much on opposing sides as they are caught up in an oscillating negotiation. The confession or apology is a backward-looking statement on the past that has a cultural capital; it is thus a valuable commodity in the memory marketplace. The acceptance of the apology by the victim, which creates an amnesty for the perpetrator and precludes the victim from taking revenge, is, likewise, a commodity. If both sides are willing to trade their commodities, the transaction is relatively smooth. The perpetrator is granted amnesty, the survivor is granted peace and, potentially, financial compensation. For any kind of social agreement to proceed, this is a necessary transaction. Yet as both plays illustrate, the confession may well be, in the end, a worthless commodity, valid only as a temporary performance; likewise, as the audience sees in *Death and the Maiden*, the victim may not be willing to trade on what she sees as the perpetrator's terms. Social agreement then remains contingent, based on the willingness of witnesses to testify and to accept the others' testimony, and whether or not they are prepared to exchange their commodity (thus relinquishing themselves to silence after the trade) for catharsis. This is particularly fraught for survivors/victims whose *only* social capital and power in these transactions is derived from the commodity of their potential forgiveness.

How Can Those Who Tortured and Those Who Were Tortured Coexist?

What do these performances of witnessing achieve? What are the outcomes? In *Ubu and the Truth Commission*, as discussed above, Taylor suggests that the perpetrators who sought amnesty from the TRC and were absolved escaped relatively freely from punishment for their crimes. When Ma Ubu asserts at the end of the play "enough of the past,"[52] she articulates the mission of the commissions themselves, which seek to hear witness testimony in order to create closure. Dorfman's *Death and the Maiden* is both more productive, in the sense that the victim gets to directly hold the perpetrator accountable, and more ambiguous in its ending. When Paulina threatens Doctor Miranda with the gun, Dorfman tests the idea of de facto revenge against de jure process. But at the vital moment of decision, the stage goes black and no shot is ever heard. The final scene, the epilogue, is set at a concert hall where Schubert's *Death and the Maiden* is about to be performed—a concert that Paulina could not previously have attended due to her association of Schubert with her torture and rape. Her presence at the concert suggests that she has found some peace and reconciliation. The scene also depicts Paulina acting as Gerardo's ideal consort—while he speaks from the stage to the audience (of the play) as if they were attendees at the concert, she buys some "candy." Notably, she is silent throughout this final scene.

Gerardo accepts imaginary thanks from the audience for his work on the commission:

> Well, I am a bit tired, but it was worth it. . . . Yes, we're very pleased with the Final Report of the Commission. . . . People are acting with enormous generosity, without the hint of a personal vendetta. . . . Well, I always knew that our work would help in the process of healing, but I was surprised it would start on the very first day we convened. An old woman came in to testify. The woman was so timid. She began to speak standing up. "Please sit down," the president of the Commission said and stood up to hold her chair for her. She sat down and began to sob. Then she looked at us and said: "This is the first time, sir," she said to us—her husband had disappeared fourteen years ago, and she has spent thousands of hours petitioning, thousands of hours waiting—"This is the first time," she said to us, "in all these years, sir, that somebody asks me to sit down." It was the first time that anyone had ever asked her to sit down.[53]

Gerardo's story summons up a world in which courtesy and respect are once more meaningful, and in which offering a chair stands in for the restoration of basic human rights ("Tell him you saw us"[54]). The woman's sobbing enacts the "healing" intended by the act of inaugurating a commission, and Gerardo thus implies that in such basic gestures as holding a chair, or being prepared to listen, their work has been achieved. Though I do not want to undermine the moment of human decency that this story relates, nevertheless it's important to note that Gerardo's story reduces the work of a truth commission to the status of a tidy anecdote, related all too easily at a social event. Using Yvette Hutchison's argument about TRCs, we might read this moment as an example of how "marginalised narratives may be used by a new ruling class to redefine a new history and collective identity" in order to shore up their own power, rather than to democratize or devolve power to the victims.[55] In other words, the commodification of the victim becomes part of the social capital of the "ruling class." Gerardo does not speak of the findings within the "Final Report," nor does he refer to the conversation that the play began with, in which Paulina objected to the commission's lack of power to actually punish the perpetrators. These absences, combined with Paulina's silence, undercut the sense that this commission has achieved significant healing at a structural level.

In his afterword to *Death and the Maiden*, Dorfman questions "How can those who tortured and those who were tortured co-exist in the same land?"[56] His play resists the "easy, even facile, comforting, answer"[57] (though this is exactly what Gerardo is articulating). Instead, Dorfman suggests that even after "healing" there are wounds that remain. As Gerardo and Paulina take their seats for the second half of the Schubert concert, "*Roberto* [Miranda] *enters, under a light which has a faint phantasmagoric quality. He could be real or he could be an illusion in Paulina's head.* . . . [*Paulina*] *turns slowly and looks at Roberto. Their eyes interlock for a moment. Then she turns her head and faces the stage and the mirror. The lights go down while the music plays and plays and plays.*"[58] There are a couple of possible interpretations here. If Paulina shot Miranda at the close of the previous scene, his appearance at the concert shows that she is still haunted by his presence and forced to live with his ghost. But if Miranda is real, then Paulina is forced to live with his presence in a different way, knowing that she extracted a confession from him but also that she has to live in a society in which he coexists. Indeed, since so many of the perpetrators went unpunished, even if Miranda is dead, since he was only one of her captors, Paulina, like so many victims, has to live in a society in which the majority of her perpetrators coexist. So what was the point of her witnessing and his confessing at all?

It is *Claudia* that stages the most hopeful answer to the question of why people witness. Claudia herself says that she sees it as part of her commitment—to politics, to her parents' legacy—that she tell her story to an audience. In following this story over a number of years, the play is able to accommodate Claudia's multiple positions, from ignorant child, to angry and experienced survivor, and the duality of being both. That duality she lived with for years, and it is only at the birth of her daughter that she feels it end. When Claudia's daughter is born, she says that she stopped believing her "appropriators" were her parents.[59] And over time, though she has only other people's stories of her real parents, she comes to feel connected to them. Claudia describes a conversation with her daughter, who is now of an age to ask about her "nonparents."[60] After Claudia explains that she was taken from her real parents and lied to for years, her daughter says of her nonparents that "they are really bad people." Claudia replies that "Yes, Guada, they did something wrong."[61] The distinction made here is important—Claudia does not identify her appropriators as "bad people" and thus does not identify them with their crime. In suggesting that crimes are actions, she sees perpetrators as performers of "something wrong" as opposed to being "bad people."

Distancing and Empathy

We never see Claudia cry, and that is a result of the perspective she has achieved over the two decades of her realization about her parents. The theatre makers go to lengths to move away from the autoperformance model, in which empathy is the most significant outcome—at points when Claudia's story becomes intense, they use video or voice-over to create some emotional distance. Both Carles and Eugenio interject their own perspectives, so that the play becomes a product of at least three points of view; Eugenio operates the production's design elements from a visible computer at the side of the stage, and Carles moves the stage furniture between scenes. All of these strategies work, like Kentridge's animations and Handspring's puppets in *Ubu*, to remind the audience of the spectacle they are witnessing, to reduce the emotional labor of the performer, and to create some intellectual space for engagement.

Ubu and the Truth Commission, as one might expect of a collaborative work between writer, animator, and puppet company, utilizes multiple representational strategies. As I have discussed above, the dynamic between the human actors and puppets creates an interesting question of empathy—how much empathy can the puppets generate, and how much physical power do the human actors have in contrast? I would like to spend some more time with these questions of representation, to consider the interaction with empathy and the motivations for avant-garde theatre to prioritize intellectual stimulation over identificatory reactions.

Kentridge and Handspring's deployment of animation and puppetry simultaneously creates moments of engagement as well as alienation from the plot/central characters. For example, the performances of both human and puppet actors are played out in front of a large screen with constantly changing animations, and these animations may be directly related to the drama onstage (for instance, the images of the dogs being hung) but often they are a counterpoint to it, dividing the audience's attention and suggesting multiple points of engagement and layers of meaning. Niles, Pa's wily crocodile advisor, is not just a puppet but a composite creature combining animal and household imagery—Niles's body is formed from a large handbag. This handbag sets Niles up as the perfect storage space for all of Pa's incriminating paperwork. Pa "feeds" the paper into Niles through his mouth, literalizing the metaphors of swallowing the truth and digesting the past. Brutus, Pa's three-headed dog, is also a puppet, freighted with the extra metaphorical weight of the image of Cerberus, the dog guarding the underworld. This combination of the actual and brutal reality of apartheid-motivated killing with puppetry and mythic stories of hell works to provoke thought, rather than identificatory reactions, from the audience.

In contrast to the hyperbolic Pa and Ma, Taylor's script also includes eight witnesses, six of whom give verbal testimony in Xhosa about their experiences under the apartheid regime. Two other "victim" puppets also appear on stage, silently, embodying the experience of exploitation; for example, one puppet tries to maintain his shop while Pa and Ma unthinkingly steal goods from him.

When I am teaching this play (as a read text, not in performance), students often comment on the choice to use puppets to deliver victim-witness testimony—many of them would, they argue, potentially feel more moved if the witnesses were human actors, displaying their emotions and performing in a more traditional sense. However, Kentridge states that the production wanted to avoid "the audience being caught halfway between having to believe in the actor for the sake of the story, but also not believe in the actor for the sake of the actual witness who existed out there but was not the actor."[62] The antipathy to appropriation was thus not Kentridge's only motivation: "The puppet becomes a medium through which the testimony can be heard."[63] In class discussions, then, we consider whether the strategy of using puppets allows the production to avoid the empathy paradox, whereby the audience overidentifies with the humanity of the actor onstage and, as a result, might not be fully cognizant of the crimes being described. However, students also express the concern that, depending on how the puppets are manipulated and how the voice-over delivering the testimony operates tonally, there is the risk that the puppets, which are diminutive in size in comparison to the human actors, may seem disempowered and weak. The counterpoint to this argument is that the relative physical smallness of the puppets may also generate greater audience empathy and visually illustrate the power dynamics of the apartheid state, as they are physically dominated/overshadowed by Pa and Ma. It is a complex debate around how different kinds of performance impact capital, particularly given that students in Ireland typically study the text without having seen a performance beyond the clips available online (a pitfall of transnational teaching and learning).

The dynamics of power and witnessing extend to the language in which the witness testifies. The puppets' testimony is delivered in Xhosa, which lends their narration veracity; yet there is also the risk for a non-Xhosa-speaking audience that the testimony becomes exoticized and remote. The script addresses this by including a direct translation, and this is performed onstage by the "translator." In an unusual move, the translator is played by the same actor who portrays Ma Ubu. This introduces additional issues of power—it is impossible for the audience to divest themselves of the idea that they are watching Ma act as an intermediary for the puppet witnesses. Does this choice of actor confuse the issue, so that the audience does not fully apprehend the witness testimony because of the corrupting or distracting presence of Ma-as-translator? Though the demeanor and voice of the actor is different in the performances of these two characters, nevertheless for an English-speaking audience, the words of the witness are filtered through the persona of one of the perpetrators (which is another layer of commentary, of course, whereby the play suggests that witnesses are always interpolated by those with more cultural capital). In using an onstage translator, as opposed to a translation voice-over, the play evokes the dynamics of the TRC itself, in which simultaneous translation was a key feature of the staging of the commission. To one side of the judges' dais, the translation booths were a visual reminder of the multiple languages within South Africa, as well as the globalized nature of this truth commission. In *Ubu*, the "translation booth" is the shower cubicle that Pa uses to wash off the blood of his victims. Again, it is hard to read the layering of meaning here—is it that the act of translation is somehow incorporated into the history of apartheid violence through the act of listening and rebroadcasting? Is it a sign that the mechanisms of the apartheid era can be repurposed for an ethical use? Or is it simply an efficient reusing of stage furniture?

There is a further dynamic to the same actor portraying both the Ma Ubu and translator roles: in the first production of the play, the actor playing Ma was a black actor in whiteface, wearing nonwestern clothing and head turban. This casting/costuming choice provokes more questions—is this a literal suggestion that race is merely a performance and that the actual color of one's skin is immaterial? Does it imply that below a thin veneer of whiteness, white South Africans were linked to black culture in ways they tried to hide? Is it a sign of the racism that is so inherent in a colonized culture that it affects black people also, as in the character of Joshua in Caryl Churchill's *Cloud Nine* (1979), who is black but played by a white actor as a sign of his cultural aspiration to be white? As Helen Gilbert points out, "At another level, this costuming technique speaks back to the profoundly raced tradition of minstrelsy, as well as disrupting precisely the kind of racial essentialism on which apartheid itself was built."[64] This strategy was largely abandoned, however, in the more recent 2015 production (with the same cast) in which the actor playing Ma only wore whiteface during one screen sequence.

These performance strategies and the questions they provoke are a quandary, I think, because, ultimately, the use of puppets and animations works as a critically distancing strategy to limit audience empathy and increase engagement with the production as a comment on the processes of witnessing. Witness testimony is always, necessarily, filtered, whether that is through the performance of the firsthand witness or how that performance is translated by mediation, translation, and representation. The use of puppets creates a defamiliarized witness who can be newly presented to the audience and thus can be newly "heard." Yet the concomitant risk is that the use of human actors to play Pa and Ma heightens the audience's impression of them as forceful, powerful characters. Indeed, Pa's posturing and direct address to the audience makes him out as a pantomime-villain who the audience loves to hate. This is central to Pa and Ma's roles as unredeemable perpetrators, but it also gives them life, and presence, and a social capital unavailable to the puppet. Additionally, the violence that is narrated by the puppet witnesses is never seen enacted onstage, and is only "performed" through Kentridge's animations, for example, in the shower scene when the animations show the skulls and bones that Pa washes himself clean of. Though these are key elements of the multimedia production, it is possible to see Pa throughout as only a *rhetorically* violent man. The puppet witnesses are poignant, but does the absence of real violence onstage, or a full confession by Pa, combined with the performance of his anxiety at his fall from grace, temper the portrait of him as perpetrator and further reduce the puppets' capital?

Of course, the invisibility of the perpetrator's crimes is a concern that should also be raised in relation to *Death and the Maiden*, especially given that the violence done to Paulina is implicit and told in fragments, rather than explicitly articulated. Miranda is, throughout, only seen by the audience as the civilized doctor, not the violent perpetrator. Though the audience hears the beginning and ending of Paulina's and Miranda's descriptions of her torture, and Paulina refers explicitly to being raped multiple times by multiple assailants, the full description is never performed or shown. The audience is thus denied full disclosure. This is a powerful strategy, leaving the extent of the violence Paulina suffered to the imagination of the audience, respecting her privacy, and prioritizing the portrait of her as a survivor, rather than a victim. Yet, equally, the strategy of nondisclosure also means that the only violence and threat performed onstage is performed by Paulina. As I've suggested above, there is a greater sense in this play of the empowerment of the victim (even if that is defined in terms of violence and revenge). But perhaps Paulina's coup and seizing of power also represents the opportunity for Miranda to be identified with sympathetically by the audience.

Who is the good victim? At the beginning of *Death and the Maiden*, Paulina follows the stereotypical behavior of someone who is marked for life by her experience of violence—she is hesitant, suspicious, tremulous. When she challenges her husband Gerardo, he dismisses her or tries to placate her, and she, eventually, allows herself to be quieted. This ends when she kidnaps Miranda, and Paulina's brusque treatment of both her prisoner and her husband suggests that she deliberately acts to throw off the performance of "good victim" by directing aggression at anyone who stands in her way. As a result, though, does she become the unsympathetic victim? And, if she does, is that necessarily a bad thing? As already argued, through her gunpoint control of the situation, Paulina achieves an agency not always granted to victims during transitional justice proceedings. As Cole argues, survivors achieve power by asserting themselves "as active agents of performed spectacle rather than passive consumers."[65] But the risk of portraying her as active is that she may lose the audience's empathy and, in a generic shift, that the play moves from being about witness testimony to the "thriller" question of whether Paulina will shoot Miranda (which is very much the nature of the film adaptation[66]). I think that Dorfman recognizes these risks, and this is another reason for the final scene in which Paulina returns to her passive role as wife, in which she is safely silent again. In this play, to actively witness one's own trauma requires, Dorfman suggests, breaking the rules of the "good victim," who is in the final scene typified by the crying woman about whom Gerardo recounts the anecdote. It is clear which kind of victim Gerardo—and the commission—prefers: the easily commodifiable one.

Throughout *Ubu*, the puppet witnesses perform as good victims. They try to go about their day-to-day lives (such as the shopkeeper trying to maintain his shop) quietly and without disruption, and when they narrate their testimony, the violent acts they describe are told quietly and with dignity. The puppets never directly challenge the perpetrator Ubu—indeed, though the puppets and actor operate in the proximate stage spaces, it is as if they exist in separate worlds. The puppets are the "righteous," yet it remains unspoken as to whether they forgive, as Niles says they must. The separation between puppet-witnesses and the Ubus means that there is never any direct confrontation between victim and perpetrator. This avoids melodramatic catharsis, but also rules out any sense by which the victim might be able to hold the perpetrator to account. Yet it ultimately also allows Taylor and Handspring to maintain the puppet-witnesses as calm and dignified good victims.

Finally, Claudia is the ultimate good victim who performs her emotional journey for the audience from an ignorant, protected, and enclosed childhood, in which she was an unwitting victim, through the phase of acquiring knowledge and a victim-identity, and eventually into her mature self who is both able to self-name and to forgive. That *Claudia* is an autoperformance—and a successful show with frequent tours—underlines the emotional labor required of the good victim.

The Witness Story Has No End

In some ways, *Claudia* functions as an example of what a truth commission can achieve by creating empathy and understanding for the victims of a terrible regime, as well as taking a measured view of how to live after the commission. As Claudia says when she describes the trial, this is the traditional point for the narrative to end: "The music rises, the credits appear, people applaud, the movie finishes."[67] But her story continues—and it is this continuation that theatre allows for, a more expansive form of witnessing than that available via any truth commission or trial.

Claudia also, of course, performs this act of expansive witnessing in a vacuum—there was no actual truth commission in Argentina. And yet it is this play that is the most optimistic about the power of witnessing and which tells the most complete story. Whereas the victim-witnesses in *Ubu and the Truth Commission* never achieve any closure or justice, Claudia does—through a criminal trial and through her own life story. And the contrast is also true for Paulina, who is the most fictional of the characters we see in these three plays, and who gets to act out an alternative truth commission as a result of her fictionality. But even in this fictional context, Dorfman cannot imagine a scenario in which Paulina can be entirely free of her past.

I am suggesting that *Claudia* performs an exemplary version of how to mourn for the crimes of the past but also live with them—as Claudia says, "Merceditas" is the past and her daughter Guada is the future. But even given Claudia's mature sense of peace with her own trajectory, the play is clear about the extent to which some people have not been able to tell their stories. One woman interviewed in the Santa Lucia segment testifies that the disappearances in her town are still "a covered up reality" and that "There are people that still do not say anything.... It is very sad to see a neighbour walk past, and know that her son has been tortured and killed ... and that his body has never been found."[68] Though Claudia was found, and she was reunited with her family, her parents' bodies have never been recovered and she reconstructs a relationship with them purely through photographs and family stories. There is no witnessing that can bring them back, and there are many witnesses who have still not been heard. There is no point at which societies can say, along with Ma Ubu, "Enough of the past."[69]

MEMORY AS COMMODITY

In *Claudia*, the performer's body becomes evidence, and she has no choice over whether to take the DNA test or not. In contrast, her testimony—how she names herself, the story she tells—is a self-determined and controlled product. When Claudia reveals her name in the original court case and, again, in the production, she generates an impact. Her story of growing up, of realizing the truth, and of coming to terms with it become the commodities she can control and trade. And yet she is also exploited: La Conquesta del Pol Sud has created a successful international production based on the credibility and cultural prestige of Claudia as "the first" of the disappeared children to testify. They deploy her testimony with skill and sensitivity—nonetheless the poetry of Claudia's suffering is how their work succeeds.

Within *Ubu and the Truth Commission* we see puppets deliver the verbatim testimony of those who gave their stories to the South African TRC. Taylor, Kentridge, and Handspring create spaces within the dramaturgy so that these stories can be heard anew by local and international audiences. Without these testimonies, however, this production would be entirely based on the criminal actions and hysteria of the Ubus and their minions—the survivor-witness testimony thus represents a valuable commodity for the play, which derives much of its moral authority and audience impact from the inclusion of their verbatim testimony.

In *Death and the Maiden*, Paulina understands the rules of the commission, given her familiarity with the law and the structures of power. Dorfman's decision to exclude her testimony protects her as a witness, illustrating how a memory play can move away from the "TRC script," as it were—deviating from the consumer-audience's expectation of trauma and empathy for the victim.

The absence of Paulina's testimony, and her reports of having falsified aspects of it to trick Miranda, suggest that through *not* publicly testifying, the survivor maintains most control over the commodity of their own memory. Gerardo's final neat anecdote about the commission's courtesy toward victims underlines exactly how official processes inevitably exploit the commodity of memory in order to create the semblance of granting power to victims, while actually reasserting the power of the status quo; illustrating the conflicting relationship between institutional need for capital and individual, emotional labor and capital. As Anna Reading writes, the "*labour* of truth-telling ... contributes to a regime of *mnemonic value* that is accumulated to form part of the *memory capital* of the emergent post-dictatorship."[70] Indeed Paulina's silence at the end of the play can be read as an acknowledgement of this uneven distribution of capital, a confirmation of the disempowerment of survivors in the face of the marketplace's need for order, and the appropriation by the institution of the survivors' voices and mnemonic capital. Alternately, we may read her silent presence (given that the audience knows what is involved in her silence) as a quiet, but constant, assertion of survival and of her retention of ownership of her own *unspeakable* memory (unspeakable, in this moment, does not mean the disempowerment of the victim, but Paulina's narrative unavailability to a top-down mode of remembering).

It is a double bind: Survivors must "sell" their testimony in the public memory marketplace in order to attain the basic recognition of their right to be remembered. But having sold their testimony they lose their power to speak in the marketplace, and the marketplace thus remains largely unchanged. The all-too-easy dissipation of the survivors' mnemonic capital is thus a salutary note on the persistence of asymmetric power relations within the memory marketplace. Another dimension to this asymmetry is the question of who is doing the consuming—as Marlin-Curiel argues in relation to South African TRC productions, these are "experimental plays with high production values [that] engage with elite liberal audiences."[71] The cultural capital of the audience thus becomes another layer to how consuming witness testimony shores up the power of certain groups.

Who are the audiences for these plays? *Death and the Maiden* and *Claudia* were both first performed in Europe for a non-Chilean/Argentinian audience; *Ubu and the Truth Commission* was first performed in South Africa, but I saw it in London. The transnational dimension to the way that spectators first encounter work has a particular effect on their reception and on the particular way that the internationalizing of local and national stories affects the commodification of memory. Transnational witnessing plays risk creating a false sense of connection between spectator and the larger subject. In other words, having seen *Claudia*, spectators (e.g., in Antwerp, where I saw the play) may believe they now "know" what happened during the Argentine dictatorship. Emerging from *Ubu and the Truth Commission* did I feel that I now understood the South African TRC? Are "truth commissions" themselves a product being sold to an international audience keen to read conflict through a framework of peace and reconciliation? The heightened singularity of these shows may seem to guard against this risk, nevertheless the danger of cultural appropriation—the commodification of the testimony of a distant "other"—still remains.

Indeed, this chapter displays these risks itself—in comparatively examining the performances of witnessing in these three plays, each from a different historical and national context (both in terms of subject and their site of production), have I unintentionally conflated them, removing their specificity and flattening their particular contexts? Certainly, in focusing on the performance of memory and identity by Paulina, Ubu, and Claudia, this chapter has overlooked other frames of interpretation, imagining their stages instead as global public spaces on which globalized stories of suffering and witnessing can be viewed and discussed, as if the main distinctions between them are formal or performative choices made by producers and directors. And yet this is, in fact, how theatre circulates as a cultural product on the same stage—I saw *Ubu* in the same theatre that I saw a Greek production of Sophocles's *Oedipus at Colonus* and the National Theatre of Scotland's *Black Watch*. As an Irish spectator, I can only ever encounter South American and South African theatre out of its original context. I see these internationally created plays, in particular national locations, which may or may not be local to my own national context, and receive them and write about them as examples of transnational witnessing in which the victims, perpetrators, and situations are universalized.

Indeed, transnationalism is written into these plays: Dorfman conceived of *Death and the Maiden* after being involved in theatre in the United Kingdom during his exile from Chile, the play is written in English, and has been performed in more than thirty countries. Taylor's play responds to experimental French theatre history, and the international audience is consistently implied—as when Ubu gives testimony to the moving microphones, it is understood that they represent the international media, indeed the TRC was not only a highly mediated and mediatized performance, it was the outcome of international as well as national pressures. And in *Claudia*, the framing of Claudia's story with Carles (a Spanish citizen) traveling to Argentina for the first time, and acting as a tourist who visits ESMA as well as other iconic sites, foregrounds the way the Argentinian dictatorship is both locally and globally narrativized and consumed.

The audiences of plays that are performed on the global stage are thus performing a "globalizing mode of ethico-political labor."[72] Kurasawa identifies the greatest risk of transnational witnessing as "incomprehension," where witnessing fails because the distance between testifier and witness is too great—the solution to this, he proffers, is "interpretation."[73] There are various potential pitfalls, however, to acts of interpretation: the risk of misunderstanding, the risk of "domesticating" or banalizing, the risk of normalizing what are highly singular and specific narratives.[74] Similarly, Hutchison warns against the risk of "consensualising" complex historical narratives through performing a single individual's testimony for an international audience.[75] Added to these critics' views, however, is the risk that transnational drama does not communicate its central message—that victims and perpetrators are not universalizable. Indeed, consistently negative reviews of the London revival of *Ubu and the Truth Commission* in 2015 declared the play "dated," while one noted that much of the play's "relevance and symbolic imagery are not always clear to a London audience."[76] And transnational productions can vary the meaning of a play hugely—as Weaver and Colleran argue, different contexts lead to radically different interpretations, as shown by the major differences between the 1991 London premiere production of *Death and the Maiden*, which stressed the "global indifference to violence," while the 1992 New York production (at a cost of $1.25 million) stressed the "sexual nature" of the play, undercutting its political critique.[77] When *Death and the Maiden* was produced in South Africa in 1992, however, the "deeply consequential historical moment" highlighted once again the "political imperatives raised by the play."[78] Each of these three international productions aimed to be the "definitive" version of the play, demonstrating how producers compete within the marketplace. We therefore have to ask what it is that travels when memory crosses borders, and how memories are shaped not by the testimonies of survivors but by the cultural gatekeepers who determine not only access to a platform within the marketplace, but also the interpretive framework.

The act of translation, or transnational movement, is necessary so that the transnational spectator may witness and grant recognition and global legitimacy to the claims of victims and survivors (which was, historically, a major factor in the rise of democracy in all three of these national contexts), but of course it loses much of the purchase of the structural and "situational violence" of the contexts of the plays.[79] As with the risk of commodification discussed here and elsewhere in this book, the question comes down to this: Does transnational witnessing create important bonds that transcend spatial, temporal, and contextual divides, producing a greater social good (such as understanding of oppression), or does it sell the survivor short? As I have argued throughout this book, I think the answer to this question will differ based on how the wished-for solidarity is produced between the audience and the oppressed subjects depicted by many of these transnational plays—where that solidarity is produced through the medium of pain, that pain then becomes a free-floating signifier of suffering, which is "deemed universally intelligible,"[80] and can be easily consumed. However, as this chapter has shown, theatrical strategies, such as the distancing devices of puppets and video screens, and the refusal to place the burden of witnessing onto the body of the victim, can trouble the definition of suffering as purely individual and can bring into focus the larger contexts—and perhaps even the structures—of injustice.

NOTES

1. Quoted in Claire Hackett and Bill Rolston, "The Burden of Memory: Victims, Storytelling and Resistance in Northern Ireland," *Memory Studies* 2, no. 3 (2009): 355–76, see esp. 363.

2. Catherine M. Cole, "Performance, Transitional Justice, and the Law: South Africa's Truth and Reconciliation Commission," *Theatre Journal* 59, no. 2 (2007): 167–87, see esp. 172.

3. Catherine M. Cole, *Performing South Africa's Truth Commission* (Bloomington: Indiana University Press, 2010), xii.

4. South Africa, Promotion of Unity and National Reconciliation Act, 1995. The text of the act is available online: https://www.gov.za/documents/promotion-national-unity-and-reconciliation-act.

5. Brenda Werth, *Theatre Performance and Memory Politics in Argentina* (New York: Palgrave, 2010), 3.

6. Caroline Wake, "Caveat Spectator: Juridical, Political and Ontological False Witnessing in CMI (A Certain Maritime Incident)," *Law Text Culture* 14, no. 1 (2010): 160–87, see esp. 164.

7. Hackett and Rolston, "The Burden of Memory," 360.

8. Hackett and Rolston, "The Burden of Memory," 365.

9. See Yvette Hutchison, "Truth or Bust: Consensualising a Historic Narrative or Provoking through Theatre. The Place of the Personal Narrative in the Truth and Reconciliation Commission," *Contemporary Theatre Review* 15, no. 3 (2005): 354–62.

10. The revival gave producers another opportunity to discuss the use of verbatim testimony, delivered by puppets. See Yasmin Sulaiman, "South African

Play Ubu and the Truth Commission Set for 2014 Edinburgh International Festival," 2014, https://edinburghfestival.list.co.uk/article/62173-south-african-play-ubu-and-the-truth-commission-set-for-2014-edinburgh-international-festival/.

11. Jane Taylor, *Ubu and the Truth Commission* (Cape Town: University of Cape Town Press, 1998), 45.

12. Richard Crownshaw's argument explores *Beloved* by Toni Morrison in "Perpetrator Fictions and Transcultural Memory," *Parallax* 17, no. 4 (2011): 75–89.

13. Marlin-Curiel writes about *That Spirit*, Mina Nawe's play based on the TRC, as representing the humanity of both victims and perpetrators, without a confrontational tone—as a way to think beyond the adversarial nature of postconflict situations. See Stephanie Marlin-Curiel, "The Long Road to Healing: From the TRC to TfD," *Theatre Research International* 27, no. 3 (2002): 275–88, see esp. 280.

14. Taylor, *Ubu and the Truth Commission*, 73.

15. See Kentridge's illustrations in Taylor, *Ubu and the Truth Commission*, 72.

16. For a discussion of the TRC in this regard, see Hutchison, "Truth or Bust," 356–58.

17. See "Report of the Chilean National Commission on Truth and Reconciliation," United States Institute of Peace, October 4, 2002, https://www.usip.org/publications/1990/05/truth-commission-chile-90, 25.

18. This is akin to the Irish case of survivors of industrial schools: in order to receive financial compensation from the Redress Board, survivors had to sign a nondisclosure agreement, thereby silencing them once more. See Sharon Commins, "Survivors of Abuse Must Be Allowed to Speak Freely," *Irish Times*, March 18, 2010, https://www.irishtimes.com/opinion/survivors-of-abuse-must-be-allowed-speak-freely-1.639465.

19. Ariel Dorfman, *Death and the Maiden* (London: Nick Hern Books, 1994), 6.

20. Dorfman, *Death and the Maiden*, 6.

21. Dorfman, *Death and the Maiden*, 7.

22. Dorfman, *Death and the Maiden*, 6

23. Dorfman, *Death and the Maiden*, 10.

24. Dorfman, *Death and the Maiden*, 16.

25. Dorfman, *Death and the Maiden*, 27.

26. Dorfman, *Death and the Maiden*, 18.

27. Dorfman, *Death and the Maiden*, 22.

28. The reason Paulina gives, however, is more personally political—when she arrived at Gerardo's house, she interrupted him in bed with another woman. This sexual betrayal meant that she refused to speak of her experience out of anger at his disloyalty to her.

29. Dorfman, *Death and the Maiden*, 25.
30. Wake, "Caveat Spectator," 167.
31. I am grateful to La Conquesta del Pol Sud for making a recording of a live performance of *Claudia* (Grec Festival, Barcelona, 27 July 2016) available to me for the purposes of this research; there is currently no published text in English, all quotations are based on my transcription from the recording.
32. *Claudia*, recording, July 27, 2016, my transcription.
33. *Claudia*, recording, July 27, 2016, my transcription.
34. "Argentina Revokes 'Dirty War' Amnesty," *Irish Times*, June 15, 2005, https://www.irishtimes.com/news/argentina-revokes-dirty-war-amnesty-1.1178726.
35. See, for example, Michal Ben-Josef Hirsch, "Ideational Change and the Emergence of the International Norm of Truth and Reconciliation Commissions," *European Journal of International Relations* 20, no. 3 (2014): 810–33; Anne Leebaw, "The Irreconcilable Goals of Transitional Justice," *Human Rights Quarterly* 30, no. 1 (2008): 95–118; G. M. Millar, "Local Evaluations of Justice through Truth Telling in Sierra Leone: Postwar Needs and Transitional Justice," *Human Rights Review* 12, no. 4 (2011): 515–35; Julie Adoch, Cheryl Keykoop, "Our Stories, Our Own Ways: Exploring Alternatives for Young People's Engagement in Truth Commissions," *Peace and Conflict* 23, no. 1 (2017): 14–22.
36. David Roman, "What We Know about Transitional Justice: Survey and Experimental Evidence," *Political Psychology* 38, no. 1 (2017): 151–77.
37. *Claudia*, recording, July 27, 2016, my transcription.
38. *Claudia*, recording, July 27, 2016, my transcription.
39. *Claudia*, recording, July 27, 2016, my transcription.
40. *Claudia*, recording, July 27, 2016, my transcription.
41. Taylor, *Ubu and the Truth Commission*, 5.
42. Taylor, *Ubu and the Truth Commission*, 57.
43. Taylor, *Ubu and the Truth Commission*, 61.
44. Taylor, *Ubu and the Truth Commission*, 67–68. As Loren Kruger points out, Pa's confession is based on the TRC statement of Eugene de Kock, head of the Vlakplaas secret anti-insurgency unit, known as "Prime Evil." See Loren Kruger, "Enlightenment, Embodiment and the Ends of Modern Drama," in *Modern Drama: Defining the Field*, ed. Richard Paul Knowles, W. B. Worthen, and Joanne Tompkins (Toronto: University of Toronto Press, 2003), 80–101, see esp. 97. See also Antjie Krog, "The Repentance of Eugene de Kock," *New York Times*, March 13, 2015, https://www.nytimes.com/2015/03/14/opinion/sunday/the-repentance-of-eugene-de-kock-apartheid-assassin.html.
45. Onur Bakiner, "One Truth among Others? Truth Commission's Struggle for Truth and Memory," *Memory Studies* 8, no. 3 (2015): 345–60, see esp. 353.
46. Taylor, *Ubu and the Truth Commission*, 67.

47. Taylor, *Ubu and the Truth Commission*, 17.
48. Taylor, *Ubu and the Truth Commission*, 17.
49. I am grateful to Brandi Byrd and her work on autobiography for this reference. Paul Ricouer, "Reflections on a New Ethos for Europe," in *Paul Ricoeur: The Hermeneutics of Action*, ed. Richard Kearney (London: Sage, 1996), 3–13, see esp. 9–10.
50. Dorfman, *Death and the Maiden*, 44.
51. Dorfman, *Death and the Maiden*, 22.
52. Taylor, *Ubu and the Truth Commission*, 71.
53. Dorfman, *Death and the Maiden*, 45–46.
54. Samuel Beckett, *Waiting for Godot* in *The Complete Dramatic Works* (London: Faber, 1986), 50.
55. Hutchison, "Truth or Bust," 355.
56. Dorfman, *Death and the Maiden*, 49.
57. Dorfman, *Death and the Maiden*, 49.
58. Dorfman, *Death and the Maiden*, 46.
59. *Claudia*, recording, July 27, 2016, my transcription.
60. *Claudia*, recording, July 27, 2016, my transcription.
61. *Claudia*, recording, July 27, 2016, my transcription.
62. William Kentridge, director's note to *Ubu and the Truth Commission*, by Jane Taylor, xi.
63. Kentridge, xi.
64. Helen Gilbert, introduction, to *Ubu and the Truth Commission*, by Jane Taylor, with William Kentridge and the Handspring Puppet Company, in *Postcolonial Plays: An Anthology*, ed. Helen Gilbert (Abingdon, UK: Routledge, 2001), 26. This strategy might also be compared to the use of the same actor to portray both the perpetrator and the victim in *That Spirit*, another TRC play, by Mina Nawe.
65. Cole, "South Africa's Truth and Reconciliation Commission," 184.
66. *Death and the Maiden*, dir. Roman Polanski (1994), https://www.amazon.com/Death-Maiden-Sigourney-Weaver/dp/B001TDNMPM/.
67. *Claudia*, recording, July 27, 2016, my transcription.
68. *Claudia*, recording, July 27, 2016, my transcription.
69. Taylor, *Ubu and the Truth Commission*, 70.
70. Anna Reading, "The Female Memory Factory: How the Gendered Labour of Memory Creates Mnemonic Capital," *European Journal of Women's Studies* (2019): 1–20 (italics in the original).
71. Marlin-Curiel, "The Long Road to Healing," 275.
72. Fuyuiki Kurasawa, "A Message in a Bottle," *Theory, Culture and Society* 26, no. 1 (2009): 92–111, see esp. 95.
73. Kurasawa, "A Message in a Bottle," 95, 96.

74. Kurasawa, "A Message in a Bottle," 97.

75. Hutchison, "Truth or Bust," 354.

76. "Ubu and the Truth Commission Review at Print Room at the Coronet, London—'Uncomfortably Yoked,'" October 21, 2015, https://www.thestage.co.uk/reviews/2015/ubu-and-the-truth-commission-review-at-print-room-at-the-coronet-london-uncomfortably-yoked/.

77. For an in depth discussion of these issues relating to the two productions, see James Weaver and Jeanne Colleran, "Whose Memory? Whose Justice? Personal and Political Trauma in Ariel Dorman's *Death and the Maiden*," *Performance Research* 16, no. 1 (2011): 31–42.

78. Weaver and Colleran, "Whose Memory?," 40.

79. Kurasawa, "A Message in a Bottle," 100.

80. Lauren Berlant, quoted in Rosanne Kennedy, "An Australian Archive of Feelings," *Australian Feminist Studies* 26, no. 69 (2011): 257–79, see esp. 265.

FOUR

THE IMMATERIAL LABOR OF LISTENING
Presence, Absence, Failure, and the Commodification of the Witness

THEATRE IS A SPACE FOR listening. Or, put another way, theatre is a space in which the immaterial labors of testimony and listening are recognized and can accumulate symbolic capital. This symbolic capital is partly derived from the understanding that theatre audiences encounter, and consume, witnesses who would otherwise be unheard in the marketplace owing to their lack of either social or cultural capital. In this context, testifying and listening function as interventions in marketplace hierarchies. In previous chapters, I have focused on the labor of performance by the onstage witness; here I shift the focus onto the labor of listening, a labor usually performed by the audience. The chapter considers how concentrating on listening makes visible both the immaterial labor of witnessing and the process of commodification, which are furthered—and subverted—through the audiences' consumption of the stories they hear.

THE UNHEARD

To ask to be listened to is a revelation of precarity—the witness is dependent on the audience to fulfill this role. Listening is not neutral.

Twilight Los Angeles, 1992 is a docu-verbatim play, compiled and performed by Anna Deavere Smith (US, 1994) in response to the 1992 riots that followed the acquittal of Los Angeles police officers charged with assaulting Rodney King in 1991. The play is a multivocal work presenting testimony that Smith gathered from forty-six witnesses who were affected by police violence and the ensuing riots. The witnesses include gang members, representatives of the police force, politicians, clergy, victims, and perpetrators. Smith embodies and enacts all these testimonies, assuming each character in turn through body language, intonation, and accent, assisted by lighting, prop, and costume changes to signal changes in witness. The play's subtitle—*On the Road: A Search for American Character*—reveals the production's attempt to come to grips with more than an event and its fallout; like the *Laramie* plays it is an excavation of how people respond to violence and what conditions precede such an explosion of hate.

> **Rudy Salas Sr.:**
> They took me to a room
> and they locked the door behind me
> and there was four guys, four cops there
> kicking me in the head.
> As a result of the kicks in the head they fractured my ear drum,
> and, uh,
> I couldn't hear
> on both ears.
> I was deaf,
> worse than I am now.
> (*He pulls out one of his hearing aids*)
> So
> from that day on
> I, I had a hate in me
> . . .
> for white policemen.[1]

Rudy Salas Sr., a sculptor and painter, has "*a hearing aid in his left ear and in his right ear.*"[2] He has been profoundly physically affected by police violence, which he attributes to being targeted as a Mexican by a racist police force. The link Salas makes between violence and deafness is not limited to the physical after effects of being kicked in the head—something else is fractured in the assault. In opening *Twilight—Los Angeles, 1992* with Salas's testimony in a scene titled "My Enemy," Smith ties several aspects of violence and deafness together: deafness is the result of violence; hatred is the emotional and political result of the physical impact of violence; hatred is a kind of deafness.

Smith takes a different approach in the second scene, "These Curious People," focusing on Stanley K. Steinbaum, the former president of the Los Angeles Police Commission. Steinbaum tries to persuade the police at the Seventy-seventh Precinct to be open to talking to the gangs, "these curious people":

> **Stanley K. Steinbaum:**
> I knew I hadn't won when they said,
> "so which side are you on?"

When I said, I said it's...
my answer was
"Why do I have to be on a side?"
Yu, yuh, yeh know.
Why do I have to be on a side?[3]

Though Steinbaum is, unlike many other witnesses in this play, an individual with high social capital and a platform to speak directly to his audience (in this case the police), his position of authority does not translate into being listened to. The mismatch between Steinbaum's social capital and the audience's reaction surprises him, evident as he stutters to comprehend their failure to listen, a response that completely undermines his usual position in the marketplace. Moreover, the police response to his suggestion of mutuality—to insist that he must pick a side—is a cultural and political deafness reminiscent of the Ubus' refusal to notice the black witnesses they share a stage with, discussed in chapter 3. Deafness in these examples can be read as an example of what Nancy Tuana calls "willful ignorance," which is "the active ignoring of the oppression of others and one's role in that exploitation," or, in other words, a symptom of the refusal of those with social capital to acknowledge the voices and experiences of those without.[4]

In setting the first two scenes of the play as a contrast between a man of low social capital, who has been deafened as a result of police violence, and a man who is, as president of a police organization, at the top of the hierarchy, which is nevertheless deaf to his arguments, Smith reveals the extent to which violence is a problem of listening. In previous chapters on docu-verbatim work, I have argued that these plays are important for the platform they give witnesses to speak about their memories. In amplifying victims' and other stakeholders' voices, docu-verbatim plays act to intervene in the marketplace of public discourse and cultural memory around social injustices, such as child abuse and sexual violence. Theatre companies use tools, such as performing shocking testimony or utilizing music and lighting, to create a dramaturgical context that will foster a connection between the stage witness and the audience so that, through empathy and understanding, the audience will take on these memories as part of their own, expanding and deepening both personal and cultural memory. But what if, despite these tactics, no one is listening?

Disempowerment is often seen as synonymous with silencing. And yet disempowered witnesses do speak out. So perhaps it is more accurate to say that disempowerment is synonymous with others' deafness, with not being listened to, because though you may speak, your reduced social capital does not entitle you to an audience. As Paul Ricoeur states, "There are witnesses who never encounter an audience capable of listening to them or hearing what they have to say."[5] Ricoeur's formulation is necessary to understanding witnessing because of how it places the responsibility (and blame) onto the audience for their role as appointed listeners. Moreover, his formulation highlights that the problem of silencing is not due to any failure on the part of the witness to speak, but rather on the part of the audience to hear or invest in what "*they* have to say." Labor is only being performed by the firsthand witness, not by the audience; the capacity to listen and hear that Ricoeur refers to may be interpreted as the difference between the audience-consumer and the audience-witness. Finally, there is a distinction between listening and "hearing"—with the implication that the latter term involves some processing. In the above case of Steinbaum, he may have been listened to by the police, but he was not *heard*. In juxtaposing testimony from witnesses with different levels of social capital, Smith exposes the structural power relations of the marketplace and attempts to balance them.

This chapter focuses on the need for witnesses to be heard. Moving on from the consideration of how testimony is performed in verbatim work (chaps. 1 and 2), I will now consider how audiences *listen* to testimony, both as producers and consumers. By discussing six plays from different moments and contexts, I seek to answer two persistent questions: What does the act of listening mean to witnessing? And what role does listening have to play in forming and maintaining memory and mnemonic capital? And, finally, I seek to consider how the act of listening may help both subject and spectator resist the alienating processes of commodification. These discussions will focus on *Twilight* by Smith, *Come Out Eli* (UK, 2003) by Alecky Blythe, *Annulla (An Autobiography)* (US, 1985) by Emily Mann,[6] and three plays by Samuel Beckett: *Krapp's Last Tape* (Ireland/France, 1958), *Footfalls* (Ireland/France, 1976), and *Come and Go* (Ireland/France, 1965). These plays give us different models for listening-as-witnessing, and ultimately suggest how *embodied* listening may act as a form of resistance to commodification.

AUTHENTICITY

Smith, a pioneer of docu-verbatim work in the United States, has developed what is now a common practice in verbatim theatre of recording interview testimony and devising a script based on these verbatim sources (what is unusual is that she performs all the roles herself—theatre companies typically employ a number of actors to take on this ensemble verbatim work). This practice raises questions about presence and authenticity, which are applicable to any play that includes secondhand testimony as a major structural element. Some plays address this separation between original witness and performer by including voice-over testimony, playing witnesses' words via a soundtrack.[7] The disembodied voice is thus given a presence, without the extra demand on the witness to have to appear publicly or to perform themselves. Another strategy is to incorporate the voice of the witness into the performer's role via headphones worn by the actor. This approach has informed the mash-up work of Alecky Blythe who, inspired by Smith's process of interview and recording, has incorporated the recorded voice directly into her performances of verbatim work but not as audio that the audience hears directly. Both strategies make the labor of mediation and of performance visible.

Blythe's first docu-verbatim play, *Come Out Eli* (2003), is based on the events in Hackney, London, around the 2002 siege standoff between police and an armed man, Eli, who held a man hostage for fifteen days, before taking his own life. Seeing the siege announced on the news provoked Blythe to go to the site itself—where she interviewed residents, police, and bystanders. In the aftermath, Blythe conducted follow-up interviews, and together these testimonies provide the raw material for *Come Out Eli*. The innovation in Blythe's work is that there is no printed script. Instead, Blythe edits the actual recordings into an audio-script, and this is played to the actors onstage via earpieces. The actors then repeat what they hear verbatim, including accents, intonations, and nonverbal noises. Actors do not have a script and they do not learn the lines—the novelty of this production is the premise of a spontaneous and instinctive performance (perhaps belying the skill involved), based on sound rather than written text, and on listening rather than learning by heart.

Blythe suggests that this process allows for greater authenticity: "By listening to the audio during performances the actors remain accurate to the original recordings, rather than slipping into their own patterns of speech."[8] Blythe further argues that a person's intonation is key to understanding their character, how they are "as a person, at that particular moment in time. . . . So that's why it's important for the actors not to embellish and just stick to copying what they hear."[9] And yet in not including the voices of the witnesses themselves, the act of ventriloquism remains a central part of the play. The gap between the performer and the original witness, an embodied gap that Blythe bridges through audio technology (what has been called, in relation to Beckett's *Krapp's Last Tape*, an "audio prosthesis"[10]), highlights the imperfection of memory performance. I say "imperfection" because of the stress that Blythe puts on the authenticity of the actors' re-recitation of the original vocal performance; it is usual in theatre to understand that the actor onstage is *not* identical with the character they portray, and this is not a fault but rather a mark of creative practice. In the case of Blythe's audio-enhanced verbatim plays, however, the leap of faith the audience takes is constantly subverted by the expectation that the audio technology creates a greater indexical link between the original witnessing subject and the actor's presentation, as if the act of mediation was less than in other kinds of theatre. And yet the script is still edited and controlled by Blythe, the actors still employ their expertise night after night, this is still a professional production and not a form of unmediated access to "the real."

The performance of *Come Out Eli* works best when audiences have a sense that in some way the performers are working in collaboration with the original subjects. If anything, for me, the production was most powerful when I could see the labor and effort involved in the actors' attempts to act as a channel for the subject, putting their own selves and egos to one side; this could be an awkward process—and all the more authentic for that awkwardness. Similar to the way that autoperformance actors can stumble over their lines, thus forcing the realization that this is *not natural* because they are not trained actors, the labor involved in this kind of memory performance creates an aesthetic of effort that perhaps inadvertently, perhaps deliberately, enriches our understanding of memory as an act of laborious retrieval and reconstruction, resulting in a potentially accident-prone performance.

Witnessing Multiplicity

Whereas Smith concentrates on one witness at a time, Blythe stages group testimony with multiple actors, and the play features regularly recurring witnesses and testimonies that are broken up so that their pieces create a collage of the event as it unfolded. Blythe combines "in-the-moment" testimony taken at the barricades around the siege, alongside retrospective interviews. Across seventy-two mini scenes, Blythe includes perspectives from bystanders, residents, local business owners, police, politicians, and even the hostage that Eli took at the beginning of the siege. The impulse toward representativeness and inclusion here makes for a multilayered and multivoiced production. It further suggests, however (much like Smith's huge collection of witnesses from across the urban social sphere), an impulse for completeness, as if performing so many voices and perspectives can grant access to what really happened, thereby achieving a kind of memory-omniscience. Yet what each of these plays really demonstrate, behind the barrage of voices, is that no such omniscience is available or even desirable. We can know that something happened, we can know some of its details, and what it meant to a particular group, but we can never know it in its totality. There are two parts to this restriction that I want to highlight: first, witnessing is only ever partial and subjective, whether firsthand or secondhand; second, witnessing is not synonymous with judging.

First, gathering together a collection of testimonies by different witnesses to an event (a riot, a siege) will always result in a muddle, because there will be conflicting accounts, contradictory details, or just too much detail. When testimonies are multiplied, the perspectives increase, and the number of insights increases too, but this does not necessarily increase the insight into the event that gives rise to the interviews and performances in the first place. Having more voices, stories, and memories only gives us more voices, stories, and memories because plenitude does not equal authority, it only equals plenitude. It also brings us back to the problem of abundance in the marketplace—creating competition for the limited supply of audience attention.

Second, Blythe understands that this is not a legal case she is building, and audiences are not there to judge what happened, only to get an insight into what each of these people felt and thought at the time and how they recall it in the present. During the "real-time" interviews, the audience gets a sense of the unfolding drama and the in-the-moment observations, as the shopkeepers and residents grow increasingly weary of the demands of having a police cordon on their street and the negative impact this has on their lives and businesses. In the reflective scenes, however, the audience can hear testimony that is shaped by larger, narrative concerns:

> Louise—Early thirties. Direct. Party/rave organiser. Sheffield accent.
> We had ten—ten officers a day out there, none of them from Hackney, some of them being quite rude about, "You must be used to this, this is Hackney, this is what's like, isn't it?" So you're like, "Well, no actually, no it's not, it's not like that, this is where we live."[11]

Louise's testimony is marked by resistance, functioning as a bottom-up (or local) response to the top-down (nonlocal), class-based narrative of the siege. The tension between the locals and the police recurs as a feature of multiple testimonies, suggesting that one effect of plenitude is not a complete version of the siege, but the emergence of an unexpected narrative—the social marginalization of an urban area.

Other witnesses are more positive, but no less subjective, partial, or, indeed, contradictory. During Mrs. and Mr. Field's first interview, they state that "We had absolutely no problem at all [with the police presence].... We felt safer- than we've felt -in a long, long time. / We only heard the sirens go once."[12] Yet toward the end of the play, they reappear as characters, and in this scene Blythe includes details of their "problems": "We hardly slept for five— two weeks in fact I hardly slept for a month because I couldn't sleep after that."[13] When the Fields make their first appearance Blythe describes them as being in their early sixties; Mr. Field is a retired solicitor and ex-naval officer with *"carefully chosen words,"* while Mrs. Field is an *"avid reader, researcher and archivist."*[14] They would seem to be ideal witnesses. Yet in their final testimony they contradict each other about the veracity of their own listening: whether they heard shots and what time of day they heard shooting. Both declare that they have forgotten the details—they did not listen well enough. Instead, what is most vivid to them is their own internal experience of excitement at the siege and the attention it brought to their neighborhood, along with the extra security of police presence. The act of talking to Blythe seems an extension of this, as their version of the event is finally being heard. They clearly relish being interviewed, and this enjoyment illustrates how valuable it is to be listened to, and to listen (even when the testimony being produced is unreliable). The Fields know that they have a limited window of cultural capital to trade their experience in return for Blythe's attention (and, by extension, the audience's attention). In some ways, their poor value as witnesses of what actually happened, which would make them less valuable in other contexts, such as a court trial, makes them more interesting to an audience, and thus more successful in the memory marketplace. They are heard because their testimony is contradictory and fluctuating, not because they are reliable.

CONSUMER DESIRE FOR THE COMPLETE STORY

The circumscribed, unreliable witness is always measured against the ideal of the perfect witness: that mythical individual who sees everything, who remembers everything, who understands what each memory *means*, and who can replay it word for word for a listening audience. As discussed in the conclusion to chapter 2, the perfect witness (the ideal audience witness) is the impossible witness. But in many ways, we now assume that technology can play the role of the perfect witness (as in *Come Out Eli*), with high-definition recording and playback, plus the constant and eternal surveillance of social media, making up for the human tendency toward imperfection. Technology also has the "advantage" of making some labor invisible.[15] But again, as with the Fields, as listening *human* subjects, is perfection or invisible labor what we want to achieve in the theatre? Is the reliable, unchanging, high-definition memory ever more authentic than the fallible, shifting human version? And which has more mnemonic capital?

In Samuel Beckett's *Krapp's Last Tape* (1958), set "in the future," each year on his birthday Krapp records an audiotape based on his observation of the year that has passed. Each tape is in turn recorded in a ledger that lists the notable events of the year, and each spool of tape is numbered and archived in a numbered box. Krapp remembers everything. Indeed, Robert Reginio points to this play as an example of the "insatiable collecting" that typifies the desire to archive memory.[16] The archive, of course, is the accumulation of mnemonic capital made material. Krapp's archival system, as a technologized form of memory, points to how much better archives are at doing the work of memory than humans—when reading the ledger, Krapp stumbles over his writing: "Memorable . . . what? [*He peers closer.*] Equinox, memorable equinox. [*He raises his head, stares blankly front. Puzzled.*] Memorable equinox?"[17] This comic moment, exposing the fallibility not only of memory but also of our judgements about what will prove memorable, also leads us to question which version has more value—Krapp's sense of the past, in which the equinox features not at all, or the ledger's/audiotape's? The archive is the "perfect" version, but meaning is generated in the play not by the ledger etc., but by the interaction of the current Krapp with his earlier selves.

Krapp is the ultimate producer-consumer whose efforts at testimony expose the alienating effects of commodification on the subject testifying (in this case, himself). Part of Krapp's annual ritual involves playing an old memory prior to recording his birthday tape. The audience watches as sixty-nine-year-old Krapp selects a spool, arranges it on the tape deck, eats a banana, drinks some beer, and presses play. In order to hear his own words, Krapp has to sit close to the tape deck, an intimate relationship in which he seems to hold the technology (if not his earlier self) close to him. The first memory he plays is his recall of his mother's death. Younger Krapp has recorded that he was in a park across the road watching, until "the blind went down" to signify her passing. As she dies, he holds a ball in his hand: "A small, old, black, hard, solid rubber ball. [*Pause.*] I shall feel it, in my hand, until my dying day."[18] Beckett measures the inconsequence of the detail of the ball against the monumentality of Krapp's mother's death, and the inconsequential detail wins out. Yet it is arguable as to whether present-day Krapp even remembers the ball, like the equinox. The value of these audiotapes, therefore, is their preservation of details that are meaningful in the moment, details that fall out of mind; at the same time, however, Beckett shows how forgetting allows *different* stories to be excavated from the archive.

As consumer, elder Krapp rejects intellectual value for emotional value. He loses his temper with his younger self, whose taped testimony endlessly records his intellectual achievements, "what I have chiefly to record this evening" (more important, then, than his mother's death), and his great epiphany that "the belief I had been going on all my life, namely— [Krapp *switches off impatiently, winds tape forward, switches on again*]."[19] The audience never learns what belief Krapp has exposed as either true or false, or indeed any other details of his intellectual development. Krapp persistently, and increasingly bad temperedly, fast-forwards the tape to exclude from his present remembrance his past epiphanies. The devaluation of these memories, what the thirty-nine-year-old Krapp believed was most significant, is explained when the elder Krapp finds what he was searching for—a memory to which he listens without interruption: "I lay down across her with my face in her breasts and my hand on her."[20] The loneliness of the elder Krapp, sitting in a pool of light on a mostly darkened stage, hugging his tape recorder for company, is pitiable as he listens and replays his memories of the end of his love affair, and then the recorded voice's assertion that "Perhaps my best years are gone. When there was a chance of happiness. But I wouldn't want them back. Not with the fire in me now. No, I wouldn't want them back."[21] After Krapp listens to this self-destructive claim, the recording ends and the tape plays on in silence as Krapp stares, lost in thought, before him. Whether or not Krapp regrets his earlier self's "Farewell to... love"[22] is never articulated. But his actions suggest deep regret—Krapp abandons the attempt to record a tape of the current year's progress and throws the new tape away, rejecting the production of new mnemonic capital, so that he can replay instead his memory from three decades previously: "my face in her breasts and my hand on her." At this stage in his life, Krapp prefers the labor of listening to that of testifying—to be an audience to himself, not a firsthand witness; a consumer, not a producer.

Krapp rejects his earlier self's judgement of how to witness his life, preferring instead the emotional investment of listening to memories of love. Through remediating the tape, Krapp demonstrates how new selves and pasts are shaped through consumer desire—the story of past-Krapp is determined by what he wants to listen to in the present. In this way, Krapp is not just a witness but also gatekeeper and consumer, embodying the circle of creation, production, and demand that characterizes the marketplace.

We might assume that we are our own perfect witnesses—both in giving and receiving our own testimony. Krapp's loneliness, however, seems linked not only to his rejection of human contact, but to the process of recording testimony itself. It is not just that Krapp's rejection of earlier versions of himself reflects the fluctuating value of different personal memories and shifting priorities; it seems as if the closed circle of witnessing (the completely privately controlled marketplace) is emblematic of how Krapp can only consume himself, and never function as a full witness of another. In the end, the play, which at first appears to extol the virtue of the archive, serves, as Reginio puts it, as "a critique of the archive."[23] In functioning as both producer and consumer, Krapp takes control of his own mnemonic capital. Yet it does not make him happy. Krapp begins the play with a *"Happy smile"* but ends brooding, in a demonstration that having total control over the personal memory marketplace is not empowering but the converse: depressing. This is arguably because in recording his memories for later consumption, Krapp *has commodified himself*—a process that Beckett reveals as deeply alienating.

Presence

Krapp demonstrates the difficulties of being in dialogue with an earlier version of the self. Listening to the tapes provides him with proof that his alter ego is himself, not an unknown other, yet rather than provoking any continuity or unity between the younger and older Krapp, listening creates disjuncture and disharmony:

> Hard to believe I was ever that young whelp. The voice! Jesus! And the aspirations! [*Brief laugh in which* Krapp *joins.*] And the resolutions! [*Brief laugh in which* Krapp *joins.*][24]

> Just been listening to that stupid bastard I took myself for thirty years ago, hard to believe I was ever as bad as that. Thank God that's all done with anyway.[25]

The first reaction, from the thirty-nine-year-old Krapp to the twenty-nine- or twenty-seven-year-old version is comical. The second reaction, from the sixty-nine-year-old Krapp to his thirty-nine-year-old self is bitter. The assertion that "that's all done with" is contradicted by the act of memory that the play represents: only by ceasing to listen can Krapp actually be "done." Far from being a success, Krapp's archive amply illustrates the danger of remembering, and the strategic advantages of forgetting, what we used to be like, how we sounded, what we thought, and what we deemed important.

Despite the "presence" of former versions of the self, Krapp is, in fact, alone onstage. This loneliness is worsened given that the only dialogue he can enter into is a closed loop, and that the responses are all predetermined by what was recorded years earlier, despite how he may manipulate them in the present. While this quandary is obviously true for any scripted drama, it seems to be a particularly acute form of entrapment for characters like Krapp who, alone onstage, are tied into a relationship with a recorded voice, whose machinery may be visible onstage but whose presence is always and unchangeably offstage. We may question what kind of witnessing, and what kind of remembering, this is—given the closed loop, Krapp may fast-forward as much as he likes, but the past cannot change, the memory cannot change (though it may change its emotional inflection), and the act of witnessing this past is, as Krapp's discarding of his current tape recording and his staring blankly into space suggest, ultimately unproductive.

WHO IS THE WITNESS?

When a character is, like Krapp, alone onstage, it becomes relevant to ask who is doing the witnessing—is the character self-witnessing, or does the audience take on a newly important role in being the only witness present? Emily Mann addresses this question in her play *Annulla (An Autobiography)* (1985). This short verbatim work is built around Mann's journey to London in 1974 where she interviewed Annulla Allen, the aunt of a friend, who came to the UK as a Jewish refugee after securing the release of her husband from a concentration camp and having herself escaped the Nazis. The conceit of the play is that it is a staging of the interview between the two women, with one major difference—Mann is absent from the stage. Instead her role is represented by a disembodied voice-over—an actor's voice, which plays over speakers. Mann thus reverses the pattern we are used to, where the presence of the interviewer/playwright onstage stands in for the absence of the interviewed subject. Instead, Annulla is, like Krapp, alone onstage, and it is the interviewer who becomes the invisible other.

Mann is present in the play through a "young woman's" voice-over, who begins by recounting how Mann initially interviewed Annulla to learn something about her own family history, otherwise unavailable to her: "I needed to go to someone else's relative in order to understand my own history because by this time my only living relative of that generation was my grandmother... and she had almost no way to communicate complex ideas. She'd lost her language.... She had *no fluent language*."[26] It is not that Mann's grandmother is beyond language, or complex ideas, but her dysfluency renders her unable to communicate. The "loss" of language means she is an imperfect witness to her own, and her generation's, experiences.

In contrast, Annulla is highly articulate and highly literate, and thus "worth" listening to; in fact, she has written a play herself, a huge sprawling script that is constantly present onstage—another example of mnemonic capital made material—that she promises to read from (but never does). Annulla's enthusiastic labor in her willingness to answer questions about the past, and to monologue about her experiences in Germany and London and elsewhere, is quite remarkable. In many ways, her willingness to divulge her personal memories (for example, her struggle to free her husband) demonstrate the enthusiasm and energetic labor of the active witness. Unlike Krapp, who sits to listen to his memories replaying, Annulla talks as she prepares tea and food and wanders around her apartment, constantly occupied and busy. The immaterial labor of housework mirrors that of remembering, and by extension the audience's work in listening.

Annulla is, however, a circumscribed witness. There are memories that she cannot, will not, narrate: "I cannot even talk to you about the death camps ... this whole affair, this whole Hitler affair ... this whole war [...] I didn't know that people were so evil until I saw it with my own eyes. I didn't believe it that people could be so evil. [*Sips tea*]"[27] We might view this refusal and the fragmentation of her narrative at this point as a reflection of what has been traditionally seen as the effect of trauma on the individual's ability to narrate their history. We might also view Annulla, however, as a more active and alert witness who puts certain aspects of her life out of the range of audience consumption and thus commodification.

Who is Annulla's audience? Though Annulla tries to be upbeat and assertive, it is hard not to notice her loneliness, heightened by her isolation onstage; the voice-over of the interviewer is a poor substitute for actual copresence.[28] While Mann cedes the stage to Annulla, so she may star in her own drama, it also leaves Annulla looking slightly lost, as if she is playing the caricature role of lonely-woman-talking-to-herself. Yet Annulla's isolation has another effect too—without an onstage interviewer, the audience becomes Annulla's only live witness, forcing them to be better listeners, as they wonder if it is them that Annulla is in discourse with.

Why does the presence/absence of the interviewer matter? So what if Annulla's stories are spontaneous and monologue-like utterances, rather than answers to a series of questions? So what if they are disseminated to an unknown audience rather than to the young woman Annulla has invited into her home? In a sense, it does not matter—the stories remain the same. But, as with so much docu-verbatim theatre, the interviewer's absence indicates a larger lack of transparency about the process—and the labor involved. An onstage listener would make clear how "the presence of listeners ... 'cue' or prompt certain ways of remembering the past."[29] In *Annulla*, as in *Come Out Eli* and *Twilight*, the interviewer has an implied presence but is effaced in order to foreground the testimony of the primary witness—but this has the result of also effacing the cues that the primary witness is following. Because memory and testimony are *not* singular processes. No one remembers, or testifies, in a vacuum. Though the audience can stand in for the interviewer, they are a very different kind of listening presence, because audiences are, predominantly, noninterventionist witnesses. The interviewer, on the other hand, is an active witness—who, as Sue Campbell argues, acts as "a second voice" in the memory testimony of the primary witness.[30]

The primary witness always performs for an audience, their testimony is shaped by two forms of expectation: First, the expectation of the active listening witness whose "second voice" intervenes to ask questions, to make statements, to demand something. And, second, the expectation that the witness has of their audience, that they will want something particular from them—the truth, or a certain segment of the truth—and always the expectation of a revelation previously ungiven and unheard. As Hank Greenspan writes in relation to Holocaust testimony, "The relationship between survivors and their listeners has always been focal, particularly the impact of listeners' expectations on what is actually retold."[31]

We know, then, that just as the actor onstage is projecting and performing for the audience sitting in the auditorium, the original witness performed just the same, if only for a smaller audience. This first "audience" between subject and interviewer, primary and secondary witnesses, is only ever a shadowy background to the play's performance as it happens in the theatre. The theatre audience can assume that the playwright or interviewer has verified the testimony of the witness. We can assume that the erasure of the interviewer's presence is not designed to mislead the audience but to give precedence to the onstage witness. Further, we can assume that the process of selection and curation of that testimony into a script has left out nothing important—indeed, that it has purposely included *only* what is important, an edited highlights reel as it were (what Mann calls "the poetry"[32]). With each of these assumptions, however, the audience cedes control over how *they* witness to the invisible playwright/interviewer.

The standing-in of the audience for the playwright/interviewer as the receiver of testimony is thus a slightly false substitution, given that the audience does not cue or control the primary witness's testimony. Let me challenge this for a moment—because of course one could also argue that the expectation of the testimony being given for the purpose of creating a play embeds the "presence" of the anticipated theatre audience in the process from the beginning, and therefore the audience *does* cue and control the testimony of the primary witness. However, in a play like *Annulla*, the testimony was not given with the expectation of a theatrical production. Though this is a verbatim play, it is more akin to a play like *Krapp's Last Tape*, in which the audience are voyeurs of a private moment of testimony given without an expectation of an external audience. In this case, the surveillant presence of the audience takes on a more sinister association.

When Annulla says at the end of the "interview"/play "I am so glad you could come to see me today. Really. But *it went by so fast*. Do you know, *everything has gone by so fast* . . . Thank you . . . It was so nice to meet you. Good-bye,"[33] she is speaking to Emily Mann. In some way, however, she has also now "met" the audience, in that their act of listening constitutes a kind of contact. Yet the audience is nevertheless intruding in what was a private moment, an intrusion made poignantly clear by the stage directions: "*(At a loss. Tentative, very vulnerable [. . .] Gets to door. Turns back. Very difficult to say)*: Good-bye."[34] As the real-life Annulla has died since the interview took place in 1974, this goodbye (like Krapp's discarding of the last tape) signifies more than a simple farewell. In this final passage, the audience sees Annulla, so confident and voluble during the play, finding it difficult to speak, revealing her vulnerability at being left alone. Mann—and the audience—have harvested what is valuable to them (testimony about the Second World War) and the relationship between testifier and listener-consumer is now over.

WHO IS THE AUDIENCE LISTENING TO? THE COMMODIFIED WITNESS

When the performer is present, but the subject is absent, how does their testimony get consumed? In *Twilight*, Smith ventriloquizes or, in her words, "reiterates"[35] the testimony she gathered and recorded with witnesses. She says of this process of gathering: "I was listening with an ear that was trained to hear stories for the specific purpose of repeating them with the elements of character intact."[36] Smith aims to bring these unheard voices to a wider public, to act as witness to them in order to broaden the scope of social witnessing. Her play is thus a theatrical performance *and* an intervention, using her cultural capital to enable these witnesses to be heard in the marketplace.

At the same time as giving audiences an insight into the stories of the powerful and the disenfranchised, Smith's work, like Blythe's too, raises questions of authentic voice and embodiment, selectivity, commodification, and listening as a mode of witnessing. The inherent function of mediation and remediation is to give theatre audiences something that is different from the original. By distilling a verbatim testimony down to its important points, performers bring those points into isolation and relief, enabling more effective witnessing by the audience. These acts of mediation are more than simply how the work gets made; the labor of mediation, much like in autoperformance, is part of what is being consumed. Part of Annulla and Krapp's attraction to audiences is their performance of labor in real-time—audiences enjoy watching performers *act* (i.e., work). Likewise, in *Come Out Eli*, the use of audio devices plays a major role not only in mediating testimony, but in marketing the play to an audience of consumers of technology. In Smith's work, her act of mediation is key to why her shows are so popular—in attending, audiences become consumers of a virtuoso performance of thirty-seven characters by one woman (in an approximately ninety-minute show).[37] In the theatre, the presence of Smith's body onstage and the absence of any other testifying body or voice foregrounds the performer herself as the originator of testimony and obscures the original witness, even as the audience listens to their words. Whose work is being seen, and heard, by the audience?

There is no doubt that Smith is performing significant mnemonic labor on the audience's behalf. Janelle Reinelt argues that this labor (not only in performance, but in the meticulous interviews she conducts) has established Smith as "a bearer of truth, accuracy and validity."[38] Sitting in the front row of another Smith show, *Let Me Down Easy* (2011, Berkeley Repertory Theater), I was struck by the extraordinary labor of this performer in occupying so many subject positions and inhabiting so many conflicting views (in this case, focusing on healthcare). But what I did not hear were the voices of the witnesses that Smith interviewed. Her sweat, her facial mobility, her body language—her mediation and remediation—*were* the show. At the end, I had a sense that I had come into contact with a panoply of memories and personalities, but I struggled to connect any of these to anything beyond the body of Smith or her political viewpoint.[39] Perhaps I was not listening hard enough.

Twilight thus manifests the problem at the heart of witnessing others' pain: the commodification of another's experience. The generation of both cultural prestige for the performer, economic rewards for the producers, and catharsis for the consumer is another layer to this problem. Though *Twilight* has a strong social-justice message, exposing structural racism and, importantly, allowing for a multitude of perspectives to be heard and creating a complex portrait of a city, it nevertheless translates all those factors into a successful cultural formula—the main outcomes of which are high box office takings and the identification of Smith as a leading figure in American theatre. It is her voice that is heard. The virtuoso performance of Smith, and the audio technology in *Come Out Eli*, thus not only make the labor behind mnemonic capital visible, but also perform the processes of *gatekeeping*, highlighting the higher cultural capital of these gatekeepers.

THE LABOR OF MEMORY, THE CONSUMPTION OF THE SELF

The idea that witnessing is a consuming process (or, rather, a process of consumption) is emphasized by Beckett in both *Krapp's Last Tape* and his later work *Footfalls* (1976), in which consumption is equated with an erosion, rather than confirmation, of presence.

In *Footfalls*, May is in need of witnessing. Like Krapp, she requires external proof of her internal existence, and external order to marshal her inner disorder. Though she is in intermittent dialogue with her mother (an offstage character conveyed through voice-over), she struggles to know herself. Pacing regularly nine steps, turning, and pacing another nine steps, wheeling and moving to and fro, May impels herself and the audience to notice her. But pacing is not enough to confirm her existence—as she tells her mother, she has removed the carpet so that she may "hear the feet, however faint they fall [. . .] the motion alone is not enough, I must hear the feet, however faint they fall."[40] May's is an embodied and performed testimony, and she further attests to the work of listening as a key part of witnessing, and demonstrates how difficult, how labored this performance is. May must strain to listen, using her body's repeated paced testimony to enable her "faint" performance to be heard. Yet still, despite her attempts at self-witnessing, she fades away.

May is a shadowy presence at best, lit dimly at the beginning and, as the play waxes on, even more dimly as the light fades at the end of each "scene." The final tableau shows *"No trace of* May"[41] in a moment that makes Krapp seem, retrospectively, a portrait of vigorous liveliness. May is only in her forties, yet her decreasing sense of presence, signified by the fading light, tallies with the sense that her endless witnessing—"revolving it all"—takes both a physical and metaphysical toll, to the point of the complete consumption of the self.

My assertion that May's pacing, listening, and monologue function as a form of witnessing can only be a tentative one because of the play's lack of definition—the audience never learns the subject of May's act of witnessing, only vague suggestions of a traumatic subject that she must "revolve":

V: Will you never have done? [*Pause.*] Will you never have done . . . revolving it all?
May: [*Halting.*] It?

V: It all. [*Pause.*] In your poor mind. [*Pause.*] It all. [*Pause.*] It all.
[May *resumes pacing.*]
[...]
V: Does she still sleep, it may be asked? [...] Still speak? Yes, some nights she does, when she fancies none can hear. [*Pause.*] Tells how it was. [*Pause.*] Tries to tell how it was. [*Pause.*] It all. [*Pause.*] It all.[42]

The lack of clarity as to "how it was" and what "it all" means is frustrating for an audience. The shadowy presence of May, and the equally indeterminate presence of her mother offstage, denoted as "V" by the script, give very little certainty as to what is being seen, what is being heard, and what is being witnessed. Indeed, when the mother recounts that May only speaks when "she fancies none can hear," and that failure ("tries to tell") is embedded in her testimony, it seems as if Beckett has created a play that resists witnessing. And yet *something* has happened, something that requires that it be testified to and, as a result, deserves to be witnessed. As with Krapp, the audience plays a voyeuristic role whereby their presence validates what is being performed onstage, and yet part of what they are witnessing (and validating) is the total isolation, the complete aloneness, and rejection of external witness by the onstage figure.

So what is being consumed and how fully is May actually consumable? In not telling her story fully, but instead turning her act of memory into a fixed ritual in which she is her own audience, May becomes, like Krapp, both producer and consumer. And, again, through these processes, over time May has *commodified herself* as a persona embodying her own pain. Beckett's depressing finale—a space without a presence for the audience to witness—suggests the danger of this process of commodification, whereby the self cannot exist outside the witness persona, and is thus entirely consumed.

VIOLENCE AS A KIND OF WITNESS

Footfalls demonstrates how difficult it is to find both language and actions suitable to fully witness "it all." And so we need to talk about another kind of witnessing—where violence takes the place of language. In *Twilight*, Smith's witnesses can be roughly grouped into two general categories: people who see the Los Angeles riots as a moment for speaking out, and people who decry the violence done (who see the riots as a kind of silencing of civilized values), as embodied by two witnesses: Paul Parker, chairperson of the "Free the La Four Plus" Defense committee, and Maxine Waters, Democratic congresswoman from California.

Paul Parker:
We spoke out on April 29.
Hoo (*real pleasure*),
it was flavorful,
it was juicy.
It was, uh,
it was good for the soul[43]

Maxine Waters:
The fact of the matter is,
whether we like it or not,
riot
is the voice of the unheard.[44]

Parker and Waters, representing the first category of witness, acknowledge the violence and injustice of the riots (both the violence and the police reaction), but nevertheless also see something "juicy" in them happening, because of the possibilities for speaking out the violence opened up. This kind of speaking out forces an audience to listen—that is its value. The second category of witness (the police; those whose property was vandalized) instead see the riots as an assault on civil order. Which group a person belongs to is often, though not necessarily, determined by whether that person has previously experienced (or was aware of) police brutality or racism. Both groups see violence as a substitute for talking.

Given this, it is troubling that Smith ends the play by emphasizing that for most people affected by the riots (a cohort not restricted to the citizens of LA by any means) the violence—physical and social—is not over. The final scene of *Twilight* stages the testimony of Twilight Bey, an organizer of the truce between rival LA gangs (and a gang member himself). Twilight Bey testifies about the "limbo" of twilight, "that time / between day and night" and makes the link between light and "wisdom," suggesting that the condition of being in LA is to be caught between ignorance and wisdom.[45] The final lines of *Twilight* do not inspire confidence as to how it will work out:

Twilight Bey:
When I'm in my own neighborhood, I'm driving through and I
see the living dead, as we call them,
the base heads,
the people who are so addicted on crack,
if they need a hit they be up all night doin' whatever they have to do
to make the money to get the hit.

It's like getting' a total dose
of what goes on in the daytime creates at night.[46]

Smith does not end the play with an optimistic sense that people will listen to each other as a route to resolving police and gang violence. Instead, Twilight Bey's testimony returns the audience to the "living dead" and the ongoing structural crisis of drug addiction, reading the impact of "crack" as the cause of the limbo that affects not only those addicts who "be up all night" but the entire city. This is a crisis not caused by drugs, but by being "unheard," by having no form of capital whatsoever.

How do we listen to violence? Smith suggests two responses, framed as different kinds of musealization of the riots. Reginald Denny is a white truck driver who was beaten and severely injured during the riots. This grievous assault was, like the police assault on Rodney King, filmed and broadcast. His testimony is relatively dispassionate; though we might expect it to be driven by anger, it is not. Denny explains that after the attack he received "notes and ... letters from faraway places" wishing him "love and compassion."[47] He plans to create a room in his house, a museum of these happy memories, "where a person will walk in / and just have a good old time in there."[48]

Denny's urge to "frame" and "place" these memories, creating a compassionate memorial, contrasts strikingly with Paul Parker's response, which is to "set aside" in his home "one room.... It's gonna be my No Justice No Peace room."[49] Parker's intention to create a memorial that he can show his sons, based on his articles and clippings about his fight for justice for his brother and the other men accused of beating Reginald Denny, points not only to their oppositional status, but also to the different role of memory in his life than Denny's. For Parker, memory is the material for a future-oriented performance of witnessing. For Denny, his memorial will enable him to reflect on the help and compassion he received, encouraging a more past-oriented act of witness. For Parker, the issues that the riots brought up are still "live" events, for Denny they are over. Both men commodify memory and testimony but with completely different messages for audiences to consume. This demonstrates that how we listen to the past, and what we choose to amplify, depends entirely on whether we access the memory marketplace with significant cultural capital (which Denny has because of having been the victim of violence that was broadcast) or as still disenfranchised (Parker). Moreover, we can also read these differences as illustrating distinct kinds of production and consumption—Denny and Parker both become producers themselves, an empowering role in which they take control of their own testimony and witness. Denny's more positive memorial will be a closed narrative enabling cathartic consumption; in contrast, Parker's dissatisfaction drives him to engage others as citizen-consumers.

"CAN'T I GET IT"

Is witnessing a mandatory performance? May's laborious and melancholy ritual suggests so, but there are ways of resisting the demand of commodification. The most striking interview in Blythe's *Come Out Eli* is with Eli's hostage, Mr. Okere. Okere is initially reluctant to testify and demands sexual favors in return for his story. Blythe foregrounds her role as producer, and the difficulty of engaging with a reluctant witness, in the play's opening scene, a phone conversation titled "Request":

> *Alecky—Blonde, middle class, thirty. Shocked and amused but tries to remain polite and business like.*
>
> Oh hello Mr Okere? . . . You are very obviously a special case which is why I'm so keen to talk to you but erm we don't have any money and like I said yesterday, I'm not, I'm not wi- willing to (*Beat*) NO! That, it's a no, I just don't—I'm not gonna, you know I'm desperate to get an interview with you but I am not that desperate.[50]

Despite Mr. Okere's offensiveness, Blythe refuses to give up, and the play stages two more phone conversations with him. Eventually Blythe is successful and scene sixty-two, "Nice to Meet You," depicts their meeting in person (their in-person conversation is also continued in two further scenes: "Undercover" and "The Sex Thing"). Including herself as a "character" in six scenes places Blythe in the drama, as part of the story, and not simply an invisible gatekeeper of others' testimony. It shows us some of the labor behind eliciting testimony, and it also suggests the personal impact of being asked, repeatedly, to do something you do not want to do—whether that is to have sex or to give testimony. The performances of reluctance and compulsion around witnessing also, of course, highlight Okere's understanding of the value of his accidental cultural and symbolic capital.

In the end, Blythe pays Okere fifty pounds for his testimony. During the interview (held in a pub), Okere (named as Hostage in the script) gives sometimes surprising testimony:

> *Hostage—Strong Nigerian accent. Not sexually threatening at all in the flesh. Enjoys the chance to talk to someone. Stutters throughout (more than can be put onto paper) trying to find the right English.*
>
> **Hostage:** [. . .] he told me to come in there to stay with him in the room—if I'm feelin a bit lonely or something like that. They-

Alecky: Did you not want to leave, did you want to leave?

Hostage: Er, I wasn't... from that second day third day it was all good, good, good, the situation was good, yeah, you know—he hasn't been getting stressed by them you know—it was just as, business as usual, normal [...]

Alecky: [...] So for the first couple of days you were kind of just hanging out?

Hostage: Yeah, yeah.

Alecky: Not—thinking it would pass / and

Hostage: /Yeah.

Alecky: Maybe they would, maybe Eli would give himself up?

Hostage: Yeah, yeah.

Alecky: That's what you were thinking?

Hostage: Yeah [...] he's not like my enemy.

Alecky: (*chewing*) In the newspaper article it says that he asked to have, he said he'd come out if he got to sleep with one of the police women. Is that right?

Hostage: Yeah that's right. Mmmm hmmm, Heather.[51]

The conversation between Blythe and Okere demonstrates the extent to which the interviewer shapes the witness's testimony, with the strong sense that she is providing the terms that he stutters to find. The sexual request that Eli makes about the policewoman, Heather, seems surprisingly like the request that Okere himself made to Blythe, suggesting an affinity between Okere and Eli (perhaps, after all, giving the audience an insight into Eli).

In the play's penultimate scene, "Tannoy," Blythe includes Hong, the owner of a Vietnamese carryout restaurant, who witnessed the siege and her tearful "*Crying*" response to Eli's death. This might have been a cathartic or universalizing ending to the play. Yet Blythe chooses not to end with this moment of emotion, but instead to end by returning to her interview with Okere. In this finale, Okere once more raises "the sex thing," saying:

Hostage: I wouldn't mind ya know (*Beat*) having it or something. But I—I—I know you are a little bit hesitant.

...

Alecky: I'm more than hesitant. (*Firm but can't help smiling at his persistence*) I'm not gonna do it with you![52]

Beginning and ending the play with her own boundaries as to what she is prepared to do to elicit testimony is a strong move on Blythe's part, allowing the audience to see her process, and to witness her own "*persistence*." The scenes with Okere, however, concentrate more on his requests for sex than on his testimony about Eli. This focus on Okere's repeated requests, "can't I get it,"[53] constructs him as an unreasonable witness. The real impact, of course, is that in harassing Blythe, Okere loses his victimhood capital. These interactions then shift the audience's focus of witnessing from the ostensible subject of the play (the hostage-taking) to the theatre maker's risk-taking in making work about violence.

While this is illuminating in making visible Blythe's emotional, as well as intellectual and theatrical, labor, I also want to note the process of resistance here: Okere's unreasonableness makes him hard to commodify (again, a feature typical of complex victims). Perhaps one of the most salient features of Okere's repeated petitions for sex is that, while it does not put him in a position of power exactly, it denotes his refusal to become a commodity for consumption—instead, he projects that role onto Blythe. That an audience will most likely not like him as a result is a salutary illustration of the exploitative relationship between commodity and consumer.

Rather than using the theatrical platform to raise the *social* capital of the victim in the marketplace, Blythe uses Okere's demands to show that the witness will *always* want something in return (what is Annulla testifying for, if not the continued promise of sympathetic listening?). Yet there is a further purpose here too—in prioritizing Okere's reluctant and obnoxious testimony, Blythe insists that the unlikeable, or unsympathetic, witness should also be listened to and witnessed. *Cultural* capital is not dependent on likeability.

Witnessing often involves audiences in uncomfortable dynamics, and this is particularly acute at the play's ending, as the labor of witnessing switches from the stage to the auditorium—whether the audience is acting as witnesses to a poignant farewell by Annulla, the limbo of Twilight Bey, the eradication of May onstage, the frozen stare of Krapp, or the sexual harassment of Blythe. What cues do these moments leave the audience to follow? How do audiences witness them adequately? What memories do they create in the audience? Though very different, each of these endings leaves the audience without an easy "message" to remediate even when (or perhaps most when) they have been actively listening. The performance of labor in these plays, therefore, does not result in either an easily consumable message or, indeed, easily consumable mnemonic capital.

EMBODIMENT AND THE RESISTANCE OF COMMODIFICATION

In *Annulla*, Mann recalls her grandmother's resistance to the challenges of witnessing. Speaking of Mann's desire to visit Poland, her grandmother asks accusingly: "Why do you want to go there? They killed us there."[54] Yet Mann undertakes the journey, though she is frustrated and cannot find what she is looking for: "We got to the town—followed the map—we found the store, but it wasn't a store anymore. The synagogue had been destroyed, never rebuilt. There was no Jewish graveyard. We went to the town hall and asked for the family records. We were told that there was no record of any of the names we asked for. There were no records. No trace. Nothing."[55] Like Beckett, despite the elusiveness of traces and meaning, Mann insists on the necessity for characters to persist in the labor of creating their own records, their own acts of witnessing. Perhaps this is the only cue that the audience can take for their own acts of witnessing after the lights have gone up.

I do not want to end, however, by suggesting that witnessing is impossible. Instead, I want to pause a moment and think about how there can be grace to withholding, and acceptance in silence. In Beckett's *Come and Go* (1965) three female characters—Ru, Vi, and Flo—meet again after many years and exchange confidences. At first it seems as if this will be another play of failure, when Vi asks a question and it is refused:

Vi: When did we three last meet?
Ru: Let us not speak.
[*Silence.*
Exit VI right.
Silence.][56]

Not only is Vi's question shut down, but Ru's response seems to force Vi from the stage. In her absence, however, Ru and Flo do speak, as Flo whispers a secret observation about Vi to Ru, who *"Appalled"* exclaims "Oh!"[57] Vi then returns and resumes sitting with Flo and Ru. This pattern is repeated until each of the women has left the stage, been whispered about, and returned. Beckett withholds knowledge here, too—the audience never learns the meaning of the whispered observations, just as each of the offstage women are also in the dark about what has been said.

When "we three" are sitting together again, Vi asks once more "May we not speak of the old days? . . . Of what came after?" only to be greeted with "*Silence.*"[58] But this time she does not leave the stage, countering instead with a different proposition: "Shall we hold hands in the old way?" and *"After a moment they join hands."*[59] The women's interwoven and clasped hands, their contorted bodies, create a sense of togetherness and renewal, as Flo declares "I can feel the rings." What "rings" these are is unclear—in notes to the play, Beckett specifies that no "rings [are] apparent"[60]—but perhaps it is the connectivity of decades of friendship since childhood that Flo refers to, and the act of feeling witnessing through embodied memory rather than verbal testimony. Though much meaning is unavailable to the audience, and though there is a spectral quality to the women (not least in their echoes of *Macbeth*'s witches), this does not seem to me to be a haunting or failed performance of witness and memory. On the contrary, in *Come and Go* the audience both listens to, and *sees*, a requited request for witnessing "the old way." Though Beckett is far from being a didactic playwright, perhaps the audience can nonetheless learn through *Come and Go* that witnessing is available to them in quiet, even silent, moments, in which they "speak" and "listen" through gentle action and reaction. Witnessing does not have to involve violence, tears, or pain—not always.

Beckett's refusal to share with the audience what the women whisper about, or what the final meaning of "rings" might be, is more than a negotiation of presence and absence, and more than a desire to frustrate the audience's quest for answers. Instead, it seems to me to acknowledge the desires of witnesses for completeness—to know everything—and yet to also insist that some experiences and knowledge remain beyond our remit. In depicting characters across his plays who perform their pain for an audience, Beckett stages the human need to witness and be witnessed. This work also produces an awareness of the audience's surveillant role, in which they voyeuristically exploit the onstage persona's vulnerability for their own catharsis. But in refusing to make everything clear, in refusing to allow the audience to hear "it all," Beckett goes further than Mann, Smith, and Blythe, who each only hint at the untold story beyond the script. Instead, Beckett's work creates spaces within which witnessing failures (and failing at witnessing) act to resist the neoliberal impulse to commodify everything, including painful experience. Though the rituals of Beckett's plays suggest the existence of characters not as full people, but rather as a series of commodified personas, in the end, his work subverts the marketplace demand that "it all" be consumable.

NOTES

1. Anna Deavere Smith, *Twilight Los Angeles, 1992: On the Road: A Search for American Character* (New York: Anchor, 1994), 3.
2. Smith, *Twilight*, 2
3. Smith, *Twilight*, 15.
4. Nancy Tuana, "The Speculum of Ignorance: The Women's Health Movement and Epistemologies of Ignorance," *Hypatia* 21, no. 3 (2006): 1–19, see esp. 11.
5. Paul Ricoeur, *Memory, History, Forgetting*, trans. Kathleen Blamey and David Pellauer (Chicago: University of Chicago Press, 2004), 166.
6. Mann is also well known for her documentary plays about public trials, and her work is thus pioneering in the docu-verbatim field. See Carol Martin,

"In Defense of Democracy: Celebrating Emily Mann," *Women & Performance: A Journal of Feminist Theory* 14, no. 2 (2005): 111–16.

7. See Emilie Pine, "Theatre-as-Memory and as Witness: Active Spectatorship in *The Walworth Farce, The Blue Boy* and *Laundry*," in *Breac: A Digital Journal of Irish Studies*, ed. Shaun Richards (July 10, 2014), https://breac.nd.edu/articles/theatre-as-memory-and-as-witness-active-spectatorship-in-the-walworth-farce-the-blue-boy-and-laundry/.

8. Alecky Blythe, "Introduction to *Come Out Eli*," in *The Methuen Drama Anthology of Testimonial Plays*, ed. Alison Forsyth (London: Bloomsbury, 2014), 125.

9. Alison Forsyth, "Alecky Blythe Interviewed by Alison Forsyth," in *The Methuen Drama Anthology of Testimonial Plays*, 120.

10. Everett C. Frost, "Audio Prosthetics and the Problems of a Radio Production of Samuel Beckett's *Krapp's Last Tape*," *Journal of Beckett Studies* 15, nos. 1–2 (2005): 1–20, see esp. 9.

11. Blythe, *Come Out Eli*, in *The Methuen Drama Anthology of Testimonial Plays*, 143.

12. Blythe, *Come Out Eli*, 137.

13. Blythe, *Come Out Eli*, 169.

14. Blythe, *Come Out Eli*, 137.

15. See Anna Reading, "Seeing Red: A political economy of digital memory," *Media, Culture & Society* 36 no. 6 (2014): 748–60 for a discussion of the ways that globalized cultures of technology erase the labor of construction.

16. Robert Reginio, "Samuel Beckett, the Archive, and the Problem of History," in *Samuel Beckett: History, Memory, Archive*, ed. Seán Kennedy and Katherine Weiss (Basingstoke: Palgrave Macmillan, 2009), 111–28, see esp. 111.

17. Samuel Beckett, *Krapp's Last Tape* in *Samuel Beckett: The Complete Dramatic Works* (London: Faber, 1986), 217.

18. Beckett, *Krapp's Last Tape*, 220.

19. Beckett, *Krapp's Last Tape*, 220.

20. Beckett, *Krapp's Last Tape*, 221, 223.

21. Beckett, *Krapp's Last Tape*, 223.

22. Beckett, *Krapp's Last Tape*, 217.

23. Reginio, "Samuel Beckett," 112.

24. Beckett, *Krapp's Last Tape*, 218.

25. Beckett, *Krapp's Last Tape*, 222.

26. Emily Mann, *Annulla (An Autobiography)*, in *Testimonies: Four Plays* (New York: Theatre Communications Group, 1997), 10.

27. Mann, *Annulla*, 24.

28. The young woman's voice, like Krapp's voice, is not recorded, thereby retaining a sense of spontaneity, the idea that her words are freshly performed in the moment.

29. Sue Campbell, "The Second Voice," *Memory Studies* 1, no. 1 (2008): 41–48, see esp. 42.

30. Campbell, "The Second Voice," 42.

31. Hank Greenspan, "Listening to Holocaust Survivors: Interpreting a Repeated Story," *Shofar: An Interdisciplinary Journal of Jewish Studies* 17, no. 4 (1999): 83–88, see esp. 83.

32. "Emily Mann: In Conversation," an open conversation with the audience at the ATHE Conference, July 29, 1999, *Theatre Topics* 10, no. 1 (2000): 1–16, see esp. 3.

33. Mann, *Annulla*, 30.

34. Mann, *Annulla*, 30.

35. Smith, *Twilight*, xxiv.

36. Smith, *Twilight*, xxiv.

37. As Janelle Reinelt writes in "Performing Race: Anna Deavere Smith's *Fires in the Mirror*," *Modern Drama* 39 no. 4 (1996): 609–17, see esp. 610; Smith has "celebrity" status.

38. Reinelt, "Performing Race," 611.

39. Reinelt argues that Smith's persona "ghosts" the show, but that she acts as a bridge to facilitate the portrayal of others' voices. Reinelt, "Performing Race," 615.

40. Samuel Beckett, *Footfalls* in *Samuel Beckett: The Complete Dramatic Works* (London: Faber, 1986), 401.

41. Beckett, *Footfalls*, 403.

42. Beckett, *Footfalls*, 400–1.

43. Smith, *Twilight*, 174.

44. Smith, *Twilight*, 162.

45. Smith, *Twilight*, 254.

46. Smith, *Twilight*, 256.

47. Smith, *Twilight*, 111.

48. Smith, *Twilight*, 111.

49. Smith, *Twilight*, 177.

50. Blythe, *Come Out Eli*, 130.

51. Blythe, *Come Out Eli*, 163–64.

52. Blythe, *Come Out Eli*, 171.

53. Blythe, *Come Out Eli*, 171.

54. Mann, *Annulla*, 13.

55. Mann, *Annulla*, 27–28.

56. Samuel Beckett, *Come and Go* in *Samuel Beckett: The Complete Dramatic Works* (London: Faber, 1986), 354.

57. Beckett, *Come and Go*, 354.

58. Beckett, *Come and Go*, 355.

59. Beckett, *Come and Go*, 355.

60. Beckett, *Come and Go*, 356.

FIVE

CONSUMERS OR WITNESSES?
Site-Specific Performance

I wait in the foyer downstairs. There is one other person sitting on the bench, and we exchange smiles. We sit facing a door. This is the right place? The door opens, the other person is summoned. I sit alone. Soon the door opens for me.

I follow the woman upstairs. At the top she half turns, holds her fingers to her lips. Quiet. She puts her hand on the doorknob, pulls the door open.

The room is dark, I wait for my eyes to adjust. She takes my hand, leads me further into the room. Now I can see more. There is a tall man by the shuttered window. He holds a long mirror, one end balanced on his feet, the other held between his hands, his head bent low towards it. I notice that he is biting the top of the mirror. He turns, slowly, shuffling his feet and the mirror to face me. She leads me further into the room. He is still turning. I see myself in the mirror, the crack of light from between the shutters illuminating us in slices. She leads me further into the room. We are at the far end now, he is behind us.

A girl sits at a desk. "Boat or plane?" she asks. I say "Boat." She takes a piece of printed paper and folds it, origami-style, into a boat. She gives it to me. I am led from the room.[1]

This is *Proximity Mouth* (Ireland, 2014), a site-responsive performance piece devised by artist Dominic Thorpe. The description of the performance is strange because the experience was strange—it is up to the spectator to connect the disparate elements (performers, mirror, space, paper, dark and light) and to devise for themselves a meaning. That meaning emerges from both the performance and its context. In some ways, the frame of interpretation is already extant. The performance is staged in Dublin Castle, once the seat of British colonial government in Ireland. The particular room that I entered was not a neutral background set randomly selected by Thorpe: this was the former Children's Court that, after national independence in 1922, heard cases brought against children by social workers, truancy officers, or the police. These children were targeted for minor social problems, the largest of which was poverty; if sentenced, they were sent to industrial or reform schools (a system of residential institutions funded and overseen by the Irish State and staffed and run by the Catholic Church). Thorpe's work has repeatedly responded to this history, most notably in *Redress State* (2010) an endurance performance piece in reaction to the 2009 Ryan Report on institutional abuse in industrial schools. So, the setting of *Proximity Mouth* is resonant.

Though the last residential school for children in Ireland closed in the 1990s, the institutional story of Ireland is not over. The performer who leads me by the hand into and around and out of the room is a woman living in a direct provision (DP) center, a network of institutions where asylum seekers are forced to live under inhumane conditions (such as multioccupancy rooms, and the outlawing of cooking), enduring years while waiting for their asylum applications to be decided upon. The girl at the table, the expert in origami, folds me a boat or a plane, the two modes of refugee travel; the paper she uses is printed with a list of DP centers across Ireland. She is a child who has grown up living in the DP system. Institutionalization still occurs, structural callousness still marks Irish society. Thorpe holds up a mirror, hoping for us to reflect on this. We are in the dark, but being led to knowledge by those who are currently being punished by this system.

I LIKE SITE-SPECIFIC THEATRE

I like theatre because it makes us do things—watch, listen, laugh, cry, applaud. I like site-specific and site-responsive theatre because it adds another layer. It moves us—literally, as well as emotionally, intellectually. In taking audiences to nontheatre sites and spaces, this mode of performance pushes us to consider the intersections between memory and place. Site-specific theatre, moreover, is (like autoperformance) a mode of *immersive* performance that jolts us out of comfortable assumptions about the divisions between art and reality, and forces a reconsideration of the roles of witness and performer—who is performing, and creating, the act of witness? And I like it because it troubles the relationship between producer and consumer. I'm not alone in this—site-specific theatre is, as Joanne Tompkins argues, "no longer an alternative or fringe genre," and its rise in commercial viability is a sign of the more general "increasing diversity in art forms."[2] We might also argue that it is a response to increasing consumer demand for experiential practices as well as for a diversification of the audience's roles as spectators.

This chapter considers site-specific theatre of two varieties: interactive and guided performance, and audio-guided (also known as self-guided while listening to audio) performance. In discussing the work of Thorpe, ANU Productions, and Kabosh Theatre in Ireland, and the audio productions *And While London Burns* and *Echoing Yafa* in London and Tel Aviv, respectively, this chapter engages with various locations and forms of performance. There are significant distinctions between these experiences, but across all of them I consider how the performances make visible the layers of memory within an urban space, how labor and capital emerge in new ways for audiences who perform actual, and not just emotional (seated), labor, and how the audience is changed (or not) by coming into contact with these mnemonic landscapes. Necessarily, this chapter will focus on my personal experience (in many cases, there is no script for me to quote or return to for verification) and will also reference performances that are unrepeatable. The ephemerality of this form will therefore be a further consideration for how site-specific performance enacts and illuminates memory only briefly or temporarily, leaving barely any trace. Does the unrepeatability—the foreclosure of future consumption—also mean this performance form resists commodification? In one way, the immersive or involved quality of site-specific work, which relies on an active audience member as a coproducer of meaning, suggests a form that works to enlist audiences as witnesses, thereby resisting the pull of consumerism and commodification. This has to be measured, however, against the fact that the co-option of audience labor turns consumers into "prosumers," coproducers not only of meaning but of the theatrical product. As Jen Harvie argues, the blurring of lines between work and culture might "compel audiences to reflect critically on social relations," but simply casting the audience as performers is not always "entirely beneficial."[3] As discussed in the chapter's conclusion, the prosumer has a particular relationship to the product, and the construction of shows around an active audience-performer may actually obscure social relations by prioritizing their experiential returns on their investment.

We Define Ourselves Spatially

We define ourselves by the spaces we are comfortable entering, and that we assume, imagine, or enact as accessible to us. We also define ourselves by the kinds of spaces we want to go to. As we have seen with the recent rise in heritage tourism to dark sites, painful memory attaches to particular locations, which become destinations that generate both economic capital for the sites and social capital for the visitors.[4] Though Dublin Castle has a difficult history related to Ireland's colonial past, it is not a space that would seem to qualify for trauma tourism. Indeed, it is one space that I regularly enter—I walk through the grounds as a shortcut between St. Patrick's Cathedral and Dublin city center, the café has a lovely balcony, the museum has a wonderful permanent collection of Asian art. Many years ago I had done a tour of the castle, paying a small fee to be given a brief history of its development as a hub of power. It all seemed to apply to a long-distant world. But during the performance of *Proximity Mouth*, I went somewhere I had never been before—into an interior room with a very specific history of administering structural and ideological cruelty against children. I also came into contact with people I had never met before, holding hands with my guide and talking to the girl who made me a boat. I was walking around this room, but subject to how they wanted me to use the space. It felt current.

The interactive dimension that is key to "live" site-specific performance requires that the spectator become not just visible but an actor in the immersive drama. Likewise, the space for site-specific requires attention, as the location shapes the performance's actions and meanings. As Louise Lowe and Una Kavanagh argue, site-specific work forces the audience "to be present."[5] Simply put, site-specific work creates new connections between bodies, spaces, and narratives. These connections are often not easy, involving bodily and mental recalibrations of norms and expectations. The effort involved in making the connections—the process of site-specific work—is, I will argue, its primary purpose—the witnessing that represents *surplus* value in other plays is an *integral* value of the site-specific product.

Thorpe's work is typical of how site-specific work brings us into spaces we would not normally enter or that we do not feel comfortable entering. In the end, the Children's Court is a banal space—a long rectangular room with tall windows along one side, and a door set into each of the walls. There is no judge's seat, there are no benches for "the accused." It is plushly carpeted. It does not feel like a space of trauma, and there are no visible traces of its bureaucratic history. This is how state violence disguises itself. Only upon being told its history did I feel curious about it as a location. In this way, the setting of *Proximity Mouth* illustrates how the performance brings meaning to the space, as well as vice versa. As Mike Pearson puts it, site-specific work "recontextualises ... sites."[6] The interior of Dublin Castle, though it was not an everyday space I encountered, felt relatively normal. This further suggests the ways that site-specific work leads spectators in "normal" activities—walking, listening, talking, watching—but also queers them so that we notice them anew. In *Proximity Mouth*, the action of taking another's hand, of watching a man hold a mirror, and of a girl doing origami became heightened and notable by being staged for an audience. Likewise, the space became less a backdrop and more a performance of memory in its own right, given the meaning the production derived from the location's invisible layers of state history. As Charlotte McIvor argues, site-specific work has the potential to perform "the ethics of memory as a lived experience of the present."[7]

Making strange is a vital part of site-specific work, which has the double impact of removing the security of the division between stage and audience, and of including everything within the frame of the staging. Unintended aspects feed into our experience—the fact that it was a sunny day when I saw *Proximity Mouth* made walking into and out of the darkened building seem more atmospheric, and made the light that glinted through the shutters seem more penetrating. The setting of the castle is a quiet space, apart from the city's main thoroughfares, and this makes attending the show feel like a serious undertaking. The performance was brief and I blinked as I left the building, reentering the everyday. I think about that room, about its historical resonances, every time I pass through the castle. The performance has changed the space for me.

In this chapter, I will think through the "rules" of site-specific work, how site-specific work creates witnesses of consumers, how it challenges boundaries between self and other, and how it both exploits and partakes in the cultural trend for commodifying pain in order to make that trend visible and, precisely through its visibility, deconstruct it.

PART ONE: THIS IS NOT GOING TO BE EASY

The process of attending an ANU Productions show is not easy. Over the past decade, ANU Productions has developed a site-specific, memory-led dramaturgy across multiple shows that are unified by the concern for hidden or suppressed gender and class histories in Ireland and the UK. This chapter considers several plays from the Dublin Monto Cycle (a four-part cycle of plays about the Monto district in Dublin), including *Worlds End Lane*, 2010; *Laundry*, 2011; *Boys of Foley Street*, 2012; *Vardo*, 2014), as well as *Thirteen* (2013) and *Sunder* (2016).[8] The first ANU show I saw was *Laundry*, the second play of the Monto Cycle, set in a former Magdalen Laundry and Good Shepherd Convent on Sean McDermott Street (formerly Gloucester Street) in the north inner-city area of Dublin. *The Boys of Foley Street* was set nearby in multiple locations around Foley Street (formerly Monto Street), a street that has been a byword for social deprivation for a century, since the Monto was the setting of Dublin's red-light district. In *Vardo*, spectators traversed the same streets again. In *Thirteen*, the locations were more varied, as thirteen linked performances were produced across the city, with the main locations concentrated on the northern side of the city (historically the part of the capital with the highest concentration of social deprivation and marginalization). And in *Sunder* the action again occurred on the north side of the city, in the streets where the 1916 Easter Rising ended.

This list of locations will enable you to find these places on the map, but they do not give much insight into the affective geography of ANU's settings. These are parts of the city in which many spectators will find themselves uncomfortable—indeed, the plays are often staged in locations where one would not usually linger: derelict council apartments, blind alleys, and public parks littered with cans and needles. Miriam Haughton calls these "alien places" that create "shell-shock" in the viewer.[9] It doesn't sound that great a destination, does it? But then part of my purpose in buying a ticket for an ANU show is exactly this—to be brought to places that I usually do not find myself in, either because of my discomfort or because they are otherwise inaccessible to me. I become a tourist in my own city, a class tourist, a consumer of other citizens' pain. But ANU knows this—and so they challenge the process of consumption. In *Laundry*, the moment the spectator enters the convent, the forbiddingly heavy door is closed behind them, blocking off any exit. In *Vardo*, you are implicated in sex trafficking. In *Boys of Foley Street*, one scene requires you as spectator to follow two actors down a blind alley. These are not easy scenes to consume, not just because they require you to think about another's pain, but also because they require you to act.

In staging work in areas of the city that are socially deprived and marginalized—both economically and historically—ANU is very deliberately intervening in social, theatrical, and historical narratives, all of which suggest that this part of the city is a no-go space, or at most a space that pedestrians should move through without stopping. But stopping, watching, and interacting are exactly what is required by these shows because these are the actions required not only to make theatre happen, but also to make social justice happen. Site-specific work like this forces spectators to consider what are "safe" spaces, what assumptions underlie their feeling of discomfort, how they normally consume images and stories of social disenfranchisement, and whether there is real danger or just projected danger in a particular location. Since we were given warnings by the cast not to have our cell phones visible (as we walked down the locally nicknamed "iPhone alley" due to the number of thefts), there was a level of risk involved. But the larger risk of perceived moral danger, a perception that still sees activities such as prostitution and poverty as a kind of contagious social dirt[10]—this perception is entirely debunked.

In the Laundry

I enter the door of the convent and am channeled into a waiting room, it is small and the paint is peeling from the walls. I watch as a tall man cradles a crying woman, then leaves her there sobbing. I say "I watch" but I am closer than that suggests—they brush past me as they move, I can hear them breathe, I back away as far into the corner as I can. This is the first time I have encountered site-specific theatre where I am the lone audience member. A woman comes to the door and brings me into a larger hallway. She takes record cards from an overflowing filing cabinet and recites women's names, asking me to remember them. I am led into a room where a woman is bathing in one of those old-fashioned stand-alone tin baths. The water is cloudy, it looks cold. Another woman sits on a high stool overlooking the scene. I stand watching as the bathing woman gets out of the water. She picks up a bandage and starts to wrap it around her breasts, she asks me, mutely, to hold one end, to help her wrap herself. Further scenes I encounter include a woman who holds my hand and tells me about her husband, a woman who dances with me in a confessional box, and a group of women beating themselves while reciting articles from the UN Convention of Human Rights. The rooms I move through are decrepit, the scenes I encounter are intense. Walking through one corridor I see piles of broken children's high chairs, testament to the women's absent children. In the last convent-scene, I meet a woman who asks me to help her escape. I take the bundle of sheets she thrusts at me and follow her, retracing my route back through the building, to the front door, and out. There is a waiting taxi, she pushes me toward it, but runs off in another direction. The taxi driver asks me if I know her and to my shame I say, "no, not really." He drives me around the block, narrating some of the history of the area and the laundry, and drops me at a modern launderette. I am put to work ironing, and I listen to a conversation as a man describes how his mother was incarcerated in the laundry. The show ends.

During the research and devising processes for *Laundry*, ANU talked to local residents about the history of the building, many of whom had had no idea of the (very recent) history of the convent and laundry. As Director Louise Lowe reports, people had not wanted to know what was behind the walls. The Ghanaian artist El Anatsui says: "Walls are meant—by the people who build them—to either hide something or sequester something or to protect something. In all cases they have to block the view. And I think that when the view is blocked, the tendency is for the human imagination to take over and leap over that thing, and start imagining things at the other side of it.... I felt that really walls, rather than conceal things, were constructs which help reveal things."[11]

As the case of the local reaction to making theatre in the Sean McDermott Street laundry demonstrates, human imagination does not always take a leap over boundaries, indeed I would generalize from this local scenario to argue that in Ireland imagination has often historically (and currently) stopped at walls. Irish history is embedded with scandals of people not looking, not noticing, not intervening, particularly when it comes to institutional abuse.[12] This does not mean that the abuse was not known about, but that that knowledge did not translate into action—this is again the distinction between, and problem with, passive versus active spectatorship. Observation is a key requirement for ethical behavior, but it is not in itself ethical in situations where observation is divorced from action.

Site-specific theatre productions like *Laundry* aim to invert that, exploiting curiosity as the driver of shows that force you to act. As will be discussed below, ANU raises many ethical questions about the norms of passive consuming. There is a point at which in site-specific work, particularly in more extreme moments, when the forced exposure of the spectator to events and performances she or he would normally avoid, or that would normally be inaccessible to him or her, are too direct. As Brian Singleton argues, spectators can be deeply uncomfortable when asked to participate and perform roles that violate their own personal boundaries.[13] There is always the risk, then, of shutting down exactly the processes of curiosity and exploration that these productions aim to provoke in the spectator. We do not always want to be confronted by what McIvor terms "the seething presence of the past" with all the shame that connotes.[14]

I was deeply affected by seeing *Laundry*. Though I was aware of this history, the production gave me some insight into the bodily experience of the total institution. How far does this insight go? Attending site-specific theatrical productions is about attaining experience and extending the witnessing of the past beyond the original witness's claim, so that the audience member can also say "I was there." What we were there for, however, needs further scrutiny. As spectators who not only see, but touch and talk to the performers, we believe that we are party to a performance of radical intimacy. In crossing boundaries of personal space, in evoking a sense of danger (both for the performer and the spectator), the site-specific performance seems to change the rules.

And yet the rules are still the same as ever—the memory performance is, as in any traditional stage-bound play, enacted by actors within a fictional frame (albeit within a "real" location). And so it is important to note that the experience derived from witnessing these shows is always necessarily a secondary form of witnessing, even as it feels as if we are transformed into primary witnesses; as Singleton argues, "at times the distinction between reality and performance was blurred to the point of spectators not knowing what was real or performative. It was a strategy that awakened in spectators a heightened sense of consciousness."[15] Because of the veracity and strangeness of these performances of memory, the spectator—especially in remediating it to others after the show—may be justified in mistaking what was experienced for the "real" thing. And, indeed, the theatrical experience is a very real and firsthand experience. But the memory must always remain at a distance, and we do well to keep that distinction in sight.

On Foley Street

In *Boys of Foley Street*,[16] the spectator is solo, illustrating again how ANU removes the division between actor and spectator. Without the security of a fellow spectator, bravery vanishes ("no, not really") along with the assurance that this is fictional. When two male actors harangued me as I hesitated to walk down an alley I felt the impact of the blurring of real and fictional. These men were not careful of my sensibilities, they were tall and big and following them down the blind alley went against every instinct I have honed over years of living in the inner city. But I went down the alley nonetheless. Unpacking my reasons for following them reveals a combination of feeling that I had no choice, curiosity about what would happen if I followed them, and not wanting to be perceived as either scared or disruptive. I also knew that any delay in my response meant a follow-on delay in the carefully timed and choreographed production in which multiple scenes were occurring simultaneously, at different locations, each for a solo spectator. All of these elements have to do with agency and dependency. To take the latter first, I realized in that moment of follower-spectatorship the extent to which the audience is dependent on the performer—to guide them (metaphorically and literally). But there is a greater dependence too: for them to be actors, for the performance to work, I have to be present as spectator; and, equally, for me to be a spectator, they have to be present. The firsthand witness defines the secondhand witness. If I wanted to be a witness (and why else was I here?), I had to walk down the alley.

What is this desire to be a witness that drove me, and that I imagine drives other spectators? As an answer, I offer descriptions of other scenes in this show. Once I had walked down the alley way, I was witness to a young man being beaten up for something related to drugs. As the two men who had led me turned and beat him, I was given a cell phone and told to film the altercation. I held the phone away from me, but since I had already given them authority over me by following them, even though I angled the phone at an uncomfortable distance from my body, I still obediently filmed it. Next I was brought to a disused car housed in a garage and instructed to sit in the back seat. As I sat there, noises and voice-over played, recounting the experience of the 1974 Talbot Street bombing, just one street away. A woman with dirt and plaster on her face and hair slid across the windshield of the car, staring in at me. It was relatively calm, even though it sought to represent an event in which twenty-seven people died (including the nearby bombings at Parnell Street and South Leinster Street). After the car, I was taken to a block of run-down apartments and ushered into the living room of one on the ground floor. A girl in a school uniform led me by the hand, invited me to sit down, and offered me a cup of tea. Around the room two women were shouting and being shouted at, a man was in the kitchen space off the room. He engaged in violent and sexual contact with the young girl. I mutely watched it all. Then I was hurried out of the room into a small bathroom off the hallway. There was a young woman in there. She turned her back to me and asked me to do up her dress. Déjà vu ensued as she asked me if I would help her escape. We edged into the hallway, but she was caught by the hand and brought into the main room, while I was pushed out the front door. Again, I did not protest. A waiting car took me back to the main street, and then the starting location. Here I was led into an exhibition space, with walls covered with photos. These photos were of the spectators of the show, and included one of me, walking down a street. This was the end of the show.

This brief overview is unable to capture the complexity of what happened in the show—the sense of multiple exchanges and overlapping dialogue, and the violence present in almost every exchange. Most of the time that I was in the apartment, even though I was surrounded by women and even though I knew it was all performance, I felt unsafe. And I felt unable to use my voice, either to object to the violence happening around me, or to leave the performance. All of which was deeply uncomfortable. Relief only came when I arrived at the gallery and felt back in my comfort zone, back in a world I knew how to navigate. The metalevel of ANU's surveillance of the spectators by photographing us as we engaged with the street scenes also reminded me that I was part of a show, and that I was just a very small part of that show. As Ciara Murphy puts it, "the immersed audience member is not only watching the performance... she is also being witnessed."[17] I was not the arbiter or decider, ANU Productions was. In the final "reveal" of my dependency, they excused my lack of agency.

But why go through any of this? What is the appeal? Are we "macabre thrill-seekers"?[18] Does the temporary contact with violence offer a particular form of catharsis, a safe way to feel unsafe? My answers to these questions are not unambivalent: we go to these shows because they allow us to differentiate ourselves from being traditional "shopping" consumers, because we want to intervene in the marketplace, because we want to be witnesses. But while this may seem "better," than simply consuming it also, of course, leads us to the disconcerting questions of whether we enjoy the temporary suspension of our own social capital within the mise-en-scène, and whether "witness" is just another identity up for purchase in the marketplace.

Vardo, *in Which I Am Still No Help to Anyone*

ANU finished the Monto tetralogy in 2014 with *Vardo*, another multilocation production focused on the history of the Monto as a red-light district. Unlike the other shows in the sequence, *Vardo* is set in contemporary Dublin and exposes the present-day crises of sex trafficking, sex work, and migration. Again, spectators navigate the show in isolation (at times meeting up with one other spectator), and again each spectator is expected to interact with the performers and to make themselves part of the show. In one scene, a woman who had been trafficked ran with me into the basement of a bus station and entrusted me with her passport, but as before with other women who asked me for help, I was no help—when a man purporting to be her "minder" turned up, I let him take the passport. In the waiting area of the bus station, I listened sympathetically as a man from Nigeria told me about his father's death and his sorrow at being so far away from his family. But I could not offer any help.

Both of these interactions highlight another aspect of agency—or the lack of it—at the heart of both spectatorship and witnessing. Due to the scripted and predetermined nature of the play, I knew that my intervention would not make any difference—had I refused or hidden the passport, there would have been no major alteration in the outcome of that scene, that eventuality had already been workshopped by the actors. And what, faced with the story of a man trapped by asylum rules, could I have done as either a spectator or a witness beyond listening? There are many ways in which "scripts" control behavior in real life as well as theatre, and this is one example of how often the witness position—the citizen-consumer—may distinguish itself from consumption-for-entertainment, but it is nevertheless still a kind of passive consumption.

The later scenes of *Vardo* moved into the private locations of a car, an elevator in an apartment block, and a one-bedroom apartment. In all of these places, I was joined by another spectator, and we moved through the scenes together. As well as viewing the actors, we were also viewing each other and our different reactions to the scenes. Where I was quiet and compliant, my fellow spectator was angry. In the car, she objected to the woman driving the car (who seemed to be the chief pimp), in the apartment she looked around and tried to leave the room, in the elevator she questioned where we were going: it became apparent that I was a follower, she was a questioner. "It's just a play," I thought, "don't get so involved." But what if it were not a play? Would she and I react as we were reacting to the performance? The absence of a historical frame, and the fact that the stories being dramatized were arguably happening in reality in similar ways and in similar locations at exactly the same moment as the performance blurred the lines between fiction and reality in a different way. What was being witnessed could not be distanced as "memory."

The observation that witnessing is often an uncomfortable experience and that it forces the witness and those being witnessed to confront the limits of what is possible through listening and seeing, returns me to the question of why it is that audiences buy tickets for these shows? And they do buy tickets—ANU is well-known for selling out a full run within days (sometimes hours) of tickets being released, so much so that attending an ANU show has significant cultural and symbolic capital, while souvenirs from the shows (e.g., soap from *Laundry*) testify to the collectability of both the theatrical experience and the symbolic capital.[19] Remediation is key to their commercial success: people who have seen one of the Monto shows will talk about it, and word of mouth is often the strongest driver of cultural consumption. The company is award-winning, and this cultural prestige also brings audiences to their work. Perhaps it is the perception that they offer something unique that is most alluring for audiences, including me. And this is where agency and desire become enmeshed in questions of ethics, and where I wonder how much labor the audience is actually performing and for what kind of payoff.

Trying Performances

In trying to understand the dynamic of audience/consumer/performer/witness, I come up against the difficulty of determining exactly the effects of prosumerism. These are performances that ask a lot of spectators, but what, as an active spectator, am I asking for in return for my labor? Access is one answer—these shows give me access to a "hidden Dublin," in particular in shows like *Laundry*, without which I would never have entry rights to the buildings of the Magdalen Laundry. When I apply the same reason, though, to *Boys of Foley Street* and *Vardo*, this motivation becomes a little murky—these are, for the most part, public locations that I can access myself (except for the two apartments). But they are equally locations I usually choose not to access myself. In visiting them as part of the performance, it is as if the show gives me a passport, and safe conduct, through an inner-city area, transforming me into a class tourist, a transformation that I think does no favors for either side of the deal.[20]

So let me try again. The ANU shows provoke me to become a "better" witness, to confront my lack of empathy, for example, toward people who are publicly violent and to think about the personal stories that lie behind that violence. The shows make me question how I witness in my everyday life and how I might seek out opportunities for ethical witnessing more effectively outside the performance. It is true that I walk away from shows that foreground social-justice concerns with a renewed sense of the requirement for every citizen to be active, not passive. But when I look at this as a motivation, it seems, at times, to have less to do with ethical witnessing and more to do with a narrative of self-improvement. In viewing others' pain as a route to improving my performance as witness, I am guilty (again) of appropriation.

Try again. In attending site-specific performances, I see theatre outside of its usual context of stage and auditorium, which leads me to recognize theatre as part of a larger ecosystem of ways of knowing the world, of which I am one element and this performance is one element. This is a more expansive view that integrates theatrical performance into everyday performance and suggests a continuum in which active spectatorship does not stop when the performance stops. This feels less appropriative and suggests a more affiliative performance of active witnessing than simply watching an abject performance happening. Perhaps consumption and witnessing are not mutually exclusive? I am still trying.

Inclusion and Exclusion

The public locations of site-specific theatre ensure that witnessing is not limited to ticket-buying spectators. On the first day I attended *Boys of Foley Street*, as I was led along the street by two actors, a small group of people sitting in an adjacent park watched us and jeeringly shouted that we were "in a play." The two actors I was walking with were costumed in dirty tracksuits, carrying a two-liter bottle of alcohol and a dirty sleeping bag. They did not look that dissimilar to the people in the park, our sarcastic audience. This moment illustrates the potential for the audience of site-specific work to be much larger, as the show intermingles with everyday life and passersby become unintentionally part of the show or part of the audience. In some ways this moment of public surveillance was later echoed in the final exhibition where it was revealed that the spectators are part of the spectacle—but it felt different. Rather than giving my money to actual homeless people, I was spending it watching and interacting with people who were pretending to be homeless from a period thirty years ago. Here again the specter of class tourism raises its head. The site-specific performance's mimicry of real social deprivation can, unlike the original being mimicked, deliver both catharsis and closure—the show produces something that is easier to consume than reality.

In the case of *Boys of Foley Street*, the people in the park were knowing commentators on the performance, well aware of what was happening and of the absurdity of people watching "a play" about a history that was, in reality, ongoing only a few feet away. Certainly this is a facet of public performance that ANU encounters regularly, and which is built into their development process as they work with local communities to reflect their stories. There are moments, however, when, as with my example, there seems to be an unintentional distance between the work that, for all its site-specificity and local reflection, is nevertheless disconnected from its roots in social justice. During a later production, *Sunder*, I also experienced such a juxtaposition. This show, which was a commemorative response to the centenary of the 1916 Easter Rising, was performed at several locations around Moore Street, the location in north Dublin of the last stand of the rebellion. The final scenes of the show were performed in a building actually on Moore Street, and depicted the civilian casualties of the Rising who were lethally affected by the rebels seeking refuge in their homes. This was an important and untold story. In order to reach the performance rooms on the upper levels, spectators walked through the ground-floor Asian food shop, selling general groceries and Halal meat, a common combination on one of Dublin's most multicultural streets. Yet the cast and, as far as I could see, the audience of ANU's *Sunder* were entirely white. The contrast between the monocultural production and the multicultural venue was marked, creating a different kind of discomfort and questioning how commemorative work, whether performed in traditional or nontraditional venues, can be disconnected from current realities and, in this case, performing national history in a form that excluded modern citizens.

PART TWO: THE LISTENING CONSUMER

Changing urbanscapes and inadvertent moments of spectatorship are part and parcel of site-specific work, and this is particularly true of audio site-specific performance work. Moving away from Dublin, this section considers the performance walks produced by Kabosh Theatre in Belfast on the production *Quartered: A Love Story* (originally produced 2016), Miriam Schickler's Tel-Aviv-set *Echoing Yafa* (2014), and Platform's London audio-walk, *And While London Burns* (2007). Though through slightly different formats, each of these three works represents an audio walk around a particular public, urban location, and through the performance of each (a performance coproduced by the listener), each walk acts to stage an intervention in that urbanscape.

Before I began to travel and take part in audio walks elsewhere, it was ANU's work in Dublin that first introduced audio-performance to me—in *Thirteen*, a series of thirteen miniature site-specific works created by the company to commemorate 1913 and the Dublin trade union Lockout. The first piece was an audio-performance on a tram. Before the show, spectators downloaded a soundtrack, then met at a Luas (tram) stop, boarded a tram, and pressed play at the same moment. The audience got off the tram at the last stop, followed a guide down the street, and watched two scenes of a young woman in a park, who then went into an office building as a cleaner, before the show finished. Having seen both *Laundry* and *Boys of Foley Street*, the audio brought a new dimension and, seeing this show, there was again a sense of mystery. Unlike other ANU shows, there was also security in the presence of other spectators.

The public setting of the tram, in which the group of spectators, though together, was separated by virtue of each of us listening to our own devices on headphones, made it feel like a performance of simultaneous connection and division. There was a curiosity to looking at the others and wondering if they were listening to exactly the same moment of commentary as I was. There were others on the tram also wearing headphones, but who were not part of the "audience" and so were listening to something else—I looked at them too and wondered what their experience was and if we each blended in to look as if we were all just commuters (as opposed to witnesses). The commentary encouraged each of us to look around at our surroundings and at the other passengers, breaking that unspoken rule of public transport in which we so often pretend we are in a private bubble. When the performance ended, there was a moment of confusion as we took off our headsets and paused, as if asking for permission to speak.

I have now, five years later, experienced several audio-performance works, but the sense of wonder and the questions about the experience have not really altered or been answered definitively. During Kabosh's *Quartered: A Love Story*, which I attended in the spring of 2018 in Belfast, these questions surfaced again. It was a Saturday afternoon and very sunny, and central Belfast was crowded with people shopping and enjoying a few drinks. Beer gardens were overflowing—a fact particularly relevant as the show began and ended in two different pubs, and pubs were the landmarks by which the performance navigated audience members around the city. Attending the performance with me were five other people who I did not know. We were met by a guide, who gave each of us an mp3 player and counted us down to pressing "play." We began standing in a vacant lot behind a pub, listening as a male voice-over described to us the end of his relationship with his boyfriend. We followed the guide as she led us out into the alleyway and down toward the street. The voice-over commented on the murals, how the street had changed since he was younger, and how he had met his partner in one of these pubs. This performance walk thus interweaves urban and personal histories as part of a tour of different gay pubs in the city quarter.

The breakup at the heart of the plot has been caused by conflict between the couple about how comfortable each of them is with public displays of affection. Within a gay pub or club the narrator is happy to hold hands or kiss. But outside that safe space, he is much less "touchy feely" and this creates a division in his relationship as his partner wants more public affection. Unable to traverse the physical distance between himself and his partner, he creates an emotional distance. As in ANU's work, this Kabosh play draws attention to hidden histories and to the fear and consequences of visibility: gay-bashing. As we followed the audio instructions, I realized that as a group of people, all listening to headphones and standing in fixed spots for several minutes, we ourselves also became visible, a target of public attention, which seemed somehow fitting. Unlike ANU's work, however, in the context of the tour group, with a designated guide/leader, the sense of being vulnerable was far less.

During *Quartered*, the group walks a fairly tight route around a small quarter of Belfast, now dubbed the "gay quarter" and known for its nightlife. The narrator comments on the intrusiveness of straight men and women coming to gay clubs, and he also points out the places that used to be gay venues and which are now gentrified and "straight." The peace dividends for Belfast post-1998 have transformed the city in various ways, in particular the gentrification of the inner city, a fact that is prominently on display as we walk through streets crowded with shoppers and drinkers. As we near the end of the tour, this is less felt and we are now on emptier, wider avenues where our visibility as a group is higher. We end in a gay pub, sitting down as the narrator declares that he wants to fight for his relationship and to learn to be comfortable with being openly and publicly gay. As we end the show and take our headsets off, one woman comments that this is a return to Belfast for her after emigrating years before and that through the show she was returning to the cityscape of her younger years; she could not believe how much the streets had changed. The guide tells us that every time they produce the show, they have to alter it as the urban streetscapes change so quickly that the narrative and route quickly go out of date.

The disappearance of urban landmarks is a particular stumbling block for site-specific work. During Platform's *And While London Burns*, first created in 2007, the participant is self-guided with an audio commentary that directs them to look for particular landmarks in London. The tour plunges the participant into the world of the unnamed narrator, who works for British Petroleum (BP, now renamed "Beyond Petroleum"), and it alternates between his internal monologue and an operatic score. The narrator is overworked and stressed and refuses to go back to work at BP. He and his partner, Lucy, are struggling to conceive, and he despairs that pollution has caused him to have fertility problems. As with *Quartered*, the subjective experience maps onto the objective urban landscape.

When I did this tour in April 2018, navigating the route was made significantly more difficult by the renovations of Bank Underground Station (the starting point location) and the rebuilding of the City area.[21] In particular, the Temple of Mithras, a ruined Roman temple, which causes the narrator of this tour to ruminate on the civilizations that preceded the current one, is now no longer publicly visible—it is encased within the new Bloomberg building (yet another frustrating example of the privatization of public spaces in cities around the world, so that they become available only to certain highly privileged consumers). For those in the know, they can enter the Bloomberg foyer and still see the temple as part of an exhibition space within the building. But the audio commentary has not been updated, so the unprepared participant of *And While London Burns* is left to ruminate on the street about the absence of the landmark, and to piece together a more subjective route. The show argues that traces of the past are always present, and that they provide signposts for those of us in the present to better navigate our way through the city (and through life). However, traces—even of the built environment—fade or are moved or destroyed, and the spatial reorganization of the city, ironically, counterpoints the show's message of layers of memory and history that are visible to the active urban witness. The map of the route that can be downloaded is further evidence of this irony: it looks hand-drawn and includes only the old names of streets and landmarks, like the now-vanished temple. It is a frustrating document to use, given how little it seems to match the contours of the current city (though it is only a decade since it was created) and how it does not match *at all* the current digital map on my smartphone!

One more feature of change affects the experience of this walk: three years after the creation of *And While London Burns*, BP was responsible for the largest oil spill in history to date. The audio's references to BP thus have even greater resonance regarding the dangers of unfettered and unwitnessed consumption. As Platform states on its website, "In order for an oil company to produce oil and transport it to the global market, it needs either the support or the silence of the population in those areas of the world where this takes place."[22] Moreover, Platform argues that companies like BP purchase "social license" by sponsoring the arts: "The sponsorship programmes of BP and Shell are means by which attention is distracted from their impacts on human rights, the environment and the global climate."[23] *And While London Burns* exposes the "carbon web," by showcasing a hidden London—the city of oil, gas, and commerce, the economic forces that "feed the global economy,"[24] drive the wealth of the city and which, in turn, pollute the world. The aims of the production are thus explicitly about consciousness-raising and activism—to highlight the exploitation and destruction of rampant consumerism, thus turning consumers into witnesses.

Given that this, unlike the other site-specific works discussed so far, is a self-guided tour, and that the participant is hampered by not being able to easily connect with the intended route, during *And While London Burns* I had a strange sense of being a flâneur, rather than a theatre spectator. In some ways this sense of being a distanced (rather than involved) observer ties into the message of this show about the corporatization of London and the erasure of the individual, who is overwhelmed by the behemoth of the city. It also, of course, makes me question what the divisions are between flanerie and theatrical spectatorship, and which position is more or less likely to resist the commodification of consumption that the anticapitalist narrative of this show projects.

Both flanerie and theatrical spectatorship are positions based on curiosity and moving through a space while watching and listening. Baudelaire described the flâneur as a "passionate spectator,"[25] while Walter Benjamin famously linked the unproductiveness of the flâneur (or flâneuse) to a critique of modernity. The Benjaminian version of spectatorship seems particularly apt in this twenty-first-century performance walk all about how people are transformed into cogs in the capitalist machine. As I walk along busy streets, with people hurrying past, I value my own relative inactivity, my unproductiveness, my leisure. Yet there is also the irony that as I look relatively idle, I am actually performing as a consumer.

And While London Burns performs a delicate balance between hope and despair. On the one hand, the narrator declares that "the city is a senseless suicide machine, plotting its own and so many others' deaths," and on the other he keeps moving through that city, looking at it, and hoping for an answer. The route is interspersed with symbols of that binary of hope/despair:

> Let's turn left at the cash points, onto the cobbles of Pudding Lane and we can really feel the valley now, let's follow it down ... towards the river ... what is it we will take through the flood, what will we leave behind. ... Lucy can see it, she can feel it in her bones. ... Stop! Look up there on the right, the monument to the fire of London, topped in gold. ... Dad took me up there when I was a child.[26]

The route is plotted around fixed points, symbols of commerce (Bank Station, the Bloomberg Building, the Bank of England, the cash machines), and history (the Temple of Mithras, the Great Fire Monument). Yet though the narrator focuses on what is destroyed and abandoned, in a sleight of hand toward the end of act 3, the narrative finishes with a hopeful reverie inspired by the Great Fire Monument:

> [*Narrator:*] The monument wasn't built to symbolise the destruction of the city, but its resurrection, it's a monument to the possibilities that disasters bring in their wake. People fled the flames and returned to the ruins, everything they owned destroyed, and yet they returned, they returned to make a new city. What an expression of love and hope.
> Let's stop here. Look up. It must have seemed so tall when it was built.
> [*Lucy's voice:*] How useless, an obstacle, it distracts us from the here and now ... climate change is not going to go away ... sea levels are rising. ...
> [*Narrator:*] I'm not leaving, not running away from this city, this valley has changed the world so much for better and for worse. We could stay here together. Desert our old lives ... but stay in this place, stay and change this city. Love London in a way that we never have before, love this city, coax it back from the brink of suicide. ...
> Go through the wooden door, as my father did so long ago, my hand in his. ...
> [*Sound of a child counting steps as we climb to the top*]
> ...
> [*Opera, lyrics include "we could build a new city"*][27])

Lucy's intervention is disturbing to the spectator, refuting our desire to look, insisting that the visible is not the most relevant object to witness, and declaring memory an obstacle to dealing with the crises of the here and now. However, the production chooses not to end on this note, but instead opts for a rising in all senses—as the spectator climbs the steps of the monument, the narrative about climate change gives way to panoramic views of London and a sense that "we" could "love this city." *And While London Burns* finishes with opera singing, with lyrics including "we could build a new city," and the sound of a young boy as he repeatedly says "go close to the edge," finally stating "and they could fly." Given the shock value of the preceding hour's narrative about rising sea levels, this ending is itself unsettling, as it seems to represent a too-easy solution of "love" as a balm for the self, with no practical wisdom to offer regarding climate change. Yet how might the conflict between the challenge of the narrative and the catharsis of the ending also be productive of meaning? As with the ending of ANU shows, when spectators are relieved to reenter their "real" lives, do site-specific productions create more than a trace meaning? Does the audiences' labor transform into more than symbolic capital?

As I descended from the monument, Lucy's difficult phrase, "how useless," stayed with me. This phrase suggests a falsity to the spectator's belief that their participation in this performance walk represents change, when in reality it produces us as passive (rather than disruptive) consumers. Though spectators engage with a different version of London through the show, and though we can argue that by moving differently thorough the city, as a flâneuse or flâneur, embodying both leisure and critical engagement, somehow changing its rhythm and subverting, even briefly, the focus on capitalist consumption and busy-ness, that argument feels flimsy in counterpoint to the scale of the problem of climate crisis. The narrator declares that he will "desert" his old life, but there is no road map for what that remaking might look like. Likewise, the memory of the Great Fire of London as an opportunity for rebirth in the wake of total destruction seems promising, but it is a false parallel to climate change. Moreover, Lucy's description of the monument to this past as a useless distraction can be interpreted as a critique of the play itself, as a sideshow that provokes questions but does not create any material change. In including its own self-critique within the narrative, the script is a knowing nod to its own limits. At the time of doing the walk, I felt that it was a missed opportunity to give audience members a better "take away," a productive message about how to affect climate change. But since then I have thought again—a take-away message produces another layer of passive witnesses. Better for us, perhaps, to produce our own message.

Acting Invisible

Part of the issue with *And While London Burns* is its invisibility as a mode of protest. Because the walk is conducted via headphones, and because walking around London is a commonplace action, there is no outward sign of the show's internal confrontation of toxic capitalism and corporate pollution. Consequently, on audio-performance walks there is often a disjuncture between the politicized act of walking and listening at sites of contested meaning, and the relative absence of impact due to the privacy of the performance. Though this is, in the case of *And While London Burns*, a possible diminution of its impact, there are cases of audio-performance walks where the contested space is actually so hostile, that the privacy of personal audio devices is what *enables* resistance, rather than detracts from it.

In a scenario where live performance is not possible and where sites are not fully accessible to all, the audio-performance walk can become a technology of opposition rather than amelioration. In experiencing *Echoing Yafa*, an audio-performance walk around the Manshiyya district in Tel Aviv, I was very aware that access to this historically Arab/Palestinian neighborhood, and to the memory narratives that make up *Echoing Yafa*'s sixteen scenes, was dependent on what I was listening to not being public. When I undertook the audio-performance walk in April 2017, it was a Saturday, and so the area, including the usually busy marketplace, was deserted. In one sense, this allowed me to move more freely and without distraction around the streets, but in another sense, it made me highly visible. I was therefore doubly grateful that the audio was only audible to me.

Established in the late 1870s, by the 1940s Manshiyya was one of Yafa's largest Arab neighborhoods. Stretching along the sea from the Yafa Old Town toward the newer Jewish settlements to the north and west, the area in 1944 had a population of "12,000 Palestinians and about 1,000 Jews, on an area of some 2,400 dunums."[28] In April 1948, the Jewish Etzel forces launched an attack on the neighborhood, expelling its Arab population. Following Etzel's "clearing" of the area, many homes were taken over by poorer Jewish families, while other buildings were razed (such as the police station). Several decades of neglect followed, until in the 1960s the remaining structures were demolished to make way for new residential and commercial developments. Today, the Hassan Beq Mosque is the only building remaining from the period when the neighborhood was an Arab quarter.

At the beginning of the audio-performance walk, the female narrator tells me "this is where they decided to draw the border line between Yafa and

Tel Aviv."[29] The narrator gives some historical background to the area, while rooting her narrative in her position as one of the neighborhood's residents. She remarks that the area was first settled by Egyptians, that for years it was under the rule of the Turkish, and "now" of the British. As she puts it, "All of this time we've been dealing with all of this shit." The temporality of the tour is unstable—the "time" is both 1948 when the district was first attacked and cleared, and *now* (the listener's time frame). This is again apparent later in the walk when the narrator shifts time frames. In 1948, the Etzel strategy in Manshiyya was to enter buildings and blast a way through each of them, driving the occupants into the streets where they were vulnerable to sniper fire. Depicting this experience, the audio soundtrack plays the sounds of gunshots and general mayhem as the residents flee their homes. Then the voice of the main female narrator cuts in to link the history of 1948 to the present. Describing Etzel's strategy she says, "That same tactic was employed by the IDF in Nablus in 2002. Seventy Palestinians died, hundreds were arrested. The operations commander referred to his tactic as inverse geometry. Turning the inside out and the outside in." Through this linking of past and present, the narrator suggests a continuation of the violent oppression of Palestinians by the Israeli forces, first Etzel and now the IDF, in a strategy that overlaps past and present. The continuities of oppression are felt again at the end of the tour, when the narrator says, "Those of us who managed to stay in Yafa . . . to move into the emptied homes in the Ajami ghetto, keep on wandering. Today five hundred families in Ajami, many of whom are refugees from '48, face house evictions and house demolitions. Once more they will be dispossessed and displaced."

The participant on this walk is asked to be an active witness, noticing these shifts and disparities. One scene is set in a park, which used to be "a built-up area," but is now the "Park of the Conquerors." In the center of the park there is an imposing stone monument, dedicated to the Jewish "conquerors" of Yafa. Those who were conquered were, of course, the Palestinian citizens of Manshiyya. As I stand at the rear of the monument, the voice in my headphones changes to the whispered tones of a man recalling that "while a mother buries her child, they keep erecting monuments . . . marble blocks of guilt." Again, as in *And While London Burns*, monumental history is a suspect cover-up of the reality of conflict that the spectator should be witnessing instead. The limits of spectator sympathy are then tested by the politicization of the narrative when it talks about the Palestinian community of nearby Yafa "mobilising" to protect the Hassan Beq Mosque. While one might assume that the majority of participants on this walk are sympathetic to the Palestinian cause, and recognize the violence of the Nakba (the expulsion of Palestinians from their homes in 1948), the narrator's references to ammunition and snipers may cause listeners to question what political—or paramilitary—actions they are tacitly supporting through their engagement with this walk.

But *Echoing Yafa* is not an incitement to violence or hatred. At several points, the narrative is careful to suggest the community cooperation between different groups before 1948. One Arab character describes how he took in his Jewish Yemeni neighbor after his father kicked him out for joining the communist youth. This scene also cites the "deep friendships" between Arabs and Jews, and notes the number of Jewish women who fled Manshiyya in 1948 with their Arab partners. A few scenes later, a young boy describes how "on Saturdays my mother sends me over to the [Jewish] neighbours' house to warm food for them ... so I help them." Given the restrictions of the Sabbath, in this instance a multicultural neighborhood had certain advantages. Yet these same neighbors advise the boy's mother, "It would be better to leave. Soon it would no longer be safe for [them]." It is unclear whether this advice is given out of genuine concern for their safety, or if it's a tactic to drive the Arab family away. The young boy says that "none of us should have to leave. We have a good life here." This character's optimism, however, is not sustainable, and at the end of the audio walk, the narrative returns to the story of the young girl as she describes her family's desperate flight, saying finally, "When we arrived, only a couple of kilometres away, we had become refugees."

The *Echoing Yafa* audio-performance walk ends on the dunes above the Yafa Beach. These dunes were created from the rubble of the Manshiyya houses, so that the spectator is actually standing on and witnessing a memory landscape. Nearby there is a sculpture to the "angel of history," which stands marking the "the Liberation of Yafa" by the IDF. Below the dunes, locals sunbathe and swim. Along the path that I stand on, heavily armed IDF soldiers patrol. The juxtaposition between what I am listening to (which feels like contraband), the memory landscape that is being evoked by the narrative, and the reality of consumption and militarization that I see, is a shocking one. The critical distance necessitated by this contrast justifies the sense that experiencing *Echoing Yafa* is a disruptive and potentially decolonizing act of site-specific performance. This awkwardness and discomfort causes us to, as Julie Salverson writes, "notice" and "implicate ... [our]selves in the picture."[30] Though this walk around Tel Aviv is very different from ANU's work in Dublin, there are resonances—both approaches reveal unknown layers of history and conflict, highlight the inequity of urban spaces, and require you to perform labor that reveals stark differences in social and cultural capital between audience/performer, then/now, and listening self/listened to others.

Opening Up?

To what extent do site-specific plays and performance walks open up urban space and memory? Do performance walks, as Sarah Gorman suggests, "Through a process of defamiliarization and disorientation ... ask the viewer to consider his or her place within the context of the changing environment"?[31] One particular critique of personal audio devices used in these walks is that using headphones in public areas "carves out a space for personal enjoyment and reflection, for being oneself: private space is 'nested' within public space."[32] Rather than sharing or becoming part of a larger community, the audio technology necessary for audio walks is actually divisive. As Fran Tonkiss argues, whether "immersed in a private soundscape, [or] engaged in another interactive scene, you do not have to be in the city as a shared perceptual or social space"[33] when using headphones. And although the same kind of separation is not involved in other site-specific works like the Monto tetralogy, we might also argue that the boundaries of the performance, and the process of ticket-buying, likewise "carve out" and "nest" the performance space within the larger public space. Though these productions are boundary-breaking in taking the spectator out of the theatre, they nonetheless create other boundaries around the performance and produce private spaces within the locations they choose to perform in. Even in relation to a politically dissident audio-performance walk like *Echoing Yafa*, the disruption it causes is invisible, limited to the direct participant. Unlike live performance, though I experienced a degree of surveillance from those onlookers who may have questioned why I was standing still on a street corner or in a park, the content of what I was listening to was private. This privacy enables this performance to happen—given the controversial nature of the Nakba and the "right to return" walks in Palestine/Israel[34]—but it nevertheless limits the effect of witnessing to the individual.

Spectators seeking out these productions also have a set of expectations—in Dublin, ANU works in socially deprived and economically marginalized areas of the city. Their shows' spectators seek out the high drama of ANU's projects, but also seek out the deprivation. In Belfast and London, the spectator participates in the performance walk out of a sense that there is a hidden story behind the gentrified facades, and in each, the spectator discovers a series of memories of pain and fear for the future. In Tel Aviv, the spectator refuses the authority of the Israeli state and walks through a memory landscape that evokes violence and oppression. Spectators of these shows are thus not satisfied with the regenerated surfaces of cities, they seek out the ruins. A spectator's agency, social capital, and relative wealth (financial, technological, leisured) are set in contrast to the lack of agency, capital, and power of the characters of these shows. It is not only the headphones and tickets that divide the spectators as subjects from the spectated as objects.

It is too disheartening a coda, however, to end by suggesting that experimental companies aiming to create interventionist work succeed only in creating yet more privatized spaces of consumption, entertainment, and individualized development. While for almost all of these site-specific performances I found myself a solo spectator, at the same time I know that each of these performances has been experienced by many. The performance thus allows me to reflect on both the social atomization of urban life, and to consider myself one of a larger cohort, unified through our shared, if separate, consumption of the same show.[35] The actual audience, as opposed to the immediately visible audience, is far greater. As Ciara Murphy also argues, since immersive site-specific work blurs the boundaries of real and performance, it can be unclear what is "in" or "out": "As I walked back through Dublin City [I had] a heightened awareness of the pulse of the city and the stories contained within it. For me the performance was not yet over."[36] Seen this way, through the labor of the witness-audience, the private space of performance becomes a new public space, occupied by multiple witnesses who have been required to perform in active ways. Each spectator thus contributes to a new understanding of the city, each spectator engages with memory, each spectator forms new memories. And, crucially, each spectator is "credit[ed] as a social agent."[37] Though site-specific work may appear to be a niche product, its symbolic impact is much greater.

And there is another ethical dimension to the privacy of the experience—unlike autoperformance, which requires the survivor to reanimate and perform their pain over and over again, site-specific work delivers an aspect of "the real," without requiring the actual victims to display themselves. The site stands in for the victim, bearing their scars. This is particularly true for audio-performance walks, which record the script once and then free both survivor and actor of the emotional labor of performing. Instead, that labor is transferred to the spectator.

Jen Harvie has raised important ethical questions about the delegation of labor from professional to volunteer and the transformation of consumers into prosumers (who help produce the product they are paying to consume). These qualifications, in most part, apply to unpaid volunteer workers, who do not receive either a salary or social benefits for their participation.[38] How then does this argument apply to audiences? I agree with Harvie when she argues for the value of involving the audience—"Everyone is an artist"—in the hope of encouraging an "expanded agency."[39] I would extend this to suggest that the audience's labor is key to the differentiation of passive consumers from active witnesses. This is not, however, to simplistically suggest that audience members attending a site-specific show are automatically transformed into social witnesses beyond the theatrical frame. Indeed, as Sarah Senk argues in relation to the New York 9/11 Memorial Museum, by soliciting audience input into the "story" or witnessing of 9/11, the museum positions visitors as "the authors and victims of a collective trauma narrative," a process that may "obscure the historical forces" behind the attacks.[40] Likewise, does the audience member in a participatory, site-specific show think beyond their own narrative? Is this actually a production of ethical witnessing, or is this another form of appropriation? Given the points that Platform makes about the role of sponsorship of the arts as another layer of distraction from the real ethics, should we also be concerned, for instance, that ANU shows are funded by state agencies (such as Dublin City Council) and private institutions?[41] Or does the participation of DCC allow theatre makers into spaces that are otherwise in private ownership, thus troubling the privatization of capital? Only through these kinds of partnerships can witnesses be brought to the places themselves; as Joanne Tompkins argues, the "logistics of devising, producing, and performing site-specific theatre today must account for occupational health and safety, crowd control, rights of way, security, and other such civic concerns that inevitably affect the work and can, in part, limit its success and effect significantly."[42] Though I agree that there are inevitably limits on the work being produced, I hold out hope that the kinds of partnerships represented by ANU, and the work-arounds created by audio performance, can nevertheless result in a democratization of urban spaces and their mnemonic capital.

There are aspects of appropriation to the class- and dark-tourist contexts of these works, which market an "other" experience of trauma to consumers; yet there is also a very strong contrast between the kind of emotional catharsis being sold by an autoperformance stage show, and the emotional unsettlement produced by the site-specific works discussed here. The violence—structural, physical, and emotional—of the ANU shows are clear examples of how an in-yer-face style of site-specific theatre can provoke audiences out of their comfort zones and refuse easy consumption (an example of resisting what Bourdieu calls "transgression without risk"[43]). At the other end of the spectrum, in the calmer contexts of the audio-performance walks and the guided room tour of Dominic Thorpe's *Proximity Mouth*, the audience is granted a surfeit of reflective space. Both of these strategies—which entail the audience in constantly negotiating and renegotiating their position in relation to the "spectacle"—juxtapose what is real and what is unreal, what we see and what we hear, who we are and who we are being asked to perform as, creating enough disjuncture to frustrate the inevitable process of commodification.

We might, finally, also argue that the limits on spectatorship and ethical witnessing made visible in these shows is exactly their point—it is not that audience members should only notice what is happening *in* the show, but also that they notice what is happening *around* the show, including their own actions and the status of the production as a commodity they are consuming. Site-specific work performs both separation and connectivity and demonstrates the city as a web or network of individual and communal stories. When spectatorship happens outside the theatre, it becomes multivalent and multidirectional. Performance is thus emulating the city itself as a networking device, linking many subjects and spectators. As individuals, in our daily lives, we only glimpse tiny aspects of how these networks function, and site-specific work enables both different and larger networks to be seen. One of the most potentially transformative aspects to this raised visibility is the way these shows force spectators to act as witnesses to the structural violence that results from these larger networks.

Within these shows, omniscience is not granted to the spectator (we can never see all the scenes of an ANU show, we can never know where the passersby are going, we can never access the bulldozed neighborhood). In chapter 4, I argued that this inevitable lack of omniscience suggests that witnessing can only ever be partial and subjective. However, in site-specific work I think this takes on a slightly different interpretation. Because while omniscience is not possible, in site-specific theatre, where spectators interact with real social spaces, accumulation becomes an alternative mode of knowledge, connection, and witness.

At the end of *The Boys of Foley Street*, the show's spectators are brought to a gallery where, as mentioned above, they see an exhibition of surveillance photos of spectators. The most automatic response is for each spectator to look for themselves on the walls. When you see a photo of yourself, however, you know that it is not really you—it looks like you, it shows you to yourself from the outside, but it does not capture who you really are, how you see yourself, or the various meanings of "you." We know that image may be consumed by others who think that it shows us, but in our sheepish acknowledgement that it is us, and our simultaneous resistance to the idea that it is us, that we are also commodifiable, we begin to question how *all* the images we see are constructed, and how we do not really understand the characters we have met, we have only seen—consumed—them from one angle. The shows, in making their edges visible (through the self-conscious use of images and technology), free us from the pressure to buy into the fiction. Instead, we have multiple fragments and bits and angles to assemble into our own story. When we build a collage of these angles and accumulate moments of witnessing, when we store the memories we have encountered and remediate the memories we have made, when we continue the labor, we perform ourselves as active witnesses.

NOTES

1. I witnessed the performance of *Proximity Mouth* by Dominic Thorpe and ensemble at Dublin Castle on July 11, 2014, as part of the *Immovable Walls* program (July 2014), curated by Michelle Brown at Dublin Castle. The ensemble members are protected by semi-anonymity due to the precarity of their status. Their first names are Selvi, Chinenye, Jane, and Collette.

2. Joanne Tompkins, "The 'Place' and Practice of Site-Specific Theatre and Performance," in *Performing Site-Specific Theatre: Politics, Place, Practice*, ed. Anna Birch and Joanne Tompkins (Basingstoke: Palgrave Macmillan, 2012), 1–20. Indeed, Fintan O'Toole declared the work of the site-specific theatre company, ANU Productions, to be "a new kind of national theatre." See Fintan O'Toole, "It's Ireland's Best Public Theatre," *Irish Times*, September 28, 2013, https://www.irishtimes.com/culture/it-s-ireland-s-best-public-theatre-and-it-needs-our-support-1.1542665.

3. Jen Harvie, *Fair Play: Art, Performance and Neoliberalism* (London: Palgrave, 2013), 39–40.

4. See, for instance, John Lennon and Malcolm Foley, *Dark Tourism* (London: Thompson, 2006); Philip Stone and Richard Sharpley, "Consuming Dark Tourism: A Thanatological Perspective," *Annals of Tourism Research* 35, no. 2 (2008): 574–95; Yaniv Poria, Arie Reichel, and Avital Biran, "Heritage Site Management: Motivations and Expectations," *Annals of Tourism Research* 33, no. 1 (2006): 162–78; Wiendu Nuryanti, "Heritage and Postmodern Tourism," *Annals of Tourism Research* 23, no. 2 (1996): 249–60.

5. Louise Lowe and Una Kavanagh, "The Work of Anu: The Audience Is Present," *Irish University Review* 47, no. 1 (2017): 115–25.

6. Mike Pearson and Michael Shank, *Theatre/Archaeology* (London & New York: Routledge, 2001), 23.

7. Charlotte McIvor, "Other Space (Non-Theatre Spaces)," in *The Palgrave Handbook of Contemporary Irish Theatre and Performance*, ed. Eamonn Jordan and Eric Weitz (London: Palgrave, 2018), 465–86, see esp. 479.

8. *Thirteen* is a cycle of thirteen plays that sought to commemorate the 1913 Dublin Lockout strike; *Sunder* is a 2016 play that commemorated the 1916 Easter Rising.

9. See Miriam Haughton's discussion of *Laundry* in *Staging Trauma: Bodies in Shadow* (London: Palgrave, 2018), 117–59.

10. See Mary Douglas, *Purity and Danger: An Analysis of Concepts of Pollution and Taboo* (London: Routledge, 1966).

11. Quoted in Susan Mullin Vogel, *El Anatsui: Art and Life* (Munich: Prestel Verlag, 2012), 125.

12. See Mary Raftery and Eoin O'Sullivan, *Suffer the Little Children: The Inside Story of Ireland's Industrial Schools* (Dublin: New Island, 1999). See also Emilie Pine, Susan Leavy, and Mark Keane, "Digital Reading as Active Witnessing: Re-reading the Ryan Report," *Eire-Ireland* 52, no. 1–2 (Spring/Summer 2017): 198–215.

13. Singleton discusses his discomfort as a male audience member placed in close proximity to performances of female vulnerability. Brian Singleton, "ANU Productions Monto Cycle: Performative Encounters and Acts of Memory," Irish Memory Studies Network guest lecture (2015), http://irishmemorystudies.com/index.php/memory-cloud/#singleton.

14. McIvor, "Other Space," 479.

15. Brian Singleton, *ANU Productions: The Monto Cycle* (London: Palgrave, 2017), 3.

16. This play is currently unique in ANU's oeuvre for having a published script. See Patrick Lonergan, ed., *Contemporary Irish Plays* (London: Bloomsbury, 2015).

17. Ciara L. Murphy, "Audiences: Immersive and Participatory," in *The Palgrave Handbook of Contemporary Irish Theatre and Performance*, ed. Eamonn Jordan and Eric Weitz (London: Palgrave, 2018), 717–36, see esp. 720.

18. David Reynolds, "Consumers or Witnesses: Holocaust Tourists and the Problem of Authenticity," *Journal of Consumer Culture* 16 no. 2 (2016): 334–53, see esp. 335.

19. See Gary S. Becker and Kevin M. Murphy with William Landes, "The Social Market for the Great Masters and Other Collectibles," in *Social Economics: Market Behaviour in a Social Environment* (Cambridge, MA: Belknapp Press, 2000), 74–83.

20. Singleton refers to the risk in ANU's work as "poverty porn," using Lyn Gardner's term. Singleton, *ANU Productions*, 5. See Lyn Gardner, "'Poverty Porn': How Middle Class Theatres Depict Britain's Poor," *The Guardian*, https://www.theguardian.com/stage/theatreblog/2016/apr/15/poverty-porn-theatre-boy-yen-rehome.

21. For a discussion of the ways that changing urban environments are both challenging and productive for audiences, see Deirdre Heddon, "The Horizon of Sound: Soliciting the Earwitness," *Performance Research* 15, no. 3 (2010): 36–42; and Misha Myers, "Walk with Me, Talk with Me": The Art of Conversive Wayfinding," *Visual Studies* 25, no. 1 (2010), 59–68.

22. "Oil and the Arts," Platform, accessed October 22, 2019, https://platformlondon.org/oil-the-arts/.

23. "Oil and the Arts."

24. "Oil and the Arts."

25. Charles Baudelaire, *The Painter of Modern Life* (New York: Da Capo Press, 1964), 9.

26. Platform, *And While London Burns*, Act 3. This text is transcribed from the audio mp3.

27. Platform, *And While London Burns*, Act 3. This text is transcribed from the audio mp3.

28. "al-Manshiyya Neighborhood (Yaffa)," Zochrot, accessed October 22, 2019, http://www.zochrot.org/en/village/56077.

29. All quotations are taken from the *Echoing Yafa* audio walking tour, transcribed by the author from the audio mp3. This tour is free to download via the website, https://echoingyafa.alllies.org/.

30. Julie Salverson, "Change on Whose Terms? Testimony and an Erotics of Injury," *Theater* 31, no. 3 (2001): 119–25, see esp. 122.

31. Sarah Gorman, "Wandering and Wondering," *Performance Research* 8, no. 1 (2003): 83–92, see esp. 87.

32. Nicolas Cook, "Classical Music and the Politics of Space," in *Music, Sound and Space: Transformations of Public and Private Experience*, ed. Georgina Born (Cambridge: Cambridge University Press), 224–38.

33. Fran Tonkiss, "The Ethics of Indifference: Community and Solitude in the City," *International Journal of Cultural Studies* 6, no. 3 (2003): 297–311, see esp. 305. I am indebted to Tom Lane for the Cook and Tonkiss references on listening, as part of our collaborative project *Echoes from the Past* audio walk, available at https://industrialmemories.ucd.ie.

34. For a discussion of the activist potential of walking, and the right to return, see Yifat Gutman, *Memory Activism: Reimagining the Past for the Future in Israel-Palestine* (Nashville: Vanderbilt, 2017), especially 37.

35. See Jen Harvie's point that "the audience member becomes a solo performer and is deliberately isolated in the city, inviting reflection on the ways that the city and communication technologies produce isolation." Jen Harvie, *Theatre & the City* (London: Palgrave Macmillan, 2009), 58.

36. Murphy, "Audiences," 720.

37. Harvie, *Theatre & the City*, 66.

38. See Harvie, "Labor: Participation, Delegation and Deregulation," in *Fair Play*, 26–61.

39. Harvie, *Fair Play*, 36.

40. Sarah Senk, "The Memory Exchange: Public Mourning at the National 9/11 Memorial Museum," *Canadian Review of American Studies* 48, no. 2 (2018): 254–76, see esp. 259.

41. Charlotte McIvor makes the point that the partnerships between theatre and "stakeholders from the non-arts sectors (particularly public agencies)" can both limit and create opportunities for theatre makers. See McIvor, "Other Space," 480.

42. Tompkins, "The 'Place' and Practice," 17.

43. Pierre Bourdieu, *The Social Structures of the Economy* (London: Polity, 2000), 12.

CONCLUSION

Activism in the Marketplace

HOW DO WE MOBILIZE THE past in more progressive ways? What aesthetic strategies can we draw on to recognize injustices and to galvanize present and future action? How can witnessing of the past, and the present, best be performed in the current marketplace? As this book has argued, theatrical witnessing—by both the performing subject and the audience—represents a point of possibility, to recognize and amplify injustice, give voice to the disenfranchised or silenced, and to positively alter the balance of power in the marketplace. Audiences, as critical consumers of performance, have the power to challenge the dominance of particular proprietors of social capital in the market, to bestow and coproduce symbolic capital, and to perform themselves as witnesses. Theatrical witnessing of painful pasts thus represents an opportunity to perform power and to direct that power ethically. Such ethically directed labor contains the potential for accumulating not only mnemonic, but also cultural and social capital. To argue, however, that consuming—even as a critical citizen consumer—is simply a tool for good would be not only naive, but would disregard the fundamental limits and distortions of witnessing. These limits are both internally and externally shaped.

THE LIMITS OF WITNESSING

When audiences witness the performance of injustice, whether it be "fictional" theatre or autoperformed verbatim testimony, they may be changed. This change might involve becoming more ethically aware, making an empathetic shift to identifying with the subject, or learning of a geographically or temporally distant event that makes them see another's history, or their own history, differently. They may feel called upon to respond through compassion or a sense of public duty, to recognize their own privilege and capital, to become witnesses. Based on their role as witnesses, audiences may change their minds and their outlooks, affecting both the reception of the stories of the past being witnessed and the audience's future actions in the marketplace.

Or none of these things may happen. The audience may cry at particularly sad moments, they may be tense at fraught moments, they may applaud and smile and say "how moving" as they leave the auditorium, have a drink at the theatre bar, and then—what? *Nothing.* Witnessing does not necessarily lead to change because the reliance on feeling, and the inevitably unbalanced power relationships between privileged consumers and producers and the victim or survivor whose story is being represented, often reproduce the structural inequalities of the marketplace rather than dismantling them. And even where an audience member considers themselves to have been changed, is that change enacted beyond the individual self and that person's sense of being more enlightened, or more alive, because of that moment of witnessing another's pain? Does the witness do more than simply accrue symbolic and social capital through their witnessing? These are difficult, if not impossible, questions to resolve.

And what of the story being performed? How does it change? Perhaps the repetition of the same story night after night shifts it from an initially urgent register to a ritualized set of words and stock emotions. This may be true whether the show is performed by professional or nonprofessional storytellers. The subjects of their stories, from historical state violence to contemporary rape, are projected to a larger audience, perhaps even touring internationally and achieving commercial, mainstream success. But whether this projection and reach results in more than passive witnessing is debatable. Inequality cannot be solved through storytelling alone. Likewise, the unfair power distribution of the memory marketplace is not overturned through increased consumption of verbatim stories of historical abuse—more likely, these stories represent new commodities that the marketplace responds to with increased production, creating further market segmentation, driven by creative destruction, rather than destabilizing the domination of wealthy, white, patriarchal, Western versions of the past.

Michal Givoni critiques the "political instrumentality" of witnessing because too often it takes the place of real political solutions.[1] Givoni links the rise of the independent or individual witness to the falling away of intervention by governments, which devolves social and ethical responsibility to the personal autonomy of the individual and the "free" market: "By providing a face and a practical framework for the moral crafting of the self, can it be that witnessing to genocide, disaster, and war unwittingly creates anchors for a neoliberal policy that transfers responsibility to private individuals in matters pertaining to both global and social injustice?"[2] As I have argued in relation to peace grants for Northern Irish theatre companies, the expectation that theatrical witnessing can deliver on social cohesion seems beyond their remit. Social justice is not the responsibility of the arts, though it may be their subject.

I make these points about the limits of witnessing despite the fact that I love theatre, that I believe passionately in its power to affect people, and that I am committed to culture being connected to, and a part of, social and civil discourse. As Emily Mann says, "I've dedicated my life to the belief that theatre is not only affected by the society we are in, but that theatre affects the society that we are in."[3] And I do believe that the world would be a better place if more people acted as witnesses. But that last point is only true, of course, if witnessing is understood as an active and agentic role and not simply as a form of consumption.

The fragility of witnessing as an interventionist tool is observed by Beckett in *Waiting for Godot*. When Vladimir and Estragon first meet Pozzo and Lucky, they are struck by the terrible conditions in which Lucky is employed. Vladimir "explodes":

> **Vladimir**: It's a scandal! ... To treat a man ... [*Gestures towards* Lucky] ... like that ... I think that ... no ... a human being ... no ... it's a scandal!
> **Estragon**: [*Not to be outdone.*] A disgrace![4]

But quickly the explosion subsides—rather than engaging further Vladimir suggests they leave (but true to form does not actually leave). Then Pozzo justifies his treatment of Lucky:

> **Pozzo**: Why doesn't he make himself comfortable? Let's try and get it clear. Has he not the right to? Certainly he has. It follows that he doesn't want to. There's reasoning for you. And why doesn't he want to? [...] He wants to impress me, so that I'll keep him.[5]

Rather than objecting to the ways that unequal power relationships determine "rights" as a privilege rather than a right, Estragon and Vladimir quickly accept this explanation and go on to sympathize with Pozzo for the oppression he suffers through Lucky's gloomy presence. So what lessons do we learn? Initial outrage does not lead Vladimir to action, Estragon's form of witnessing is competitive and relational, only the aggressor has the power to speak freely, and despite evidence to the contrary, Pozzo's speech is viewed as reasonable (as opposed to Lucky's later stream-of-consciousness tirade against the kind of "reason" that Pozzo employs). Thus we see how empathetic witnessing, far from challenging the status quo, serves to reinstate the aggressor who now, in turn, assumes the more sympathetic role of victim.

Beckett sounds the warning for the limits of witnessing, and it is no coincidence that *Godot* was written in the years after the Holocaust. The co-option and complicity of the original witness through reasonable argument and the exertion of self-interest (Estragon wants to claim the bones that Lucky does not eat) illustrates the pitfalls of devolving social justice to individuals, even those who consider themselves both intellectual and fair-minded.

But surely it does not have to be this way? Can we so easily give up on the utopian promise of both individual and collective witnessing? Can we not rather persist and, through witnessing, change collective memory of the past and collective visions for the future? Can our labor not accumulate more than internal or simulated change? Recent developments in the social performance of witnessing seem to offer some hope.

#METOO AS COLLECTIVE WITNESSING AND COLLECTIVE MEMORY

The #MeToo movement has been explosive, not least for its embodiment of the idea that the utopian possibilities of witnessing might actually come to pass. Using #MeToo, women and men have created a transnational collective force that, through the combination of individual strength and group solidarity since late 2017, has challenged the widespread former tacit acceptance of sexual harassment and assault of women in the workplace. Though this movement has been marked by some of the same features we see in Beckett's play—competitiveness, the performance of outrage, a countering "be reasonable" argument that asserts that the victim is not a victim but chooses not to exert their rights—it has also demonstrated the transformative power of speaking truth and suggests that the market *can* be reshaped, and unequal structural power relations challenged, through collective labor.

The scale and speed with which #MeToo took off in October 2017 was extraordinary, though it should be noted that this followed decades of inaction. The scale of the uptake on that particular hashtag, in fact, mirrors the scale of past failures of witnessing. Tarana Burke set up the Me Too activist group to support survivors of harassment and violence in 2006; it took celebrity buy-in for it to go viral in 2017. Indeed, the eleven-year gestation points to the slow burn of social movements, as the explosion in 2017 results not from a single moment but represents the apex of a reinvigorated feminist movement, and a turn toward using social media as a new platform for the performance of civil rights issues. Because though storytelling cannot change inequality, it can draw attention to it, shifting social and symbolic capital away from those assumed to be powerful, toward those who can express their mnemonic capital through these new channels. The #MeToo movement therefore acutely illustrates the conjunction between major shifts in social attitudes, developments in global communications, and watershed moments in collective memory.

Does #MeToo represent a new form of *collective* memory? Given that there has been no avoiding this movement in the Western media, we have to answer yes. Now that these stories have emerged, the past has been reexamined, the archive has been reoriented—the same photographs that used to depict smiling colleagues, now depict abuser and victim. The narrative has changed. In another sense, however, the understanding of "collective" needs to be interrogated—who do these stories, these new memories, belong to? No doubt they capture all our attention, but are they really "ours"? As Moira Donegan argues, within the #MeToo campaign, "One approach is individualist, hard-headed, grounded in ideals of pragmatism, realism and self-sufficiency. The other is expansive, communal, idealistic and premised on the ideals of mutual interest and solidarity."[6] One critique of #MeToo is that it does not so much alter the marketplace as merely further benefit the interests of an already pretty successful, vocal group. The "collective" remains shaped in these instances by a top-down archive of stories that bear only a tangential relationship to more individual or local situations.

If we read #MeToo as creating a new collective memory, which actively rewitnesses both private and public pasts, then there are further relevant questions about mutuality. Who gets left out of this new online, social archive? Who is not on Twitter? When a social movement restricts access to those who are able to engage online, there are inevitably exclusions at play. This brings us back to the privilege of the consumer. How in the twenty-first century are even "ethical" consumers exploiting the labor and mnemonic capital of the less privileged? As Anna Reading and Tanya Notley argue, because of the globalized labor market, we also have to consider the environmental and labor exploitation behind digitization as part of the activist event, a joint human and environmental cost that is all too often invisible due to the even lower social capital of those performing that labor.[7]

And there are other, obvious, questions too, about the status of this movement as a kind of collective archive. Who, for example, will curate the archive as it develops and when it ceases to be active? Who will do the labor to create activist mnemonic capital? In the 2018 referendum to repeal the constitutional ban on abortion in Ireland, the hashtag #Repealthe8th became a popular way for activists to highlight the issue online. Now archivists and historians are working to preserve the materials generated by both sides of the campaign—yet one issue already raising its head is the extent to which this will be a "balanced" archive. One official body suggested that it would archive websites associated with the campaign, and in order to depict balance it would include an equal number of "yes" and "no" sites, despite there being a greater number, and arguably a greater range, of "yes" sites and testimonies.[8] Historians also caution that there is a risk of focusing too exclusively on recent, digital history and that archives need to include and represent materials from the thirty years of reproductive rights activism since abortion was banned in Ireland.[9] This point relates to the ways the #MeToo campaign was criticized for obscuring the hashtag's foundation by Tarana Burke, as the intellectual property of a black woman became co-opted by rich, white women. The history of campaigns is hence an important part of the story, and as the shaping of these particular archives is still ongoing, they signify an opportunity to raise important questions regarding collective memory and the risk of exclusivity/exclusion. Does it matter if an archive is biased because its principle for inclusion of material is based on the volumes available? Or does the archivist always have to maintain balance? The fact that the "yes" campaign is more socially progressive does not automatically entitle it to more archive space. And we also need to acknowledge that whether the archive is balanced, biased, or fully inclusive, the potential of an archive to act as witness to a history is only ever realized when the archive is used, when it becomes a part of future performances of witnessing. Those performances will shape and reshape the material into new narratives that serve the moment of the performance.

How do those future performances happen? One of the negatives of the #MeToo campaign, like any form of autoperformance, is that it requires the victim to reanimate painful memories of the past for others' consumption. Indeed, though #MeToo demonstrates a model of public witnessing that shows great solidarity with victims, it also maintains the model in which victims take on the emotional labor of publicizing these painful memories. In order to take part, the victim must display themselves in repeated performances of distress. As with plays that focus on abuse and rape, this leads us as critics to the ethical question of how activism can itself be punishing for the victim. The potential that speaking out further penalizes the victims is made worse by the possibility that announcing their sexual harassment on a global social media platform may lead to massive personal, as well as professional, ramifications. The inherent irony here is that after the negative effects of silencing, we also have to consider the negative effects of witnessing.

One further negative effect of witnessing one's own experience of sexual violence is the consumer expectation of a performance of trauma. In late 2017, I was asked by a group of graduate students to discuss the #MeToo phenomenon. In this group, many were taken aback by the scale of #MeToo, and some said they felt as if it were becoming compulsory for them to add their story. They may not have had an experience of sexual violence or harassment, but they felt that the expectation was there that they *should*. Moreover, of those students who said that they did have an experience that would justify using the hashtag, they were wary not just of the potential attention but of the homogenizing effect of the hashtag. These students wanted to be witnessed but also wanted the specificity of their experience to be recognized. They suspected that the group-witnessing driving #MeToo would not serve them as individuals, and they were doubtful that their voices would aid anyone else. Finally, they were suspicious that #MeToo was just another manifestation of trends in social media, which would soon dry up, leaving no trace of any tangible change, but leaving a digital trail of their performance of pain.

I agreed with so many of their points: about the risk of historical flattening, the compulsory aspect of it as a new performative, and the risk of reducing violence to a likeable narrative. I agreed with them because I have written about my own experience of sexual violence and the silence I kept for twenty years after being raped as a teenager. While I am proud of how I have now told my story, I am only too aware of the emotional labor involved, and that in revealing myself as a victim, I was risking my own social capital. I have never used #MeToo. I was also dismayed by the #MeToo public display of suffering as yet another manifestation of how women have to perform their bodies publicly in order to be heard or seen, and the further expectation that their stories should then be judged by a jury of their social media peers.

As many feminists have pointed out, #MeToo is not in itself an adequate response to violence, and the energies that went into promoting it could, in some cases, be better aimed at reforming the criminal justice system so that infractions of women's bodily autonomy would be punished by law in more than the current number of instances. Again, we return to the problems with compassion, in which an audience's empathic response actually takes the place of efforts toward achieving social justice. When any critique of #MeToo or #IBelieveYou resulted in a public shaming via Twitter (see the reaction to critics such as Margaret Atwood suggesting alleged abusers be assumed innocent until proven guilty[10]), that seemed even more problematic. Then, the backlash to #MeToo that started in early 2018 showed not only the antifemale sentiment lurking just under the surface, but also the risk to those victims who had posted using the hashtag. Cultural violence became a further risk of public witnessing.

The worry that the social media campaign benefited only a small cohort, and that it would not lead to tangible benefits, was addressed by a group of activists who subsequently launched "#TimesUp," a campaign and legal defense fund to support women without the economic or social capital to challenge sexual harassment in the workplace. The campaign was begun by women who work in film, television, and theatre and who recognized their relative privilege and aimed to address it. #TimesUp also addresses the question of how to replicate and sustain grassroots activism. The slow temporality of social and legal change requires not just continued labor, but also money (not least because labor needs to be fairly recompensed). This both addresses that major limit of witnessing—acknowledging the limited transformative impact of consciousness-raising—and distributes responsibility for witnessing away from the victim. #TimesUp finally also acknowledged the limitations of short-term online action, and pointed out the risk of confusing that with institutional change, or the institutionalization of change, answering the question so many of us were asking ourselves in the months since #MeToo went viral: after witnessing, then what?

The #TimesUp campaign would seem a counter to many of the criticisms of #MeToo, as it embodies the principles of idealism and mutual interest that Donegan holds up. Yet, still, as Kathy Davis argues, hashtag campaigns struggle to be truly collective:

> [#MeToo is] a very different kind of activism than, for example, *Take Back the Night* rallies in the USA, the collective protest in India around the ubiquitous harassment of women in public (called "eve teasing") or OpAntiSH (Operation Anti Sexual Harassment) in Cairo where women and men support women's access to political demonstrations and religious festivals and rescue them from situations where they are being harassed or assaulted. This kind of activism does not focus on the testimony of individual woman [*sic*], but frames sexual violence as a collective issue facing all women, which requires raising public awareness and involving both women and men in grass-root activism as well as transforming institutions which condone violence against women.[11]

Davis prioritizes embodied collectivity over the virtual solidarity of online campaigns, suggesting that online witnessing and testimony will always be individualistic rather than the collective of grassroots social activism. Davis's point is also germane for performance scholars, who may question the extent to which individuals and groups can perform activism in online forms. Given these critiques, should we prioritize "live" performance? Should we return to older forms of engagement, like theatre, which have been creating "'publics' that stretch across geographical and cultural distance and involve individuals with widely different experiences and life positions"[12] for far longer than social media? Is the communal setting of spaces like the theatre, with its social guidance of witnessing, a better forum?

COLLECTIVE MEMORY WORK AS THE FOUNDATION FOR ACTIVISM

Paradigm shifts in collective memory, and major shifts in social attitudes, often coincide. Though Ireland's "Decade of Centenaries," a ten-year program (2011–2021) to mark one hundred years of national progress, may seem a world away from the #MeToo campaign, it has been inflected by many of the same foundational questions around gender inequality. Initially, the Decade of Centenaries program was dominated not only by a patriarchal version of Irish history but was also shaped by an almost exclusively male panel of experts. Slowly, however, through the concerted efforts of feminist scholars and activists, the narrative has shifted so that the focus of the decade has become about the memory work needed to reinstate, rather than obscure, women as central players in the nation's history. As Charlotte McIvor states, the decade represents "the most sustained period of official state-led reflection in modern and contemporary Irish history, on Irish history itself."[13] The centenary focus and sense of meta-reflection thus inevitably—though inadvertently—created an occasion for changing the narrative. Fintan Walsh remarks of this period in Irish culture that audiences to these reflections have been encouraged "not only to encounter the past, but to question their responsibility for the events presented."[14] The next step of this questioning is to consider how, as Mark Currie puts it, "The present is the object of future memory."[15] The commemorative moment is thus set up as a self-conscious process of witnessing; the inadvertent aspect has been the extent to which the present, as well as the past, has become the subject of these acts of witness. This has not always been a comfortable process. Though often the commemorative gaze can position the present as a more advanced version of the nation, affirming a progressive version of history,[16] the identification of past inequality has, in this case, only served to highlight the stultification of progress relating to gender in present-day Ireland.

Recent responses by activists in Ireland to gender inequality provide two archetypes that answer the question of how we can mobilize the past in more progressive ways. As Linda Connolly argues, commemoration provides an opportunity to claim internal social injustices: "A key challenge for public intellectuals in centennial Ireland is to acknowledge and consider both the *achievements and failures* of the State and society in the wider 100-year period."[17] To acknowledge failures is a vital step in transforming commemoration from a triumphalist or progressivist narrative into a performance of ethical accountability. However, because of the institutionalization of commemoration as a pillar of the conservative nation-state, this kind of transformation and move toward accountability often has to be enforced.

On Wednesday, October 28, 2015, the Abbey Theatre announced its 2016 program, Waking the Nation, to commemorate the centenary of the 1916 Irish Easter Rising and the insurrection against British rule. The Waking the Nation program included ten plays, yet *somehow* only one was written by a woman, and only three were to be directed by women. There was no self-consciousness about this gender imbalance, as demonstrated by the theatre's press release:

> To commemorate and acknowledge the major historical events of 1916, the Abbey Theatre extended an invitation to artists and audiences to reflect on our past, the Ireland of today and of the future. We are proud to be part of the Ireland 2016 Centenary Programme with Waking the Nation, a season featuring an exciting roll-call of new Irish voices alongside major revivals of some of the great plays from the Abbey Theatre repertoire.
>
> ...
>
> In Waking the Nation, our intention is to interrogate rather than celebrate the past. For over 110 years now the Abbey stage has been a platform for the reflection of Irish society through theatre. Plays have the power to ask questions that resonate for generations. I believe that we should listen to and reflect on what our playwrights have written, whether it's Sean O'Casey, Tom Murphy or Frank McGuinness.

This announcement provoked many theatre professionals, led by Lian Bell, to call out the Abbey Theatre for celebrating a male-dominated program and a complete failure to "interrogate" its own performance of inequality. First on Facebook and then on Twitter, the objections swelled, swiftly adopting the hashtag #WakingtheFeminists and #WTF to unify the protest.[18] As critic Helen Meany noted, "Irish theatre abounds with brilliant Irish women, unlike the Abbey's programme."[19]

The imbalance of programming at the Abbey—and indeed across Irish theatre—was nothing new. In fact, as the follow-on Waking the Feminists 2017 *Gender Counts* report shows the Irish theatre sector was marked by significant gender inequality.[20] The outcry provoked by Waking the Nation had, clearly, been building for a long time. The intensity of the response to the Abbey's program, though, vividly illustrates how commemoration functions as a flashpoint. While in many ways the national centenary commemorations initially served as a conservative assertion of the primacy of the nation as a container for identity, the Waking the Feminists bottom-up movement exploited the market's current focus on national history, and the social and cultural capital available to those remembering it, to highlight past inequalities and simultaneously reinforce an agenda for change.

We know that power is stabilized "by the successful establishment of a supposedly teleological and linear historical narrative," and, further, that marketplace hegemony is the result of one discourse being "elevated above others not because it is superior but because the most powerful group put it there."[21] In the Waking the Nation program, and the resulting WTF protests, we witness the theatrical and historical narratives being fundamentally challenged. As with many of the plays discussed in this book, this challenge rests on the issue of gatekeeping. As Bell said, "Who gets to tell the stories of our nation, and what kind of stories do they get to tell? Whose voices are being given a chance to be heard, and who makes these choices?"[22]

Commenting on the Waking the Nation program, Irish senator Ivana Bacik argued that the Abbey's decisions were not taken in a vacuum, but rather mirrored "women's invisibility in the public sphere and public life, their exclusion from politics and other areas of public life."[23] Bacik's point is compelling because it suggests that as critics we should not separate "culture" or "commemoration" from other aspects of society; these are overlapping marketplaces. Making the link between the disenfranchisement of certain social groups in society, to their equal marginalization in commemorative culture—how low social and economic capital is paralleled by low cultural and mnemonic capital—demonstrates that memory culture is not immune to structural discrimination and inequality.

The memory marketplace is shaped by power. That power, as I have suggested in this book, can be both top-down, compelling the market to reflect the memories of the social elite, and bottom-up, driving it to reflect the memories of the disenfranchised. Different forms of capital are mobilized by these opposite forces, and consumers equally respond to, and make demands on, both sets of producers. In this, as in other forms of social change, the power of the consumer in the marketplace is key as patterns of consumption can shift the balance of power and elevate minority interests to the mainstream. Movements like #MeToo and WTF indicate a major shift in what stories are being demanded by consumers and how they are being consumed.

It is, of course, always bizarre to describe women as a "minority" who have been silenced when women not only make up half the population but also have been far from silent. The idea that including women in the Irish centenary program was somehow a radical idea, or a great move toward diversity, is also counterpointed by the fact that other minorities were also excluded from the Decade of Centenaries. In line with this, the Abbey's program was not only patriarchal but based on a white, nationalist history, without any input from, or reference to, the experiences of nonwhite and migrant Irish residents and citizens. In response to these exclusions, the WTF movement drew attention to multiple intersectional forms of inequality, for example highlighting disability rights, the exclusion of Travellers, and including perspectives from international theatre makers both within and outside Ireland. Nevertheless it was striking that the 600-strong crowd at the first WTF meeting was, as far as I could see, exclusively white (reflecting the whiteness of Irish theatre more generally). The questions that were raised by WTF of the structural blocks to accessing theatre work—to women, generally, and to mothers, in particular—thus also apply to other social groups too, and should be more widely shared and applied. Social biases and privilege also mark activist movements; indeed, we need to consider the activist space as a marketplace itself.

What WTF most fully demonstrates is the necessity to move beyond consciousness raising toward real structural change. To return to Jen Harvie's point raised in chapter 2, the risk of cultural interventions is that "they sometimes offer a spectacle of communication and social engagement rather more than a qualitatively and sustainably rich and even critical engagement."[24] Culture can highlight inequality but at the same time risks operating "insidiously as a distraction . . . which can only ever be temporary and limited."[25] As this book has highlighted, art can engage with social justice, but it can't deliver structural change—nor should it be the burden of art to do this. Having said that, it has been artists who have led the call for greater gender equality in their profession and the arts as a sector. By disrupting the assumed acceptance of the Waking the Nation program, the women-led campaign worked to ensure not only that the *past* story of Ireland being depicted was more balanced but also "in anticipation of the story" they wanted to tell in *future* years.[26] Reframing the present hence affects both past and future narratives, and witnessing, in this case, is closely linked to structural activism.

The WTF movement therefore positioned itself as more than a distraction. Moreover, it used the question of representation to highlight the lack of justice and to galvanize the theatre sector to visible change. Indeed, the success of WTF as a movement illustrates just how challenges in the marketplace can change the power balance in more widespread ways. The first change was signaled by Abbey Director Fiach Mac Conghail's roll back on his views about the absence of women in the program. Mac Conghail's initial reaction to Bell and others' objections on social media was to tweet: "I don't and haven't programmed plays or productions on a gender basis. I took decisions based on who I admired and wanted to work with," and "Also, sometimes plays and ideas that we have commissioned by and about women just don't work out. That has happened. Them the breaks."[27] The protest that greeted these responses led to a more pragmatic view a few days later. Recognizing his mistake, Mac Conghail offered an apology and agreed to Bell's request for the Abbey, as a venue for a public meeting, to engage with the topic of women in Irish theatre (tickets sold out in seven minutes).[28] Though coming to the end of his tenure as director, he also oversaw (alongside the incoming directors Graham McLaren and Neil Murray) the announcement of progressive and forward-looking gender equality policy in August 2016.

And it was not just one theatre that was at issue. Though the Abbey, as the National Theatre, is the figurehead for the sector, gender bias was evident across many theatres and companies. The WTF movement decided to dedicate a year (November 2015 to November 2016) to work toward researching and changing gender equality in the sector. This was later extended, with the benefit of Arts Council of Ireland funding, so that the campaign finished in June 2017. The concentrated time frame was an important aspect for two reasons: first, it lent the proceedings an air of urgency and finitude; second, it recognized the enormous energy required for activist work like this, and the fact that the people undertaking this labor were precariously employed and yet still devoting both their personal and professional resources to improving the sector for everyone. When social justice is devolved to those who are in less secure positions, it can be not only exhausting but also exploitative, and the WTF campaign strongly recognized the need to limit the extra, and often excessive, labor required of a few individuals by a nationwide campaign. Despite that, reading the timeline of events on the WTF website is an exercise in wondering how such a small group managed to undertake so much work.

Meetings with the Arts Council and the boards of theatres and companies started in January 2016. In July, the Arts Council granted €20,000 to continue the research begun by Brenda Donohue, Tanya Dean, and Ciara O'Dowd into gender equality in the sector. Headline findings were presented at the November 2016 meeting, "One Thing More" (again held in a sold-out Abbey auditorium). The full report, which covered ten of the highest-funded theatres and companies in Ireland, with additional research by Ciara Murphy, Kathleen Cawley, and Kate Harris, was published in June 2017 as *Gender Counts: An Analysis of Gender in Irish Theatre 2006–2015*.[29] The study's data show that the four highest-funded organizations have the lowest female representation, that only 28 percent of authors employed are female, and that there is clear gender disparity in particular roles with, for example, the roles of sound designer and costume designer, gendered male and female respectively.[30] The relationship between public funding and gender inequality is striking; the study importantly backs up with hard data the subterranean knowledge that many theatre makers and audiences have long held about gender, power, and the uneven distribution of economic and cultural capital.

Change comes in stages. Since the release of *Gender Counts* and the "end" of the Waking the Feminists movement,[31] what has altered? The addition of female-authored plays and the introduction of gender-blind casting suggests a new sense of inclusion, but as WTF originally pointed out, "inclusion ... does not represent equality."[32] The real change has come with the adoption of the campaign's aims by the government ministers overseeing the arts in Ireland. In March 2017, then-Minister for Arts, Heritage and the Gaeltacht Heather Humphreys officially asked all national cultural institutions to have a gender equality policy in place by 2018, the centenary of women's suffrage. In January 2018, the Arts Council made equal opportunities, including gender equality, a condition for funding, and in July 2018, ten organizations announced policies to improve gender equality across the theatre sector.[33] Of course, as discussed in chapter 1, "we shouldn't be naive": legislation and policy change do not necessarily equal the ending of inequality. Nevertheless, it is a sign of something starting to change. Witnessing is the starting point, social and institutional change is the goal.

The Waking the Feminists movement changed other kinds of power imbalances in Irish theatre too. Grace Dyas, a theatre maker and activist, was inspired by the movement to look at how she had been affected as a woman working in the theatre sector; as a result Dyas spoke out about her experience of harassment by Michael Colgan, a sexually predatory and hot-tempered man, who had been director of Ireland's second largest theatre, the Gate Theatre, for decades. When Colgan made offensive comments in person and by phone to Dyas about sex and her body, she publicly spoke back to him, first in the bar they were in (with witnesses) and subsequently in a blog post.[34] That post, like the #MeToo movement, sparked other stories, by other women who had been harassed, bullied, or abused by Colgan. Colgan's resignation followed soon after, and an internal review was set up.

The risk that a few totemic men who (close to retirement) are sacrificed in order to purge the system, but keep it largely unchanged, troubled some within the theatre industry. As a result of Dyas's blog post and subsequent reports by other women, the Irish Theatre Institute (ITI) created an initiative to establish a code of behavior within the sector. On March 21, 2018, the ITI held a day of public talks and sessions to discuss the draft code, "Speak Up and Call It Out," which was attended by three hundred people involved in theatre. Dyas spoke at the event, giving an overview of her reasons for objecting to Colgan and her experience in the aftermath of speaking out. Dyas commented that she is often told that she is brave, but this is a label she rejects: "Bravery is doing something without feeling any fear."[35] Dyas acknowledges that self-witnessing requires courage to face fear, and she further acknowledged the cost—of fear and other emotions—of being a public witness. As JD Peters asserts, "You can be marked for life by being the witness of an event."[36] As a footnote to that remark, it's troubling to see that there are other costs to worry about too: Dyas has recently begun a crowdfunding campaign, with herself as beneficiary, so that she can "get on with trying to change power in our society."[37] Though Dyas has enormous cultural capital, she still struggles to pay her rent. Dyas's Patreon page thus represents an (increasingly popular) mode of encouraging audiences to support not only art but also activism, through witnessing and, more importantly, subsidizing the artist as well as the art.[38]

Dyas's work on gender equality is not limited to present-day concerns. As director of Theatre Club, she created and performed in *We Don't Know What's Buried Here* (2018), which powerfully (and angrily) highlighted the historical oppression and incarceration of women in Irish Magdalen laundries. On this issue, Dyas has worked alongside Councillor Gary Gannon,[39] an independent councillor in Dublin City Council, who has been at the forefront of the campaign to save the last Magdalen laundry in Ireland—on Dublin's Sean McDermott Street—from being sold for commercial redevelopment.[40] When news broke that the site would be sold to a Tokyo-based hotel chain, it seemed as if commercial interests really were the most powerful agents in the marketplace. But recently, survivors, alongside Gannon, Dyas, and campaigners from Justice For Magdalenes, have successfully persuaded councillors to vote against the sale and to consider the site's partial preservation.[41] Though this was a significant achievement in forcing political agendas to consider social and historical issues, the campaign must now continue to fight for the site to be developed instead as a Site of Conscience, which would include a memorial to Ireland's institutional past, education facilities, and social housing.[42] This memorial project, if successful, will bring together in solidarity survivors of different institutions (from industrial schools to mother and child institutions to the laundries) in a performance of mutual witnessing that may overcome some of the historical and current divisions in Irish society, and that has the potential to show how we can prioritize social justice over commercial growth. That the history and significance of this built environment first came to prominence with ANU's production of *Laundry* at the Dublin Theatre Festival in 2011 (which preceded by two years the state's report and apology for the abuse of women in those institutions), illustrates just how much theatrical witnessing and activism overlap, and the long-term impact when bottom-up producers, in partnerships with gatekeeping state agencies (*Laundry* was funded by Dublin City Council), work to recognize the cultural capital of socially marginalized people and their memories. Perhaps also, finally, it is only through institutional partnerships that activism can find sustained, and sustainable, outcomes, given that in a longer temporal view we cannot expect the victim, or the precariously employed/bottom-up activist to continue to contribute their labor and capital to the task. However, as the argument about archiving illustrates, the shift toward institutionalization may also risk losing the important individual voice and of forgetting the labor of the activist.

Where to Now?

There are many questions to be resolved in relation to performances of witnessing: Who gets to speak? How can it be sustained? What really changes? What is the cost? The performances discussed in this book—those performances that happen on and off stages, performed by professional and nonprofessional actors, and by audiences—create situations that illustrate both the limits of witnessing and its radical potentialities. Acting as a witness to past injustice, by giving testimony and by actively listening to others' testimony, may be limited, but I hope that by raising critical questions I have not overstated the case—because despite these questions, I passionately believe that uncovering hidden histories, and creating platforms for silenced or marginalized voices, is one of the most fundamental and vital roles that culture makers and audiences can play. Through this work, we change the cultural memory marketplace. And hopefully we can see those changes reflected in and by society too.

Activism, of the kind performed in #MeToo, #TimesUp, WTF, and "Speak Up and Call It Out," is the clearest example of how active witnessing can lead to social change. The utopian possibilities here are sometimes held back by the difficulties of creating change, but these obstacles do not invalidate the nobility of the motivation, instinct, and effort involved in trying to perform ethical witnessing. What these movements have achieved is a rewriting of the past to acknowledge the mnemonic capital of previously unseen and unheard individuals and groups, leading to a reshaping of cultural memory and, as a result, a reshaping of the future. I hope beyond hope that this is more than a temporary kind of power.

Silence is not a condition, or a history, that I or many women want to lay claim to—but sometimes silence is the starting point of witnessing, the beginning of voice, the opening of solidarity. That solidarity, whether it is directed from the audience to a lone performer onstage, or whether it is the kind of solidarity generated by raising our voices together, is both inspiring and impactful. The "what now?" question that trails activist movements is also present here, and there are many directions in which this activism may go. But perhaps the simplest answer is this—we keep on witnessing. Keeping on keeping on can be exhausting, and we do need to question what the tangible outcomes are and whether activism (whether for social rights or memory rights) ever really ends. McIvor frames this continued work as *effort*: "Effort quite simply names the need and value of keeping going especially when an approach doesn't yield the desired outcome."[43] Against the often emotional difficulty of effort, however, we can set the knowledge that the engagement involved in witnessing can sometimes be its own reward and can sometimes lead to unforeseen and positive outcomes.

In writing this book I have implicitly also been reflecting on academic work as a form of witnessing. In watching shows and reading scripts, I attempt to do more than simply consume—I aim to be both a compassionate and critical witness, to seek out the utopian moments, and to be aware of how often we all fall short. This is also true of how I try to act as a witness outside of theatre and memory. Focusing on the need for witnessing to move from reflection to activism has made me more determined to try to show leadership within the spheres available to me. The shift toward neoliberal policies in universities, in which so many are precariously employed, and which create a culture of overwork and a constant expectation of "impact" over and above depth of engagement and creativity, prioritizing funding over teaching and student welfare, means that those of us with tenure need to move on from simply being passive witnesses. Currently, we—by which I mean I—grumble but accept what is happening. But if we—by which I mean I—do not start to act as active witnesses of our present, university management teams will continue to fail to uphold or enact the values of the university: values like equality and respect that to so many of us are a vital part of why we want to work as researchers and teachers. The moment that we see ourselves as active rather than passive witnesses, is the moment that we begin to show leadership, to take back our disciplines, and to occupy our jobs and roles for, and into, the future.[44]

The market is a stratified sphere in which those without social and cultural capital struggle to have their voices heard. Those of us with platforms to speak, whether in theatre, academia, or the media, can act and work beyond the competitive principles of the marketplace that are embedded so firmly and deeply in our societies. We can use our labor to create change, we can notice how inequality in mnemonic and social capital overlap, and we can intervene in the marketplace. We do not have to settle for simply consuming but can be producers ourselves. We can, in other words, be witnesses.

NOTES

1. Michal Givoni, *The Care of the Witness* (Cambridge: Cambridge University Press, 2016), 7.
2. Givoni, *The Care of the Witness*, 25.
3. "Emily Mann: In Conversation," an open conversation with the audience at the ATHE Conference, July 29, 1999, *Theatre Topics* 10, no. 1 (2000): 1–16, see esp. 6.
4. Samuel Beckett, *Waiting for Godot*, in *Samuel Beckett: The Complete Dramatic Works* (London: Faber, 1986), 28.
5. Beckett, *Waiting for Godot*, 31.
6. Moira Donegan, "How #MeToo Revealed the Central Rift within Feminism Today," *The Guardian*, May 11, 2018, https://www.theguardian.com/news/2018/may/11/how-metoo-revealed-the-central-rift-within-feminism-social-individualist.
7. Anna Reading and Tanya Notley, "Globital Memory Capital: Theorizing Digital Memory Economics," in *Digital Memory Studies*, ed. Andrew Hoskins (London: Routledge, 2018), 234–50.
8. The National Library of Ireland could only archive thirty-seven "no" websites, and therefore capped the "yes" websites at thirty-seven, also. See Natalie Harrower (@natalieharrower), "The @NLIreland could only find contacts and permission for 37 No side websites, so they capped the total at 37 per side," Twitter, July 16, 2018, 2:21 a.m., https://twitter.com/natalieharrower/status/1018787583868981249.
9. See Archiving the 8th (@archivingthe8th), Twitter, https://twitter.com/archivingthe8th?lang=en for threads of discussion about Archiving the 8th. See also Alex Marshall, "Posters, Banners, Boarding Passes: Museums Try to Get

a Head Start on History," *New York Times*, June 18, 2018, https://www.nytimes.com/2018/06/18/arts/design/rapid-response-collecting-ireland-berlin.html.

10. Ashifa Kassam, "Margaret Atwood Faces Feminist Backlash on Social Media over #MeToo," *The Guardian*, January 15, 2018, https://www.theguardian.com/books/2018/jan/15/margaret-atwood-feminist-backlash-metoo.

11. Dubravka Zarkov and Kathy Davis, "Ambiguities and Dilemmas around #MeToo: #ForHowLong and #WhereTo?," *European Journal of Women's Studies* 25, no. 1 (2018): 3–9, see esp. 5.

12. Gabriel Tarde, "The Public and the Crowd," in *Gabriel Tarde on Communication and Social Influence*, ed. T. Clark (Chicago, 1969), quoted in Adam Arvidson, "Brand Management," in *Consuming Cultures, Global Perspectives*, ed. John Brewer and Frank Trentmann (Oxford: Berg, 2006), 71–94, see esp. 75.

13. Charlotte McIvor, "Other Space (Non-Theatre Spaces)," in *The Palgrave Handbook of Contemporary Irish Theatre and Performance*, ed. Eamonn Jordan and Eric Weitz (London: Palgrave, 2018), 465–86, see esp. 479.

14. Fintan Walsh, "The Power of the Powerless: Theatre in Turbulent Times," in *That Was Us: Contemporary Irish Theatre and Performance* (London: Oberon, 2013), 13.

15. Mark Currie, *About Time: Narrative, Fiction and the Philosophy of Time* (Oxford: Oxford University Press, 2006), 5

16. For a discussion of antinostalgia as a narrative in which the present is set up as preferable to a grim past, see Emilie Pine, *The Politics of Irish Memory* (Basingstoke: Palgrave Macmillan, 2011).

17. Linda Connolly, "Negotiating the Past: Reflecting on Women's 'Troubled' and 'Troubling' History in Centennial Ireland," in *Women and the Decade of Centenaries*, ed. Oona Frawley (Bloomington: Indiana University Press, forthcoming).

18. For a full discussion of the Waking the Feminists movement, see Carole Quigley, "#WakingTheFeminists," in *The Palgrave Handbook of Contemporary Irish Theatre and Performance*, ed. Eamonn Jordan and Eric Weitz (London: Palgrave, 2018), 85–91.

19. Helen Meany, "Irish Theatre Abounds with Brilliant Women—Unlike the Abbey's Programme," *The Guardian*, November 9, 2015, https://www.theguardian.com/stage/2015/nov/09/irish-theatre-women-abbey-programme.

20. Brenda Donohue, Ciara O'Dowd, Tanya Dean, Ciara Murphy, Kathleen Cawley, and Kate Harris, *Gender Counts: An Analysis of Gender in Irish Theatre 2006–15* (June 6, 2017), #WakingtheFeminists, http://www.wakingthefeminists.org/research-report/. The *Gender Counts* report was funded by the Arts Council of Ireland.

21. Berthold Molden, "Resistant Pasts versus Mnemonic Hegemony: On the Power Relations of Collective Memory," *Memory Studies* 9, no. 2 (2016): 125–42, see esp. 126 and 128.

22. Lian Bell, "Waking the Feminists One Year On—Change, in Stages," RTÉ, February 10, 2017, https://www.rte.ie/culture/2016/1110/830647-wakingthefeminists-one-year-on/.

23. Sara Keating and Kitty Hollan, "Abbey Theatre Urged to Play Role in Seeking Equality in the Arts," *Irish Times*, November 12, 2015, https://www.irishtimes.com/culture/stage/abbey-theatre-urged-to-play-role-in-seeking-equality-in-arts-1.2427102.

24. Jen Harvie, *Fair Play: Art, Performance and Neoliberalism* (Basingstoke: Palgrave Macmillan, 2013), 3.

25. Harvie, *Fair Play*, 3.

26. Currie, *About Time*, 5.

27. Sara Keating, "Beyond the Abbey: The Trouble for Women in Theatre," *Irish Times*, November 7, 2015, https://www.irishtimes.com/culture/stage/beyond-the-abbey-the-trouble-for-women-in-theatre-1.2419983.

28. Sara Keating, "Abbey Director 'Regrets Exclusions' in Programme," *Irish Times*, November 6, 2015, https://www.irishtimes.com/culture/stage/abbey-director-regrets-exclusions-in-programme-1.2419782.

29. Donohue et al., *Gender Counts*.

30. Donohue et al., *Gender Counts*, 7.

31. I say "end" because the campaigners have not stopped working as advocates and critics, though the campaign is officially over.

32. http://www.wakingthefeminists.org/about-wtf/timeline/

33. Deirdre Falvey, "Yes We Did," *Irish Times*, July 14, 2018, https://www.irishtimes.com/culture/stage/yes-we-did-irish-theatre-s-gender-equality-revolution-1.3563784.

34. Grace Dyas, "I've Been Thinking About Michael Colgan lately," Tumblr (blog), October 27, 2017, http://gracedyas.tumblr.com/post/ive-been-thinking-about-michael-colgan-a-lot.

35. Grace Dyas, "Speech at Speak Up and Call It Out," Tumblr (blog), March 21, 2018, http://gracedyas.tumblr.com/post/ive-been-thinking-about-michael-colgan-a-lot.

36. JD Peters, "Witnessing," in *Media Witnessing: Testimony in the Age of Mass Communication*, ed. Paul Frosh and Amit Pinchevski (Basingstoke: Palgrave Macmillan, 2009), 31.

37. See Grace Dyas's Twitter account: https://twitter.com/gracedyas/status/1053671467462877184.

38. See Grace Dyas's Patreon page: https://www.patreon.com/gracedyas?utm_medium=social&utm_source=twitter&utm_campaign=creatorshare2. It is humbling to note that though Dyas has a voice in the marketplace and markers of social capital, such as over five thousand followers on Twitter, she is far from achieving her fund-raising target.

39. Dyas also supports Gannon in other ways, for example by asking her Twitter followers to support Gannon's Go Fund Me campaign, https://twitter.com/gracedyas/status/1061359654507290624, and Gannon's Go Fund Me page, https://www.gofundme.com/gary-gannon-dublin-central.

40. See Emilie Pine, "We Need More Than a Plaque to Commemorate this History," *Irish Times*, April 14, 2018, https://www.irishtimes.com/culture/heritage/we-need-more-than-a-plaque-to-mark-ireland-s-history-of-cruelty-1.3452991.

41. Aine McMahon, "Dublin Councillors Vote to Block Sale of Magdalene Laundry," *Irish Times*, September 13, 2018, https://www.irishtimes.com/news/social-affairs/dublin-councillors-vote-to-block-sale-of-magdalene-laundry-1.3628671.

42. See https://www.sitesofconscience.org/en/home/ for more on this organization and classification. Paramatta Girls School in Sydney, Australia, is an important comparator here, as a former institution for children that is now a Site of Conscience. See Bonney Djuric and Lily Hibberd, "At the Stroke of a Pen, My Life Changed Forever," accessed October 24, 2019, https://www.sitesofconscience.org/en/2016/03/living-traces-parramatta-female-factory-precinct-memory-project/. I am indebted to Anna Reading for drawing my attention to this project.

43. Charlotte McIvor, "Moving from Efficacy to Effort" (keynote address, Irish Society for Theatre Research Conference, University of Lincoln, May 2018).

44. I am grateful to Jen Harvie for raising this topic at a "Feminist Storytelling" event at National University of Ireland Galway in January 2018.

INDEX

Abbey Theatre (Ireland), 34, 50–53, 66, 86, 91n52, 228–32
abuse: awareness of, 60; of children, 12, 15–16, 43, 45, 50–67, 85, 89n15, 89n19, 90n31, 124, 158n18, 164, 190, 196, 234; emotional, 62; of power, 45; sexual, 34, 62, 96, 101–2, 107, 224. *See also* rape
activism, 219–39
Adorno, Theodor, 8, 116
aesthetics/aesthetic strategies, 16, 23, 25, 27, 33, 51, 96, 108, 167, 219
agency (of audiences), 8, 17–18, 22, 29, 48, 117, 197, 199, 200, 221. *See also* consumer; spectating; witness/witnessing
Ahmed, Sara, 64–65, 87, 110
alienation, 94–95, 106, 147, 170, 172
amnesia, 75. *See also* forgetting
And While London Burns, 35, 191, 203, 205–10
Angels in America (Kushner), 68, 85, 91n56
Annulla (Mann), 34, 165, 173–77, 184
ANU Productions, 35, 191, 193–208, 211–12, 214–15, 216n2, 217n13, 217n20, 234
apartheid (South Africa), 127–57
applause, 31, 65, 87, 152, 190, 220
appropriation, 25, 29, 32, 148, 155, 201, 214
archive of experience/feeling, 43–87, 223–24; of memory, 170
Argentina, 123–57; amnesty in, 136
Artane Industrial School (Ireland), 57–67
Arts Council (Ireland), 231–32

asylum seekers, 28–29, 65, 190, 199
audience: alienation of, 94; as consumer, 165–86; as labor, 191; relation to performer, 197–218; responsibility of, 164–65; role of, 45–87; 94–122; as witness, 165–86, 191–218
audio devices/performance, 35, 166–67, 170, 177, 191, 212; walks, 203–218
Australian stolen generation, 40n81, 90n27
authenticity, 5, 12, 15–18, 22, 24, 45, 165–67
autoperformance, 26–28, 34, 45, 88, 93–122, 125–26, 135, 167, 177, 190, 213–14, 219, 224; and narrative, 88n4
avant-garde, 18, 127, 147

Banciu, Caremen-Francesca, 2–4
Banville, John, 57–58
Baudrillard, Jean, 4, 9, 13, 17
Beckett, Samuel, 5–6, 23, 34, 165, 170–72, 178–79, 185–86, 221–22
Belfast, 27, 203–5, 212; "gay quarter," 204–5
Bell, Lian, 228–29
Benjamin, Walter, 13, 206–7; on spectatorship, 206
Berlant, Lauren, 28–29, 115
betrayal, acts of, 128, 133, 158n28
Bhavnani, Sapna, 107, 113, 117
"Bloody Sunday." *See* Northern Ireland
Blythe, Alecky, 34, 165–69, 182–84
borders/boundaries: crossing, 2, 24, 87n4, 137, 156, 183, 193, 196, 209–10, 212–13

241

Bourdieu, Pierre, 7–8, 12–13, 20, 214
Boys of Foley Street (ANU), 193, 197–99, 201–2, 203, 215
British Petroleum, 205–6
Burke, Tarana, 222–23
Butler, Judith, 23, 81, 118
By Heart (Rodriguez), 30–32

capital: cultural, 8, 10, 24, 28–29, 34, 52–53, 94–95, 113, 115, 126, 154, 169, 176, 178, 181, 184, 200, 211, 229, 233–34, 236; economic, 9–10, 14, 33, 46, 60, 77, 80, 130, 192, 226, 229; mnemonic, 169–70, 177–78, 214, 223–26; political, 14, 126; social, 10–11, 14–15, 24–25, 42, 45, 47, 51–52, 57–59, 62, 74, 76, 80, 82, 85–86, 94, 100, 110, 112, 123–24, 126, 130, 132, 134, 139, 144, 146, 150, 164–65, 184, 192, 199, 212, 219–20, 223, 225–26, 236, 238n38; symbolic, 162, 200, 219–20; in victimhood, 183. *See also* memory
catharsis, 8, 13, 16, 20, 49–50, 65, 95, 110, 117, 124, 127, 144, 152, 177, 182–83, 186, 199, 202, 208, 214
Catholic Church: Ireland, 15–16, 51–67, 101, 104, 190; United States, 90
Chile, 66, 123–57
Christian Brothers (Ireland), 59. *See also* Artane Industrial School (Ireland); institutions (Ireland)
Cia Ludens Company, 66
citizen consumer, 45, 128, 182, 199–200, 218–19. *See also* consumer
civil rights, 82, 98, 223
class tourism, 201–2
Claudia (La Conquesta del Pol Sud), 34, 123–57
closure, 64–65, 83–87, 117, 202
Cloud Nine (Churchill), 150
Colgan, Michael, 232–33
colonized culture, 149–50, 189, 192
Come and Go (Beckett), 34, 165, 185–86
Come Out Eli (Blythe), 34, 165–86
commemoration, 9, 11–12, 77, 202–3, 216n8, 227–29
commodification of witnessing, 123–57, 191, 214

community/communities, 11, 20–21, 62, 64, 66–67, 68, 70, 72–78, 83–84, 97, 117, 210–12; ethical, 22; of memory, 58–9, 65–66, 116; in the theatre, 31, 63, 110–11
compassion, 28, 220, 225, 235
competition, 13–14
consumer, 1, 8–10, 12, 14–31, 35 38n47, 42n120, 43–87, 93–94, 113, 164–65, 177, 179, 189–217, 218, 220, 224–25, 229–30; desire and expectations of, 153, 169–72; disruptive, 208; ethical, 123; passive, 35, 200, 208; power of, 127; and the self, 178–79; sympathetic, 106–119; and tourism, 36n17. *See also* citizen consumer; prosumerism (Harvie)

"Darkest Corner" (Abbey Theatre), 66
Death and the Maiden (Dorfman), 34, 123–57
Decade of Centenaries (Ireland), 11, 227–28
Department of Education (Ireland), 54, 59, 64. *See also* institutions (Ireland)
Derry/Londonderry (Northern Ireland), 95, 119n6; Playhouse, 95–97
direct-address, 56–67, 112–119
direct provision (Ireland), 65, 190
"disappeared," the, 102, 135–57
disenfranchisement, 45, 47, 49, 63, 66, 95, 126–27, 154, 164, 194, 219–39. *See also* marginalized people; silence/silencing
docu-verbatim theatre, 43–87, 94–119, 123, 164. *See also* direct-address
Dolan, Jill, 21, 24, 30, 70–71
Dorfman, Ariel, 34, 123–57
Dublin Castle, 189, 192
Dublin City Council, 214, 233–34
Dyas, Grace, 232–33, 238n38

Echoing Yafa (Schickler), 35, 191, 203, 209–11
Edinburgh Festival/Fringe Festival, 95–96, 114
editing texts, 48–49, 53, 57, 69
El Anatsui, 195–96
emotional capital, 94–122, 126; labor, 105, 123, 134
empathy, 9, 26, 28, 50, 65, 125–26, 147–52, 201, 219–20, 225; empathy paradox, 95, 116–119, 148

INDEX

entertainment, 8, 32–33, 200, 213
ephemeral theatre, 191–218
escapism, 11, 46
ESMA (Argentina), 137–57
ethics, 10, 14–15, 18, 20–21, 31–33, 43–46, 50, 63, 66, 87, 117, 122, 124, 149, 196, 200–1, 213–14, 220–24; and accountability, 228; and community, 22; of memory, 75, 86,193; of production, 124; and witnessing, 57, 74, 112, 117, 214, 235
European Union Peace III grant scheme, 97, 114, 116, 221
Evidence I Shall Give, The (Johnson), 66
expectation of audiences, 167–86

Farber, Yael, 34, 94–122
Favorini, Attilio, 21, 23
Feldman, Allen, 23, 70
feminism, 33, 35, 96, 223, 227–29; and memory, 7; and performance, 33, 35, 42n126
festivals (theatre), 10, 12
fiction theatre, 45, 48, 55, 219–20
Fitzpatrick, Lisa, 19, 25, 100–1
Footfalls (Beckett), 34, 165, 178–79
forgetting, 13, 62–63, 74–80, 170, 172, 234. *See also* amnesia; witness/witnessing
forgiveness, 101, 138–44
free market, 13. *See also* capital, economic
Friel, Brian, 13, 49
fringe theatres, 11, 190. *See also* nonmainstream theatre
funding (of theatre), 4, 10–11, 14, 37n23, 96–97, 114–16, 214, 231–32, 234–35, 237n20

gatekeepers/gatekeeping, 7, 8, 10, 24, 43, 45, 48–49, 94–95, 97, 124, 171, 177–78
Gate Theatre (Dublin), 232–33
gay rights, 70, 83
gender, 22,193; as a factor in violence, 81; equality, 231–32; imbalance, 219–39
Gender Counts (Ireland), 229, 232
Giua, Carles Fernández, 134
Givoni, Michal, 26, 29, 95, 220–21
"Good Friday" peace agreement. *See* Northern Ireland

Hamilton (Miranda), 31–32
Handspring Puppet Company, 34, 123–57
Hare, David, 46, 88n9
harrassment, sexual, 222–27. *See also* abuse, sexual
Harvie, Jen, 8, 9, 18, 117, 191, 213–14, 230
hate crime, 70–87
hegemony, 12, 86, 229
heritage, 7, 9, 12, 15, 137; and tourism, 191–92
hidden history, 193, 204, 212, 234
hierarchies, 2, 58, 81, 112, 129, 162, 164
Hirsch, Marianne, 21, 23, 96
history theatre, 69
Hlaczik, Claudia Poblete, 123–57
Holocaust, 7, 114, 175, 222
Holywell Trust (Northern Ireland), 97
homophobia, 70–87
homosexuality, 72–87
Howard, Aideen, 52–53, 66
Hutchison, Yvette, 127, 146, 156
hyperreal, 4, 35n3. *See also* "real"

icon, 68, 81, 84, 155–56. *See also* images; symbol
identity, 5–6, 16, 18–19, 23, 38n48, 53, 130, 134–9, 142, 155, 199; collective/communal, 62, 66, 146; Irish, 12, 67; of victim, 152
ideology, 48, 67, 74
images, 9, 44, 63, 148, 156, 194, 215; "intolerable," 44, 63–64, 105
industrial schools (Ireland), 53–4, 57–60, 66, 190, 234. *See also* institutions (Ireland)
insecurity, 45
institutions (Ireland), 52–67, 158n18; and abuse, 196; and change, 226. *See also* Christian Brothers (Ireland); industrial schools (Ireland)
intervention, 53, 68, 96, 102, 124, 162, 164, 194, 199, 213, 230
I Once Knew a Girl, 34, 94–122
Ireland, Republic of, 11–12, 15, 34–5, 44, 50–52, 56–67, 91n51, 99, 149, 190–96, 224, 227–28, 230–34; Irish War Memorial, 11. *See also* Northern Ireland
Irish Republican Army (IRA), 97–106

Irish Theatre Institute, 233
irony, 74, 127, 129, 205–7, 224–25

Jagannathan, Poorna, 106
Jarry, Alfred, 127
Johnson, Richard, 66
justice, 138–44

Kabosh Theatre Company (Ireland), 27, 35, 191, 203–4
Kaufman, Moisés, 67–87
Kennedy, Rosanne, 13, 21, 28, 112
Kentridge, William, 127–57
King, Rodney, assault on, 162–66
Krapp's Last Tape (Beckett), 34, 165, 170–73
Kushner, Tony, 68

labels, 18, 61, 64, 71, 73, 83, 116, 233
labor, emotional, 9, 143, 184, 191, 225; immaterial, 4, 94, 143, 162–86; intellectual, 9, 184; mnemonic, 9; physical, 9
La Conquesta del Pol Sud, 3, 34, 123–57
Land Full of Heroes (Banciu), 2–4
Landsberg, Alison, 9, 29, 63–64, 110
Laramie Project, The, 34, 50, 67–87, 163
Laramie Project Ten Years Later, 34, 50, 67–87, 105, 163
Laundry (ANU), 193, 195–7, 201, 203, 234
Let Me Down Easy (Smith), 177
listening, 49, 63, 107, 111, 128, 162–86
Lowe, Louise (ANU), 192, 195–202

Mac Conghail, Fiach, 231
Magdalen laundries (Ireland), 193, 201, 233–34
Mann, Emily, 34, 165–86, 221
marginalized people, 34, 43–87, 113, 115, 194, 229
marketing, 9, 14, 115–119
Martin, Carol, 10, 22, 26, 44–45, 47
McBrinn, Róisín, 51, 53
McGuinness, Frank, 228
McIvor, Charlotte, 193, 196, 227, 235
#MeToo movement, 35, 222–36
mediation, 9, 19, 44–87, 102, 124, 166, 177. *See also* remediation

memorials, 77–78, 234. *See also* commemoration; monuments (commemorative)
memory: and change, 83; collective, 222–34; as a commodity, 126, 144, 153–57; communities, 68; cultural, 2, 42n122, 52, 58, 164, 234; entrepreneurial, 7; diversity of, 86; ethical, 32–33; future, 227; landscape, 211; multidirectional, 13, 117; multiplicity of, 84; ownership of, 5; and place, 190–218; and power, 126; prosthetic, 29; social, 110; subjective, 57; tourism, 78. *See also* remembrance; witness/witnessing
memory capital, 43–87, 154
Miranda, Lin-Manuel, 31–32
misery-memoir, 108
mnemonic capital, 2, 6, 43–87; labor, 82–83, 86; landscapes, 191; value, 154. *See also* memory
mobilisation, 3–4, 27, 30, 35, 44, 95, 118, 210, 219–39
"Monto Cycle" (ANU), 193, 212
monuments (commemorative), 44, 210
moral blindness, 128; capital, 25; consumer, 43; crises, 45; judgments, 105; privilege, 28; status, 85, 153; witness, 20–21, 23, 28, 32
Murphy, Ciara, 198–99, 213, 232
Murphy, Tom, 228

narrative: challenged, 229; closed, 181–82; collective, 62; creation, change, and control of, 2, 4, 15, 17, 45, 67, 72–73, 80, 83, 174, 192, 210–11, 223–24; editing of, 62, 79, 100–119; historical, 7, 11–12, 51, 194, 207–8, 229; marginalized, 146; of memory, 5, 10, 12, 25, 82, 209; of self, 94–122, 123–61; social, 59; of suffering, 13, 52; and trauma, 109, 214; and violence, 225. *See also* autoperformance; consumer
National Theatre (Ireland), 34, 50–54, 231. *See also* Abbey Theatre (Ireland)
National Theatre of Scotland, 155
national theatres, 11, 34, 116, 216n2
9/11 Memorial Museum (New York), 214
1916 Rising (Ireland), 11, 194, 202, 216n8, 228
1913 Lockout (Dublin), 11, 203, 216n8

INDEX

Nirbhaya (Farber), 34, 94–122
No Escape (Raftery), 34, 50–67, 68, 69, 74, 76, 85, 103, 105, 124
nonmainstream theatre, 44. *See also* fringe theatres
Northern Ireland, 28–29, 34, 96–106, 221; power-sharing in, 114; sectarianism in, 97–119
Norton-Taylor, Richard, 52
novelty in theatre, 15–16, 28–9, 33, 47, 94, 166

Obama, Barack, 83
O'Casey, Sean, 228
oral history and testimony, 46, 49, 51–87
"other" and self, 110–11, 115, 128

pain, 1–35; commodification of, 118, 124, 193; of the other, 105, 201; as a signifier, 157
painful memory, 43–87, 94–122, 191–92, 219, 224
Pandey, Jyoti Singh, killing of, 96–119
parades, 9. *See also* commemoration
Paramatta Girls School (Australia), 239n42
participatory theatre, 117, 189–218
passivity, 23, 29. *See also* consumer
patriarchy, 29, 227–29
perception, 6, 21, 52, 58, 72–3, 195, 200
performance, 3; audio, 203–9; and narrative, 62, 100–19; immersive, 190; reaction to, 200; creating relationship, 6; site-specific, 201–2; strategy/style, 48, 98, 100; trying, 200–1
Peters, John Durham, 17–18, 23–24, 28, 233
Pierotti, Greg, 70–87
Platform (theatre company), 35, 203, 206, 214
Police Service of Northern Ireland (PSNI), 105
politics/political contexts, 2, 9, 51, 82, 86, 109
power of audience, 17; of institutions, 7, 117–18, 124; limits to, 134; in marketplace, 10, 74, 219–39; power plays, 3; relations, 8, 70; of survivors, 152; "borrowed power," 126
production of plays, 44, 49, 94–122. *See also* editing texts; narratives, creation of; scripting of plays
prosthetic memory, 63, 110

prosumerism (Harvie), 18, 191–218
"Provos" (IRA). *See* Irish Republican Army
Proximity Mouth (Thorpe), 35, 189, 214
puppets, 123–57

Quartered: A Love Story, 35, 203

race as a factor in violence, 81
Raftery, Mary, 34, 50–67, 103
Rancière, Jacques, 17, 21, 63, 105
rape, 49, 80, 95–119, 220, 225
Reading, Anna, 6–7, 154, 223
"real," the, 16, 22, 24, 45, 47, 77, 87, 197, 208, 213
reception theory, 18, 48. *See also* perception
reconcilation, 117, 139
Redress State (Thorpe), 190
referendum, constitutional (Ireland), 224
refugees, 14, 173, 190. *See also* asylum seekers
religious congregation (Ireland), 51–67. *See also* Catholic Church, Ireland
remediation, 6, 26, 28–29, 64, 79, 171, 184, 200. *See also* mediation
remembrance, 11–14, 18, 24, 30, 38n37, 55, 61, 67, 77–8, 86, 104, 171
representation, 22, 24, 43–87
Rettig Commission (Chile), 129
Ricoeur, Paul, 18, 62–63, 164–65; and forgiveness, 142
ritual, 20, 23, 44, 186, 220
Rodriguez, Tiago, 30–31
Rokem, Freddie, 23, 69
Romania, 3
Rothberg, Michael, 13, 28, 38n37
Ryan Report, 51–67, 190

Sanctuary, 28, 120n14
Saville Inquiry, The (Norton-Taylor), 52
Saville Report (Northern Ireland), 98
scripting of plays, 46, 48–49, 98, 165, 199
Sepinuck, Teya, 23, 25, 94–122
sex trafficking, 194, 199
shame, sense of, 43–87, 112–19
Shepard, Matthew, killing of, 50, 67–87, 105–6

silence/silencing, 12, 22, 29, 33, 60, 70, 102–119, 129, 154, 219–39. See also testimony; unspeakable experience; witness/witnessing
Singleton, Brian, 196–7, 217n13
site-specific performance, 189–218
Smith, Anna Deavere, 34, 46, 162–86
social capital, 2, 43–87, 94, 123, 130; change, 8, 23, 72; exploitation, 17; justice, 194, 201, 221, 230–31; media, 87, 115, 225–26, 231; relations, 191 mediation, 21; responsibility, 117, 220–21
society as bystander, 108, 202
South Africa, 123–57
"Speak Up and Call It Out" (Ireland), 35
spectating, 6, 63, 65–66, 128, 189–218; active, 17, 86–87, 111–119, 196, 199; and actor, 197; ethical, 117; limits to, 215; passive, 17, 196; solo, 189–218
sponsorship, 9, 214. See also funding (of theatre); subsidised theatre
Spotlight (film), 89n15, 90n31
"starving man," 46–48, 96
States of Fear (Raftery), 53
subjectivity, 23–24, 57. See also memory
subsidised theatre, 4, 9, 14, 34, 97, 114–15
suicide, 55, 61
Sunder (ANU), 193, 202
surveillance, in site-specific theatre, 198, 202, 215
survivors, 25, 51–87; as witness, 52, 60, 104, 123–57
Swzarcer, Eugenio, 134
symbol, 68, 82, 84, 106. See also icon; images
symbolic capital, 9, 70; community, 4; functions, 1, 2; space, 5

taboo, 49, 60, 100–1
"Take Back the Night" (USA), 226
Taylor, Jane, 34, 123–57
Tectonic Theater Company, 34, 50, 67–87
Tel Aviv, 191, 203,
television documentaries, 47
testimony, 20, 22, 27, 44, 48, 108–199, 224; difficulty of, 60; four functions of, 140–41; "selling" of, 154; verbatim, 153; as voice-over, 166. See also witness/witnessing

That Spirit (Namew), 158n13, 160n64
theatre as a communal space, 21, 85, 227
Theatre Club (Ireland), 233
"Theatre of Memory" (Ireland), 86
Theatre of Witness, 28–29, 34, 94–122
therapeutic value, 111
Thirteen (ANU), 193–94, 216n8
Thorpe, Dominic, 35, 189, 214
#Times Up, 226, 234–35
torture, 12, 127
totalitarianism, 13
tourism, 36n17, 78
tours, value of, 10, 29, 220
transformation, 6, 12, 26, 30, 45, 70, 85, 87, 117, 124, 128–30, 133, 136, 197, 201, 208, 213, 215, 222, 226
Translations (Friel), 13
transmission of culture, 8–9; of heritage, 12; of memory, 10, 116; of trauma, 116
transnational movement, 154–57, 222
trauma, 9, 16, 19, 25–26, 29, 43–87, 104; as a dramaturgical tool, 105–119; tourism, 192
travellers (Ireland), 230
trend scouting, 9
tribunal theatre, 46, 105
Tricycle Theatre (UK), 46, 52
"Troubles." See Northern Ireland
Trump, Donald, 32
Truth and Reconciliation Commission (TRC, South Africa), 123–57
truth commissions, 123–57
truth in theatre, 123–57
Twilight—Los Angeles, 1992 (Smith), 34, 162–65
Twitter, 223, 225, 228

Ubu and the Truth Commission (Taylor), 34, 123–57
Ubu Roi (Jarry), 127
Ulster Defence Army (UDA), 104. See also Irish Republican Army
UN Convention on Human Rights, 195
unspeakable experience, 58. See also silence/silencing
urban landscape, chages in, 205–6
utopian theatre, 50, 65–66, 85, 87, 222, 235

value/valuation, 9–10, 192–218
Vardo (ANU), 193, 199–201
veracity, 16. *See also* "real"
verbatim theatre, 165, 173, 219–20
Via Dolorosa (Hare), 88n9
victims, 24, 28, 34, 43–87, 94–122; complex victims, 184; victim-witness, 123–57
video, 123–57
violence, 6, 18; cultural, 226; domestic, 100; paramilitary, 97–106; and personal stories, 201; response to, 163–66; rhetorical, 150; sectarian, 114; sexual, 12, 24, 43–87, 96–119, 164, 225; of the state, 192, 220; as witness, 179–82
voiceless, the, 47, 115. *See also* silence/silencing
voyeurism, 3

Waiting for Godot (Beckett), 5–6, 8, 31, 221–22
Wake, Caroline, 20, 51, 124, 134
"Waking the Feminists" (Ireland), 35, 228–29, 234–35, 238n31
"Waking the Nation" (Ireland), 228–29
walls, 195–96. *See also* borders/boundaries
We Carried Your Secrets (Sepinuck), 104
We Don't Know What's Buried Here (Dyas), 233

Widgery Report (Northern Ireland), 98
Winter, Jay, 18, 33
witness/witnessing, 3, 6, 17, 19–21, 27, 43–87, 88n8, 94–119; absent, 107–8; as academic work, 235; circumscribed, 174; collective/group, 62–63, 85, 103–119, 124, 134, 222–27; commissioned, 123–57; commodification of, 162–86; emotional, 118; ethical, 117, 215; firsthand, 197; forgetting, 74–76; and judging, 168; limits of, 219; moral, 20, 28, 32; and multiplicity, 167–69; mutual, 234; negative effects of, 225; passive, 208, 220, 235; of pain, 177, 220; public, 224; relationships, 46; secondhand, 197; status of, 59; subjective, 168; successful, 111; synechdochical, 124. *See also* audience; spectating
"witness theatre," 3, 11
women's suffrage, 11, 232
Worlds End Lane (ANU), 193
World War I, 11–12
World War II, 176
Wyoming state legislature, 82–83
Wyoming, University of, 67–87

Yafa, 209–11

EMILIE PINE is Associate Professor of Modern Drama at University College Dublin. She is author of *The Politics of Irish Memory: Performing Remembrance in Contemporary Irish Culture* and the multiple award winnning *Notes to Self*, which has been translated into fifteen languages.

www.ingramcontent.com/pod-product-compliance
Lightning Source LLC
Chambersburg PA
CBHW030120240426
43673CB00041B/1346